TAX GUIDE
2007/2008

JANE VASS

PROFILE BOOKS

For my family, Ian, William and Jessica,
who have survived their constant exposure to tax with grace and humour.

In memoriam W.J.D.V.

This edition first published in 2007

First published in Great Britain in 2003 by
Profile Books Ltd
3A Exmouth House
Pine Street
Exmouth Market
London ECIR OJH
www.profilebooks.com

Typeset in Plantin by MacGuru Ltd
info@macguru.org.uk

Printed and bound in Great Britain by
Clays, Bungay, Suffolk

A CIP catalogue record for this book is available from the British Library.

ISBN 978 1 86197 849 3

Contents

Acknowledgements

Writing about tax has many challenges and I have been fortunate in having skilled and enthusiastic colleagues. My thanks go to Jonathan Harley, Tony Hazell, and Penny Williams. And I have been grateful to Stephen Brough at Profile Books throughout for his guidance and support.

Special thanks are due to Jane Moore, who reviewed the book on behalf of the Low Incomes Tax Reform Group (LITRG). The LITRG aims to help people on low incomes to cope with their tax and campaigns for a simpler and more accessible tax and benefits system. Jane's keen technical eye and practical experience of the problems people face when grappling with their tax have been invaluable.

However, all errors remain my own, and I welcome comments, via the publisher.

Jane Vass

NOTE

Everyone's personal circumstances are different and tax rules can change. This book has been carefully researched and checked. If by chance a mistake or omission has occurred I am sorry that neither I, the *Daily Mail*, nor the publisher can take responsibility for any loss or problem you suffer as a result. But if you have any suggestions about how the content of the guide could be improved, please write to me, care of the publisher, Profile Books, 3A Exmouth House, Pine Street, London ECIR OJH.

Introduction

Gordon Brown delivered his 11th and probably his final Budget on 21 March 2007. In ten years this Chancellor has had an extraordinary effect on our personal finances, raising taxes with one hand and dishing out credits with the other.

But the fact is that more of us are paying more tax than when he walked into Number 11 Downing Street. And for this reason alone it is vital that we shelter every penny we can, use every allowance available, offset every legitimate expense and claim every credit to which we are entitled.

Just consider these facts. In the year to April 1997, just before Mr Brown became Chancellor, £69 billion was raised in income tax. In the year to April 2007, HM Revenue & Customs was expecting to haul in more than £141 billion in income tax.

The annual take on stamp duty has soared by 417 per cent from just under £2.5 billion a year to more than £12.75 billion. Anyone buying a property worth more than £500,000 will now pay £20,000 stamp duty compared with £5,000 in early 1997.

It doesn't stop there. Inheritance tax is raising ever larger amounts of money as property prices continue to rise faster than the threshold for paying the tax. This tax raised less than £1.56 billion in 1997; now it raises £3.56 billion.

Meanwhile the number of higher-rate taxpayers has soared, rising from 2 million to 3.5 million as tax allowances have failed to keep up with salary increases.

Then we can add in all those other tax increases around the periphery such as air passenger duty, insurance premium tax, fuel duties and those on 'sins' such as smoking and drinking.

So what are we to do? Well, this book is your armour against these tax attacks. It will help you reduce your tax bill to the minimum by explaining how best to organise your financial affairs and where you can shelter your money and make the most of your allowances.

Married taxpayers or those in civil partnerships can make a good start simply by making sure that whichever partner is in the lower tax bracket keeps the savings and investments. So if one partner is a higher-rate taxpayer and the other pays at the basic rate any savings should go with the basic-rate payer. This could boost your interest by 25 per cent.

There are other simple ways to avoid paying too much tax on your savings. Non-taxpayers should fill in a form R85 at their bank or building society to make sure interest is paid without tax being deducted. Make sure the form is filled in for children too. Those who should only pay tax at the lower 10 per cent rate can reclaim some of the tax charged on their interest.

It's also important to use ISAs and pensions to maximum effect. ISAs pay tax-free interest while pension contributions benefit from tax relief at your top rate. With the higher annual and lifetime allowances for pension contributions it is now possible to put sizeable sums away for your retirement and cut your tax bill at the same time.

Pensioners can further benefit from ISAs because income from them isn't taxable, so by using them it could be possible to avoid losing your higher tax allowances in the so-called 'age allowance trap'.

At the other end of the scale, sizeable numbers of people still don't claim tax credits, often because they think their income is too high. So it's vital to understand that not all income is taken into account when assessing your eligibility.

This book is your handy companion to batter the taxman. It's not just here to help you with your tax forms, it's a year-round companion that will help you fight whichever politician moves their suitcases into 11 Downing Street.

Tony Hazell
Editor, *Money Mail*
April 2007

How this book can help you

Some people worry unnecessarily about tax. Others could do with paying it a bit more attention. Most of the time, your tax affairs tick along in the background, but every so often they demand your attention – when the deadline for sending in your tax return approaches, or you suddenly realise that your company car has been costing you thousands of pounds in tax each year.

This book is designed as your road map to the tax system. You're unlikely to need every chapter, so each one starts out by telling you whether or not it is likely to be relevant to you.

You can use the book to help you:

■ *Make sense of the tax system* – Chapter 1 gives you an introduction to the different types of tax covered in this book, and advises you on trouble-shooting and where to get more help. If tax is deducted from any of your income before you get it, see Chapter 2 for how it is worked out and collected on a day-to-day basis, whether or not you get a tax return. Chapter 3 explains how tax credits work. Chapter 4 applies only if you get a tax return: it explains how the system of self-assessment works. Chapter 5 helps you save tax: it covers tax allowances and tax reliefs.

■ *Understand your tax affairs* – Chapters 6 to 11 each cover particular situations, e.g. work, investment, property. Chapters 12 and 13 explain capital gains tax and inheritance tax and whether you need to worry about them. Each chapter guides you through what counts as tax-free income and explains how the tax is worked out, what to tell HMRC, the records you need to keep and what forms you may need to fill in.

■ *Keep your tax bill down* – watch out for the tips throughout the text. Each chapter ends with a summary of tax-planning hints.

■ *Fill in your tax return and other tax forms* – each chapter illustrates key sections of tax forms and explains how to fill them in or check them, with worked examples. If you want to know which chapter covers a particular form or a particular question in the self-assessment tax return, use the 'Form finder' in the Fact file at the end of the book.

■ *Keep up to date* – Budget 2007 tax changes have been incorporated throughout the book. There is a summary of key changes inside the back cover, and a table of the new tax rates and allowances inside the front cover.

■ *Organise your papers* – you have a legal duty to keep records to back up your tax return or tax claim for a minimum length of time. The 'Record-keeping' section in each chapter covers the records you should keep.

■ *Find out more* – the Fact file at the end of the book summarises some key facts and figures, gives you a checklist of tax-free income, and has lists of useful leaflets, HMRC helplines and addresses for all the organisations mentioned in the book.

Dealing with your tax is a necessary chore. We hope that this book makes it a bit easier, a bit less mystifying, and helps you keep your tax bill as low as possible.

1

A quick tour of the tax system

The mammoth government department that administers our taxes is Her Majesty's Revenue & Customs, or 'HMRC' for short. It was only formed in 2005, following a merger of the Inland Revenue and HM Customs and Excise, but it already touches virtually every area of our lives. It collects our taxes, National Insurance contributions and student loan repayments. It administers VAT and customs and excise duties and enforces the National Minimum Wage. And it is responsible for paying out tax credits, child benefit and Child Trust Fund vouchers.

This chapter introduces all the various forms of tax covered in the book and tells you which chapter to go to for further information. If you're having problems, or need further help, see 'Troubleshooting' on page 7.

How tax is collected

You pay tax on your income or gains made in a 'tax year'. The tax year starts on 6 April and runs until 5 April in the next year. In this book, the 12-month period starting on 6 April 2006 and ending on 5 April 2007 is called the '2006–07 tax year'.

Rates of tax for each tax year are usually set in the budget (traditionally March). However, announcements about tax changes may be made at any time (such as the pre-budget report before Christmas). HMRC also announce Statements of Practice from time to time, and Extra-statutory Concessions (when they agree not to collect tax that is legally due).

Watch out for changes

Tax allowances and bands are automatically increased in line with inflation each year, even if a general election intervenes, unless a positive decision is made to change them by a different amount. Other budget proposals become law only when the annual Finance Act is passed, usually in July. These proposals may be rejected or amended, so do not count on a proposal going through – particularly when a general election is imminent.

The tax system aims to collect as much tax as possible from your income before you get it, by requiring:

- employers to deduct tax from your salary under the Pay As You Earn (PAYE) system
- building contractors to deduct tax from some subcontractors' pay
- insurance companies and employers' pension schemes to deduct tax from pensions they pay you, usually under PAYE
- financial organisations and companies to deduct tax from savings interest, dividends and so on.

Not all your tax may be collected this way – e.g. if you have profits from a business or letting out property. If so, or if your affairs are complex, you will probably be sent an annual self-assessment tax return. However, HMRC try to avoid bringing people within the self-assessment regime unnecessarily.

You may receive a variety of other forms. In particular, if you receive tax credits, you will be sent an annual review form.

The sort of contact you have with HMRC differs:

- If any of your tax is deducted from your income under the PAYE system, or you want to claim a tax refund, see Chapter 2.
- Child Tax Credit and Working Tax Credit are covered in Chapter 3.
- If you get a tax return, see Chapter 4.

Income tax

Most of what counts as income is obvious: earnings, pensions, business profits, rents, interest and dividends. However, income tax applies to some items that you might not regard as income, such as the proceeds of life insurance policies, and in some unexpected circumstances – for example, there may be an income tax charge if you benefit from items you gave away as long ago as 1986 (see page 283).

Some types of income are completely tax-free, such as maintenance from an ex-spouse and tax credits. Even when income is taxable, you can deduct various reliefs, such as your pension contributions.

After deducting tax-free income and reliefs, your income from all sources is added up. The first slice of your total income is not taxable – your personal allowance. This is £5,035 in the 2006–07 tax year, £5,225 in 2007–08, but you may get extra allowances if you are aged 65 at any point in the tax year, or if you are blind.

- For more information about allowances and reliefs, see Chapter 5.
- For a checklist of tax-free income, see the Fact file, page 296.

Any remaining income is split into tax bands as shown in Figure 1.1 on page 5. The income in each band is taxed at a particular rate, but the rates vary depending on the types of income, as shown in Figure 1.1. The rates for earnings and pensions are currently 10%, 22% and 40%. From 2008–09, the 10% tax band will be abolished for earnings and pensions (with personal allowances for pensioners, but not others, increased to compensate), and the 22% rate will fall to 20% – but this won't affect your tax for 2006–07 or 2007–08.

The detailed rules are explained in the following chapters:

- If you are an employee, or a director of a company, see Chapter 6.
- If you are a sole trader, or in a partnership, see Chapter 7.
- If you receive taxable state benefits, or a pension, see Chapter 8.
- If you receive income from letting land or property, see Chapter 9.
- If you receive income from abroad, see Chapter 10.
- If you have savings, investments or life insurance, see Chapter 11.

Capital gains tax

This is a tax on gains you make when you dispose of an asset such as investments, land, property, businesses and valuables. You pay tax on the proceeds of the transaction, after deducting the original cost, any expenses and exemptions and reliefs such as taper relief (which reduces the taxable gain in line with the length of time you have owned the asset).

In practice, however, most people do not have to grapple with capital gains tax because the first slice of taxable gains made in each tax year is tax-free. The tax-free amount is £8,800 in 2006–07, £9,200 in 2007–08.

Your capital gains are added to your taxable income for the year and taxed as if they were your top slice of income (see Figure 1.1).

➡ For more information about capital gains tax, see Chapter 12.

National Insurance contributions

You have to pay National Insurance contributions on earnings from employment, profits from self-employment and wages you pay employees. The rules for what counts as income for the purpose of National Insurance contributions, and what expenses can be deducted, differ from those for income tax, although the differences are gradually disappearing.

There are several types of contribution:

- If you are an employee, you pay employees' Class 1 contributions on your earnings.
- If you are an employer, you pay employers' Class 1 contributions on your employees' earnings, and Class 1A and possibly Class 1B contributions on taxable benefits you give your employees. An employee does not pay National Insurance on employment benefits.
- If you are self-employed, you pay Class 2 contributions at a flat weekly rate (£2.10 in 2006–07 and £2.20 in 2007–08), as well as Class 4 contributions on a percentage of your profits.
- If you have not paid enough Class 1 or Class 2 contributions, you can pay voluntary Class 3 contributions at a flat weekly rate (£7.55 in 2006–07 and £7.80 in 2007–08). (See page 6 and HMRC form CA5603 *To pay voluntary National Insurance contributions*.)

Figure 1.1: Income and capital gains tax rates for 2006–07 (2007–08)

The first slice of your income or gains is tax-free. The remaining taxable income fills up your bands in this order:

■ Earnings (including pensions, rents and business profits)
■ Interest
■ Dividends
■ Life insurance gains
■ Capital gains

Tax rates for 2006–07 (2007–08 rates in brackets)   *Example*

No tax	**Personal and blind person's allowances** Minimum £5,035 (£5,225)

Bill's income in 2006–07 was £38,600, made up of business profits of £33,000, interest of £3,000 and gross share dividends of £2,600.

His business profits of £33,000 use:
■ all his personal allowance (tax-free)
■ all his starting-rate band (tax at 10% is £215)
■ £25,815 of his basic-rate band (taxed at 22% i.e. £5,679)

Taxed at 10%	**Starting-rate band** First £2,150 (£2,230)

Tax: £215 + £5,679 = £5,894

Taxed at 20% if income is interest or capital gains, 10% if dividends, otherwise at 22%	**Basic-rate band** Next £31,150 (£32,370)

His £3,000 interest fits in the rest of his basic-rate band, and is taxed at 20%. His bank deducts the tax.
Tax: £600, paid at source

£2,335 of his dividends fits into his basic-rate band, taxable at 10% (£233). The remaining £265 falls in the higher-rate band, taxed at 32.5% (£86).
Tax: £233 + £86 = £319, of which £260 is paid at source

Taxed at 40%, or 32.5% if dividends	**Higher-rate band** Anything above £33,300 (£34,600)

Bill has capital gains above the annual tax-free amount. His £4,000 of taxable gains all fall in the higher-rate band, taxable at 40%.
Tax: £1,600

Bill's tax is £5,894+ £600 + £319 + £1,600 = £8,413, but £860 was paid at source. He has £7,553 to pay, plus Class 4 National Insurance on his business profits.

You do not have to pay National Insurance if your income is less than the personal allowance (£5,035 in 2006–07 and £5,225 in 2007–08), or for Class 2 contributions less than £4,465 in 2006–07 (£4,635 in 2007–08), or if you are over state pension age. And if you are liable to pay more than one class of contribution (because, say, you are self-employed as well as having a job), there is a maximum payment. See the Fact file for useful leaflets.

➡ For details of contributions for employees, see pages 24 and 122.
➡ For details of contributions for self-employed people, see page 157.

Check your National Insurance record

Your entitlement to state retirement pension and some other state benefits is reduced if you haven't paid National Insurance for enough years in your working life. Mistakes by your employer or HMRC may also affect your record. To check, contact HMRC's National Insurance Contributions Office. You can also get a State Pension Forecast from the Pension Service (addresses in the Fact file). If you have not paid enough in one year, you can make Class 3 contributions to boost your entitlement, provided you act within six years of the year in question. But the government propose to reduce the number of years' payments needed to qualify for a full pension, and if this goes ahead you may not need to pay extra.

Student loan repayments

Repayments on student loans taken out after August 1998 are collected by HMRC along with your tax. These loans are known as 'income-contingent' because your repayments are related to your level of income.

The Student Loans Company notify HMRC when you leave university. If you have a job, your employer will be required to deduct the repayment along with your PAYE; otherwise, it will be collected through your tax return. The repayments normally start in the April after you have finished your course, subject to your income exceeding a minimum level.

The loans are repaid at a rate of 9 per cent of your income above £15,000 a year. Taxable employee benefits, such as a company car, and investment income of £2,000 or less are ignored.

➡ For more about student loan repayments, see pages 25 and 130.

Inheritance tax

This is a tax on the value of what you leave when you die (your estate). Tax may have to be paid during your lifetime if you make a gift to some types of trust. Most other lifetime gifts are 'Potentially Exempt Transfers', which means that they will be counted as part of your estate only if you die within seven years of making them. However, the first slice of your estate is tax-free, and some gifts are completely tax-free. The tax-free amount is £285,000 in 2006–07, and is scheduled to rise to £300,000 in 2007–08, £312,000 in 2008–09, £325,000 in 2009–10 and £350,000 in 2010–11.

➡ For more about inheritance tax, see Chapter 13.

Value Added Tax (VAT)

VAT is a tax on money you spend. The tax (usually 17.5 per cent) is added to the price you pay for most goods and services. The trader hands over the tax to HMRC – but can deduct VAT paid on things that they have bought for their business. As a private individual, opportunities to save VAT are very limited. The main exception is if you buy from a small business with an income below the threshold for registering for VAT (a gardener, say). Disabled people can also buy some goods VAT-free (see the Fact file).

➡ For more about VAT if you are in business, see Chapter 7.

Troubleshooting

HMRC are committed to:

■ treating your affairs in strict confidence
■ asking you to pay only the right amount of tax
■ providing clear and simple forms, and accurate and complete information
■ handling your affairs promptly and accurately

- keeping your costs to the minimum necessary
- being accessible and taking reasonable steps to meet special needs
- courtesy and professionalism.

All HMRC offices have targets for customer service and work to various codes of practice (see the Fact file). For example, if tax has been deducted from your savings income, but you are not liable for tax, they aim to repay the tax within 28 days of receiving a claim. If they fail to meet any of their service commitments, or you are dissatisfied with their service, you can complain.

You will have a better chance of sorting out problems amicably with HMRC if you can show that you keep accurate and up-to-date records, pay on time, tell your tax office if your circumstances change, and provide correct and complete information when asked.

Getting a repayment

Even if all your tax is deducted from your income before you get it, it is worth checking that the right amount of tax has been deducted. If you get a tax return, this will happen automatically when you send in your return – see Chapter 4. If you do not get a return, you may get a repayment through the PAYE system or you may have to send in a claim form – see Chapter 2.

How to complain

First give the person you are dealing with a chance to put things right. Write 'Complaint' clearly at the top of any letter. If you have no joy, ask for it to be reviewed by a manager (usually the Complaints Manager). HMRC Code of Practice 1 *Putting things right: How to complain* gives more information, but it is no longer necessary to go to the area director before taking your complaint further. For VAT, see Notice 1000 *Complaints and putting things right*.

If you are still dissatisfied, there is an independent Adjudicator whose services are free. You must normally apply to the Adjudicator within six months of receiving a response. See leaflet AO1 *The Adjudicator's Office for complaints about HM Revenue & Customs and Valuation Office Agency*.

You may also be able to complain to the Parliamentary Ombudsman. However, note that while the Ombudsman can investigate complaints that the Adjudicator has already considered, the Adjudicator cannot handle complaints that have been investigated by the Ombudsman. Complaints to the Ombudsman must be made through an MP within 12 months of the cause for complaint arising.

While a complaint is under way, you still have to pay any tax you owe. HMRC may agree not to pursue the tax you are disputing during the investigation, but interest will build up on any tax that turns out to be due.

Keep track of costs

You can claim any reasonable costs you have had to pay as a result of HMRC mistake or delay, such as postage, phone calls, travelling expenses, professional fees and interest on overpaid tax, so keep receipts. You can claim earnings lost as a direct result of having to sort things out. You may also be entitled to compensation for worry and distress.

Complaint or appeal?

Do not confuse your right to complain about shoddy treatment with your right to make a formal appeal against an HMRC decision. The appeals procedure is laid down by law, and covers things such as your tax assessment, a penalty, a claim for tax relief, and a tax credits award.

Your tax office will tell you if you have a right of appeal against a decision, and should automatically send you information about how to appeal and an appeal form. Check this information carefully, because you have only 30 days in which to appeal, unless you can give a good reason for any delay. Be prepared to pay any disputed tax in the meantime – you may be able to postpone paying it, but interest will usually be added from the date the tax was due if your appeal is unsuccessful.

If you make an appeal, your tax office will try to settle it by agreement. Failing this, the case will go before commissioners who will hear it and make a decision. (See the leaflet *Tax Appeals*, available from HMRC offices and their website.) The decision of the commissioners is final on a point of fact, but can be challenged in the courts on a point of law.

Made a mistake?

If you have paid too much tax because of a mistake in your tax return, for example you forgot to deduct an expense, you can correct it without question within one year and ten months of the end of the tax year. After that – or if you did not complete a return – you can still claim back tax within five years and ten months of the end of the tax year – so, by 31 January 2013 for 2006–07. However, this does not override specific time limits set for making claims in a tax return, such as claiming a business loss.

Unexpected tax bills

You should not face an unexpected bill if you keep your tax affairs in order and give HMRC the necessary information. If HMRC then tell you that something has gone wrong and you have paid too little tax, they may agree to waive the tax, under Extra-Statutory Concession A19 (concessions are listed on the HMRC website or ask any tax office). This concession applies only if you were notified of the arrears more than 12 months after the end of the tax year in which you supplied the relevant information, and if it was reasonable for you to think that you had paid enough tax.

If you do face a bill that is correct but you cannot pay, you may be able to negotiate a 'time to pay' arrangement. You will still incur interest on the unpaid tax.

Enquiries and investigations

If you have to complete a tax return, HMRC have one year after the latest date for submitting it within which they can start a formal 'enquiry' (see page 54). An enquiry does not necessarily mean that they think something is wrong with your return – some are chosen at random. But you can still be investigated after the one-year period if they suspect fraud or negligence, or if you have not supplied full and accurate information.

If you are faced with an HMRC investigation, co-operation is your best bet, but HMRC are limited in what they can ask for and what they can do. Consider getting professional help. If the investigation finds that you do owe tax, you may have to pay what is owed, plus interest, plus a penalty. But HMRC will reduce the penalty if you are co-operative and depending on the seriousness of the case. See HMRC Code of Practice 11 *Self Assessment. Local office enquiries* and Codes of Practice 8 and 9.

Failed to declare taxable income or gains?

We tell you what you need to declare at the end of each chapter. If you have broken the rules you can get advice on a no-names basis on how to sort matters out by ringing HMRC's tax and benefits confidential helpline on 0845 608 6000.

Tax avoidance – a dirty word to the government

Tax evasion is illegal and dodging your income tax can land you with an unlimited fine or up to seven years in prison. Tax planning – arranging your affairs so that you pay the least tax legally possible – is not in itself illegal. But in an attempt to stamp out 'tax avoidance', there are rules that require 'promoters' of some sorts of scheme to notify HMRC, and the people who use them to make an entry in their tax returns. The rules won't affect most people, and none of the tax planning hints in this book are caught under the rules as they stand at the time of going to press, but see page 68 for more information.

Getting help

Help from HMRC

- *Pros:* Free, and will have access to your tax records.
- *Cons:* Variable standards. You have to do the legwork. No help with tax planning.

If you are an employee or receive a pension, your tax office will be that of your employer or main pension payer. If you change jobs you will be transferred to a new tax office. Self-employed people are dealt with by a tax office in their area.

If you become unemployed, you stay with your existing tax office. But if you do not have a job or pension and have claimed tax repayments in the past, your records may find their way to one of the HMRC offices that specialises in repayments. And if your affairs are complex, you may be dealt with by one of their complex personal returns teams.

These days, however, your records are held on various computer systems and you don't necessarily need to contact your own tax office. If you need help about something specific to you, phone the telephone number given on any relevant paperwork. For general queries look in the phone book under 'HM Revenue & Customs' for useful phone numbers and the addresses of HMRC enquiry centres that can arrange face-to-face meetings. You can always ask tax offices to call you back to save on phone bills and if you are housebound you can arrange for a home visit. Enquiry centres also have facilities for people with disabilities or special needs.

There are a number of specialist tax offices and departments, covering, for example, tax credits, National Insurance and non-residents. They have their own helplines, listed in the Fact file. HMRC also have a range of leaflets and a comprehensive website – again, see the Fact file.

Keep reference numbers handy

When you contact HMRC, you will be asked for your reference number. A ten-figure 'unique taxpayer reference' (UTR) will be on the front of your tax return, if you get one. Tax offices can also track your records down if you quote your National Insurance number.

In doubt about the tax treatment?

HMRC will not help with tax planning, but you can ask for information about their interpretation of tax law, and their internal guidance manuals are published on their website. If, after a transaction, there is genuine uncertainty about the tax treatment – because it was an unusual transaction, say – you can ask for a 'post-transaction ruling'. Rulings about inheritance tax are not available. (See HMRC Code of Practice 10 *Information and advice*.)

Help from a professional

■ *Pros:* Independent. Good professionals can do the legwork for you, provide help with tax planning and negotiate with your tax office if necessary. Advice could pay for itself.
■ *Cons:* Cost. Variable standards. You are still responsible if things go wrong – though you might have a claim against your adviser.

If you want someone to deal with HMRC on your behalf, you need to give your tax office written authorisation to treat that person as your 'agent'. You may be asked to complete form 64-8 *Authorising your agent*.

Many accountancy and law firms offer tax services. Lists of firms specialising in particular areas are available in libraries or from their professional body (see the Fact file).

Alternatively, you can go to a specialist 'chartered tax adviser', with the 'ATII' or 'FTII' or 'CTA' qualifications awarded by the Chartered Institute of Taxation. A lower-level qualification is run by the Association of Tax Technicians (ATT). ATT members who meet requirements such as having insurance and up-to-date knowledge are described as 'Registered with the Association of Taxation Technicians as a Member in Practice'.

There are also two charities – TaxAid and TaxHelp for Older People – that offer free advice to people who cannot afford to pay an accountant or tax adviser. Their details are in the Fact file.

Record-keeping

The law requires you to keep records if you get a tax return. You must keep records for at least 22 months from the end of the tax year to which they relate, or for five years and ten months after this date if you are self-employed or let property. You need to keep them longer if you received a late tax return, or if your tax office is enquiring into your return. (See HMRC leaflet SA/BK4 *Self Assessment. A general guide to keeping records*.)

If you don't need to complete a return, there is no legal requirement to keep records, but it is wise to do so in case you get a return later on, or you want to claim a tax repayment. As you can usually claim repayments up to six years in arrears, it makes sense to keep records for six years.

The law does not say which records you must keep, but suggestions are in leaflet SA/BK4, and examples are given in each chapter. If you keep your records on computer you can only discard your paper originals if your system captures all necessary information (using microfilm or optical imaging, say) and can reproduce it in legible form. But all vouchers and certificates of tax deducted from your income must be kept.

Tax-planning hints

1 Watch out for tax changes – you may need to reassess your tax plans.
2 Check your National Insurance record (see page 6 for how to do this). If you have not paid enough National Insurance, your entitlement to a state retirement pension or other benefits may be affected.
3 If you have a job and are also self-employed, there are rules to cap the amount of National Insurance contributions you have to pay.
4 You have a legal obligation to keep records to back up your tax return or tax claim. Make a habit of keeping key documents.
5 Make a note of your taxpayer reference or National Insurance number. It will save time if you quote it in correspondence or in phone calls to your tax office.
6 Keep a record of any phone calls to HMRC offices, including the date and time and the name of the person you spoke to.
7 If you have to complain because your tax office has made a mistake or been slow, make a note of any costs you incur – you may be able to claim them back. Keep receipts, if possible.
8 HMRC will sometimes waive tax if you are faced with a late and unexpected tax bill, due to their error – ask whether Extra-Statutory Concession A19 applies to you.
9 Don't be afraid to ask your tax office for help. As well as your own tax office, there are general enquiry centres and specialist helplines.
10 Anyone can set themselves up as a tax adviser. Look for professional accountancy qualifications, or those from the Chartered Institute of Taxation or Association of Tax Technicians, and check that an adviser has up-to-date expertise that is relevant to your needs. Make sure that you get a clear letter of engagement explaining their fees and what they will do for you.

2

Pay As You Earn (PAYE)

Wherever possible, tax is collected 'at source' – by deducting it from income before it is paid. In many cases, this means that you do not need to fill in a tax return.

There are two main ways of collecting tax at source:

- through the Pay As You Earn (PAYE) system, if you have a regular source of taxable income, such as a job, private pension or employer's pension (no tax is deducted from state pensions, although in many cases they are taxable).
- by requiring financial organisations to deduct tax from some types of savings and investment income.

PAYE applies to income tax, but your employer also has to deduct National Insurance contributions and, possibly, student loan repayments.

This chapter explains how to check the amount of tax and National Insurance deducted and how to claim a tax repayment.

➡ For what happens if you get a tax return, see Chapter 4.
➡ For the tax rules relating to income from a job see Chapter 6; for pension income and state benefits see Chapter 8.
➡ For how tax is deducted from savings and investments, see Chapter 11.

Check your tax even if you don't get a tax return

Even if all your income is taxed before you get it, you may be paying too much or too little tax. Keep an eye on what is being deducted, particularly if your circumstances change.

Around 3.8 million taxpayers are estimated to have paid the wrong amount in 2004–05 because of problems with PAYE. So even if everything appears to be working smoothly, you should still check your tax code, which tells your employer (or pension provider) how much tax to deduct.

Tax deducted at source from savings and investment income is usually at 20 per cent (10 per cent on dividends). This means that:

- If your income is low, you may be able to claim tax back (but not the 10 per cent deducted at source on dividends). If so, you may have to fill in a Tax Repayment form (form R40, described on page 33).
- Alternatively, you may have more tax to pay on savings income. This is collected through PAYE if you have income from a job or pension, in which case you will see an entry on your coding notice (explained below). If it is not, you will have to fill in a tax return (see Chapter 4).

Keeping below the tax threshold

No PAYE or National Insurance contributions are payable if your earnings are below the level of the basic personal allowance. In 2006–07 this was £5,035 a year, £97 a week or £420 a month. For 2007–08, the figures increase to £5,225 a year, £100 a week, or £435 a month.

How your income tax is worked out under PAYE

PAYE is a way of spreading your tax bill over the tax year by deducting tax from every salary or pension payment. Your tax office notifies your employer (or the pension payer) how much of your pay to give you tax-free. It does this by giving you a 'tax code'. Using special tables, your employer can then work out how much tax to deduct from the rest of your pay.

PAYE is normally cumulative. It takes into account the amount of pay and tax deducted since the start of the tax year, so that the correct proportion of the annual lower-, basic- and higher-rate tax liability is deducted on each pay day. If your income goes up, more tax will be deducted; if your income goes down, too much tax may have already been deducted and the excess tax will be refunded in your pay packet.

At the end of the tax year

By 31 May following the end of the tax year, your employer must give you a form P60 telling you how much pay you have received, how much tax has been deducted and what your tax code is. (If you leave your job, your employer must give you a form P45 with this information.) By 6 July, your employer must also give you a form P11D or P9D with details of your taxable expenses and benefits (if you had any).

This information is copied to your tax office, and enables them to check your tax bill, even if you do not get a tax return:

■ *If too much tax has been deducted*, the overpayment will first be set against any other tax you owe. You should be sent a cheque for the rest – though not if the amount is £10 or less.
■ *If you have underpaid tax*, this will usually be collected by adjusting your tax code for a future tax year (see Chapter 1 if the underpayment arose due to an HMRC mistake). For example, tax underpaid in 2006–07 will usually be recovered through the 2008–09 tax code. You can ask for the amount collected to be limited to the amount of your PAYE bill for the current year (with the rest collected through the next year's code), or less in case of hardship. You will be asked to make a repayment direct to HMRC if the amount is above £2,000, or if you no longer have income taxed under PAYE.

Checking your tax code

Your tax code shown on your payslip will look something like this: 522L. This is all your employer sees – not how the code is made up.

In January or February each year, you will be sent a P2 coding notice, which explains how your tax office has arrived at your code for the next tax year. The rates of state pensions and benefits and the next year's allowances are usually announced in time to be incorporated into your tax code for the coming year. The letters in the code allow your employer to make automatic adjustments for some budget changes. If you are affected by other budget changes, or if your own circumstances change, you may be sent a new tax code after the start of the tax year.

To work out your tax code, your tax office starts with the total allowances (and other reliefs) you are entitled to. But your tax code is also used to collect tax on non-cash items such as a company car, or on other income that has nothing to do with your job, such as a state retirement pension or untaxed interest. You can ask your tax office not to do this, but if so you will probably have to complete a tax return (see page 50).

Your code is calculated by deducting estimates of taxable income from your tax-free allowances:

- *If your allowances come to more than the deductions*, you will have some allowances left to set against your pay (see Example 2.1 on page 20).
- *If your deductions come to more than your allowances*, any remaining amount is treated as additional pay for the purposes of working out how much tax to deduct. The letter in your code will be K (see Example 2.2 on page 22).

A new style of coding notice has been introduced. It follows the same principles as the old notice, but it should be easier to understand because it includes personalised notes explaining each entry in your code. (See Figure 2.1 for common entries on a coding notice, Figure 2.2 for what a coding notice looks like and Chapter 5 for more information on allowances.) Note that payments to your employer's pension scheme or payroll giving scheme do not appear on your coding notice, even though they qualify for relief, because they are deducted from your pay before PAYE is worked out.

The number in your tax code is simply the value of all your allowances, minus the amounts taken away, with the final digit knocked off (the PAYE tables round in your favour). The letters in codes mean:

- **L, P, V** or **Y** codes help your employer to adjust your code easily to account for budget changes – your letter will be:

- **L** if you get only the basic personal allowance
- **P** and **V** if you get the full personal allowance for people aged 65 to 74, plus (in the case of a **V** code) the full married couple's allowance, and are a basic-rate taxpayer
- **Y** if you get the full personal allowance for people aged 75 and over.

■ The **BR** or **D0** codes mean that all your pay from this job or pension should be taxed at the basic rate or higher rate respectively (used for second jobs, for example).

■ The **K** code means that your deductions come to more than your allowances, so you are regarded as receiving additional pay for the purposes of working out your PAYE deduction. However, not more than 50 per cent of your pay can be taken in tax this way.

■ The **T** code is used for any special cases not covered by the codes above, or if you ask your tax office to use it (e.g. because you do not want your employer to know what allowances you get).

Figure 2.1: Possible coding notice entries

Your tax allowances
- Personal allowance
- Married allowance
- Blind person's allowance
- Maintenance payments
- Loan interest (if it qualifies for tax relief)
- Job expenses
- Personal pension relief (higher-rate relief only – see page 177)
- Charity gifts relief (higher-rate relief on Gift Aid payments – see page 81)

Deductions
- State pensions and benefits
- Other pensions not taxed at source
- Jobseeker's allowance
- Incapacity benefit
- Benefits and expenses provided by your employer (e.g. car or car fuel benefit)
- Part-time earnings/tips/commission
- Other items of untaxed income (e.g. property income, interest)
- Tax underpaid

Allowances minus deductions gives the number in your tax code

Allowances for married couples or people paying maintenance

You may get these allowances if you, or your partner (or ex-partner, for maintenance payments), were born before 6 April 1935. Unlike the personal allowance, which gives you tax relief at your top rate of tax, they give restricted relief, worth just 10 per cent of the full amount. So if you qualify for the maximum married couple's allowance of £6,365 in 2007–08, it reduces your tax bill by £636.50. For full details, see Chapter 5.

If the full allowance was given in your tax-free pay you would get too much tax relief, so the amount shown in your tax code is restricted. To check that it is right, multiply the amount shown by your top rate of tax. It should give the same result as the full allowance multiplied by 10 per cent. See Example 2.1 below.

Note that in the old-style coding notice, the full allowance and an 'allowance restriction' were shown separately – in the new notice, you will see only the allowance after deducting the restriction.

Example 2.1: **If allowances are more than deductions**

George is retired with a pension from his previous employer. His coding notice for 2007–08 (shown in Figure 2.2 opposite) includes his age-related personal allowance. The full allowance is £7,690, but George's allowance is reduced to £7,150 because his income exceeds the £20,900 limit for full age-related allowances (explained in Chapter 5).

However, George gets the maximum married couple's allowance – £6,365. This means that he gets £6,365 × 10% = £636 deducted from his tax bill. But in his tax code he sees £2,894. This is correct, because when multiplied by his top rate of tax (22 per cent) it produces the same amount: £2,894 × 0.22 = £636.

The notice also shows that the tax on George's state pension of £7,540 will be collected through PAYE on his employer's pension. To achieve this, the value of his state pension is deducted from his allowances: £7,150 + £2,894 − £7,540 = £2,504. This means that he can get £2,509 of his employer's pension tax-free each year (the last digit is always increased to 9), or £2,509 ÷ 12 = £209 each month. Tax is deducted from the rest.

The letter in George's code is T because he gets a reduced personal allowance. His tax code is therefore 250T.

Figure 2.2: PAYE Coding Notice (see Example 2.1)

HM Revenue & Customs	**PAYE Coding Notice**
	Tax code for tax year **2007 - 2008**

Please keep all your coding notices. You may need to refer to them if you have to fill in a tax return. Please also quote your tax reference and National Insurance number if you contact us.

010000:00000080:001   491/1

MR G PETROS
THE LARCHES
9 THE AVENUE
LONDON   SW25 2NR

H M INSPECTOR OF TAXES
NORTH WEST MU1
5 ABBEY FOREGATE
SHREWSBURY
SALOP
SY2 6AD

Inland Revenue office phone	Date of issue
01567 3456789	13 FEB 2007

Tax reference	National Insurance number
491/G7070/HD	CE 00 00 30 A

Dear MR G PETROS

Your tax code for the year 6th April 2007 to 5th April 2008 is 250T

You need a tax code so Rich Pension Fund can work out how much tax to take off the payment they make to you from 6th April 2007. We have worked out your tax code but need you to check that our information about you is correct. The wrong tax code could mean you pay too much, or too little tax. Please keep your coding notices, you may need them if we send you a tax return.

Here is how we worked it out		
your personal allowance		£7150
married couple's allowance		£2894
state pension	-£7540	-£7540
a tax free amount of		£2504

If we have got this wrong, or if your circumstances have changed and you think it could affect the tax you pay, please tell us. Our telephone number and address are above. We turn £2504 into tax code 250T to send to Rich Pension Fund. They should use this code with the tables they receive from HM Revenue & Customs to take off the right amount of tax each time they pay you from 6th April 2007. Rich Pension Fund do not know the details of 250T or how it is worked out – that is confidential between us.

Estimated amounts

PAYE coding notices are usually sent out in January or February for the tax year starting in April. So if your tax code includes an allowance for an item on which you get tax relief (such as a pension contribution) or a deduction for other taxable income (such as untaxed interest), your tax office has to make an estimate of how much the item is likely to be. The estimate may be based on information from your employer, or information in your last tax return (for example, regular claims for tax relief on gifts to charity), or you may be sent a Tax Review form (P810) to check the figures.

Check estimates

Always check any estimated amounts in your PAYE coding notice. If the amount has changed substantially, let your tax office know, or you could pay too much or too little tax.

Example 2.2: If deductions are more than allowances

Halina is a 40% taxpayer. Her coding notice for 2007–08 (shown in Figure 2.3) includes her personal allowance of £5,225. She also makes a regular Gift Aid payment to charity of £192. She has already had 22% basic-rate tax relief on this by handing over less than it is worth to the charity (£246), so she is only due £246 × 18% = £44 extra relief. She gets an allowance of £110 – which will produce the £44 relief due when multiplied by her top rate of tax of 40%.

Halina's tax office is using her tax code to collect tax on the rent she receives from letting out her holiday cottage (£1,750) and some unpaid tax from the previous year. The unpaid tax is £422, but the amount deducted is £1,055 because, when multiplied by her top rate of tax, this will collect £1,055 × 40% = £422. She also has a company car with a taxable value of £3,250. Her total deductions are £6,055.

Halina's deductions come to more than her allowances (£5,225 + £110 – £6,055 = minus £720). Her tax code is K72 which means that each month her PAYE is calculated as if she received £720 ÷ 12 = £60 more pay than she actually does.

Figure 2.3: PAYE Coding Notice (see Example 2.2)

HM Revenue & Customs

PAYE Coding Notice

Tax code for tax year | 2007 - 2008

Please keep all your coding notices. You may need to refer to them if you have to fill in a tax return. Please also quote your tax reference and National Insurance number if you contact us.

010000:00000080:001   491/1
MISS H HARPER
10 GRANGE ROAD
FULFORD
TAXSHIRE   TX3 4HQ

H M INSPECTOR OF TAXES
NORTH WEST MU1
5 ABBEY FOREGATE
SHREWSBURY
SALOP
SY2 6AD

Inland Revenue office phone 01567 3456789	Date of issue 13 FEB 2007
Tax reference 491/G7070/HD	National Insurance number CE 00 00 30 A

Dear MISS H HARPER

Your tax code for the year 6th April 2007 to 5th April 2008 is K72

You need a tax code so Giveus Abreak Ltd can work out how much tax to take off the payment they make to you from 6th April 2007. We have worked out your tax code but need you to check that our information about you is correct. The wrong tax code could mean you pay too much, or too little tax. Please keep your coding notices, you may need them if we send you a tax return.

Here is how we worked it out		
your personal allowance		£5225
Gift Aid payments		£110
car benefit	-£3250	
property income	-£1750	
reduction to collect unpaid tax £422	-£1055	-£6055
a tax free amount of		-£720

If we have got this wrong, or if your circumstances have changed and you think it could affect the tax you pay, please tell us. Our telephone number and address are above. We turn -£720 into tax code K72 to send to Giveus Abreak Ltd. They should use this code with the tables they receive from HM Revenue & Customs to take off the right amount of tax each time they pay you from 6th April 2007. Giveus Abreak Ltd do not know the details of K72 or how it is worked out – that is confidential between us.

More than one job or pension

If you have more than one source of income within PAYE, you will probably get a separate tax code and coding notice for each source of income, but your allowances will be given against the main source. If any allowances are left over, you will see the remaining allowances given in your code for the second source.

Your tax office may instruct whoever pays your second income to deduct tax at just the basic-rate or higher-rate, using a BR or D0 code, but may include an adjustment in your code if you have not used all your starting-rate band against your main source of income. If too much of your income is taxed at the starting or basic rates, you may also see an adjustment.

You can ask your tax office to distribute your allowances in any way you choose. So if, for example, you have two part-time jobs, rather than having your allowances set against your main source of income, you could ask for them to be split between your two jobs.

Checking how much PAYE has been deducted

Because PAYE is worked out on a cumulative basis, you need to use HMRC tables if you want to check the amount deducted on your payslip during the tax year. These tables, and other guidance, are included in HMRC's annual Employer's Pack (available on the HMRC website) or contact your tax office or local tax enquiry centre.

Checking your National Insurance contributions (NICs)

The National Insurance contributions paid by employees are called Class 1 contributions. These are not payable on pension income, nor are they payable by employees aged under 16 or over state pension age (currently 65 for men, 60 for women). However, employers still have to pay contributions for employees over state pension age.

Class 1 NICs are not affected by your tax code, because there is no adjustment for individual allowances and deductions. Employees pay contributions only on their earnings, not on benefits in kind, but there is no deduction for pension contributions you make (see Chapter 6). Also, unlike income tax, National Insurance is not worked out on an annual basis. Each pay period (e.g. week or month) is treated separately – so if your earnings dip below the earnings threshold in one earnings period, you cannot carry the unused amount forward to the next period.

Unless you are a woman who chose before 11 May 1977 to pay reduced-rate contributions, or are claiming a deferral (see page 30), you can use Figure 2.4 on page 26 to check the amount shown in your payslip.

Married women paying reduced contributions

If you are a married woman who opted for reduced National Insurance contributions, the rate you pay is currently 4.85%. These contributions do not entitle you to a state pension in your own right and you should consider switching to the full rate. (Details are on HMRC's website, see the Fact file.)

Checking your student loan deductions

Repayments on student loans you took out after August 1998 may also appear on your payslip. The amount of the repayment is related to your level of income, so they are called 'income-contingent' loans.

If you have one of these loans, the Student Loans Company will notify your employer – they will not appear on your PAYE coding notice. Student loan repayments are based on the same earnings (i.e. excluding employee benefits) as NICs. Investment income is ignored unless it exceeds £2,000. You do not have to make repayments on the first £15,000 a year of income (£288 weekly, £1,250 monthly). The repayments are 9 per cent of anything above these figures.

HMRC help sheet IR235 *Calculation of student loan repayments* includes a calculator for loan repayments (available on the HMRC website).

Like National Insurance contributions, student loan repayments are non-cumulative and each pay period is treated separately. If, at the end of the year, you have paid too much, you can get a repayment from the Student Loans Company. If you want to pay more, you must pay the Student Loans Company direct.

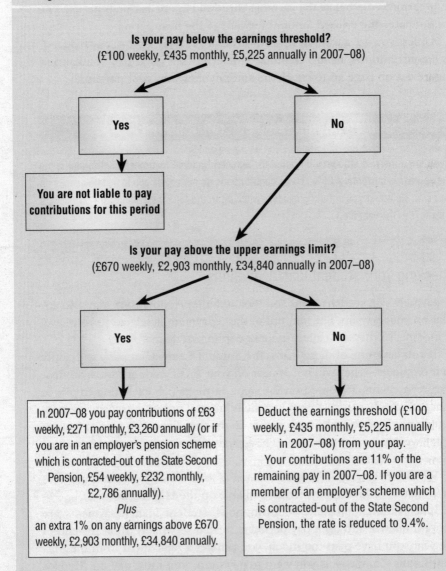

Figure 2.4: Checking the National Insurance on your payslip

Is your pay below the earnings threshold?
(£100 weekly, £435 monthly, £5,225 annually in 2007–08)

Yes

No

You are not liable to pay contributions for this period

Is your pay above the upper earnings limit?
(£670 weekly, £2,903 monthly, £34,840 annually in 2007–08)

Yes

No

In 2007–08 you pay contributions of £63 weekly, £271 monthly, £3,260 annually (or if you are in an employer's pension scheme which is contracted-out of the State Second Pension, £54 weekly, £232 monthly, £2,786 annually).
Plus
an extra 1% on any earnings above £670 weekly, £2,903 monthly, £34,840 annually.

Deduct the earnings threshold (£100 weekly, £435 monthly, £5,225 annually in 2007–08) from your pay.
Your contributions are 11% of the remaining pay in 2007–08. If you are a member of an employer's scheme which is contracted-out of the State Second Pension, the rate is reduced to 9.4%.

Example 2.3: **Checking National Insurance contributions**

Amina received total pay of £2,500 for the month of July 2007. Her employer does not offer an employer's pension scheme.

To check the National Insurance on her payslip, she deducts the first £435, which is the amount below the earnings threshold £2,500 − £435 = £2,065. As this all falls below the upper earnings limit of £2,903, she pays 11 per cent National Insurance, which works out at £2,065 × 0.11 = £227. (See Figure 2.4 opposite.)

In December Amina receives commission that brings her earnings up to £3,500. As this is above the upper earnings limit she pays 11 per cent on the amount between the earnings threshold (£435) and the upper earnings limit (£2,903), i.e. £2,468 × 0.11 = £271. She pays 1 per cent on her remaining earnings of £3,500 − £2,903 = £597, i.e. £6. Her December contributions are £271 + £6 = £277.

Who to contact about student loans

HMRC collect your student loan repayment, but it is administered by the Student Loans Company. HMRC only tell the Student Loans Company after the end of the tax year the amount of repayments deducted, so keep your payslips in case you need to query something. The Student Loans Company have a repayment helpline on 0870 240 6298.

Checking your deductions when things change

Starting or leaving a job

When you leave a job, your old employer is obliged, by law, to give you a form P45 which tells you (and your new employer) how much pay you have received in the tax year so far, how much tax you have paid, whether you are liable to pay student loan deductions and what your tax code was at leaving. You should give this to your new employer so that the right amount of tax can be deducted straight away.

If you don't have a P45 – either because this is your first job, or for some other reason – your new employer will ask you to fill in a form P46 which is sent off to your tax office (unless you are earning below the PAYE threshold and this is your only or main job). Your tax office will try to trace your records so they can give you your proper code. If they can't, they will send you a form P91 asking for details of your previous jobs. Until a correct code is issued for you, your employer will usually give you the 'emergency code' (see below).

The minimum wage

Employers must pay most employees at least £5.35 an hour, or £4.45 if aged under 22, or £3.30 for school-leavers under 18. From October 2007, the rate rises to £5.52 (£4.60 if aged 18–21, £3.40 if under 18). HMRC are responsible for enforcing this, and have a helpline (see the Fact file). Also see Department of Trade and Industry leaflet *National Minimum Wage: A short guide for workers*.

Avoid the 'emergency' code

If your employer does not know what your tax code is, you will be taxed on the 'emergency' code of 522L in 2007–08 (503L in 2006–07), or on code BR. Code BR gives you no allowance, while the emergency code gives you only the basic personal allowance for someone aged under 65. Unless this is your first job, the emergency code ignores any tax-free pay that might have built up before you started your new job. So it is in your interests to give your new employer your P45 or, if you do not have one, to get your tax code sorted out quickly.

Sick pay

Statutory sick pay, and any sick pay from an insurance scheme paid for by your employer, is taxable. However, if you pay the premiums for sick pay insurance yourself, the payouts are tax-free.

Your employer will deduct PAYE and National Insurance from any taxable sick pay, but because your sick pay is likely to be less than your normal pay you may get a refund of some of the tax paid so far. If you receive incapacity benefit for more than 28 weeks, the Department for Work and Pensions (DWP) may also deduct tax from that (see Chapter 8).

Maternity or paternity leave

Maternity and paternity pay, including statutory maternity, paternity or adoption pay, is taxable and your employer will deduct PAYE and National Insurance. If you do not have the right to return to work after the birth, your employer will give you a P45. Any payments made after receiving your P45 will have basic-rate tax deducted, so you may be able to claim a tax refund. When your child is born you may be entitled to Child Tax Credit (see Chapter 3).

A student with a holiday job

If you think your income over the year is likely to be below the basic personal allowance (£5,225 in 2007–08), your wages can be paid without deduction of tax. Ask your employer for form P38(S). Note that you cannot fill this in if you are on an overseas course, unless special arrangements apply, or if you are working part-time outside normal holiday times. (See the special pages for students on the HMRC website.)

Form P38(S) does not affect your National Insurance, which will be worked out in the normal way (although no contributions are due on earnings below £100 a week, £435 a month, in 2007–08).

Getting work through an agency

If a UK agency pays you direct, it will normally be responsible for operating PAYE and deducting NICs. If an employer pays you, it should operate PAYE. There are special rules for some types of worker, notably entertainers, models and homeworkers. (See the employment status section of HMRC's website.)

Having a second job

You will get a second tax code for the second job – see page 24.

Under the normal Class 1 National Insurance rules, you could end up paying contributions at the full rate of 11% on each job, even though overall your income is above the limit on which this rate is payable. So there is an annual maximum contribution, worked out as if all your earnings came from one job. If you expect to pay contributions on earnings of at least £670 a week from one job (or combination of jobs) throughout the 2007–08 tax year, you can ask to put off paying some of the contributions on your second job. You can settle up, or get a refund, when it is clear, at the end of the tax year, what you have earned.

If you are employed in one job and self-employed in another, you can apply to defer Class 2 or Class 4 contributions. Details are given in HMRC forms CA72A *Deferring employee Class 1 National Insurance contributions* and CA72B *Deferring self-employed National Insurance contributions*.

Becoming unemployed

If you are claiming Jobseeker's Allowance, you should give your P45 to the Jobcentre Plus when you claim. Jobseeker's Allowance is liable to income tax (up to a maximum), but no tax is deducted when it is paid.

Instead, when the claim ends or at the end of the tax year, the JobCentre Plus works out the tax on your total pay and Jobseeker's Allowance in the tax year so far. This may result in a refund of some of the tax you paid before stopping work. Any refund is paid either by the Jobcentre Plus, or by your new employer. You will get a P60U at the end of the tax year, or a P45U to hand to your new employer.

If you are unemployed but not claiming Jobseeker's Allowance or taxable incapacity benefit, you may also be entitled to a tax rebate. You can use repayment claim form P50 (from tax offices or the HMRC website), but you must wait four weeks after leaving your job before returning it.

Retiring

If you are retiring on an employer's or private pension you will receive either a P45, or a similar form (P160) or letter notifying you of your pay and tax in the tax year to date.

Your pension will be paid using your existing tax code until the end of the tax year or until your tax office reassesses your code, but you will not have to pay National Insurance. If you receive a P45, be sure to give it to the pension payer or you will be taxed on the emergency code.

To help your tax office reassess your code, you might be asked to complete a 'pension enquiry' form (P161). This asks what sources of income you have, and how you expect this to change in retirement.

Under your new code more tax may be deducted from your pension than you expect. This is because your code will also collect the tax on any state pensions, which are paid out before tax. But you may be entitled to a higher age-related allowance if you are aged 65 or over – see Chapter 5.

Being widowed

When somebody who is being taxed under PAYE dies, their P45 is sent to their tax office. If their widow or widower is entitled to a spouse's pension from an employer's or private pension scheme, the pension scheme will notify the widow or widower's tax office, and will pay the pension with tax deducted either as before, or at the basic rate from the whole amount (i.e. code BR), until a new tax code is issued.

You may be sent a 'pension enquiry' form (P161) to help your tax office decide what your new code should be.

What to tell HMRC

Your tax office will get most of the necessary information from your employer or pension payer. After the end of the tax year, they must tell HMRC how much they have paid each employee, how much tax they have deducted, and what taxable expenses and benefits they have paid you. Your employer must also tell your tax office during the tax year if you have changed your company car.

However, HMRC have other sources of information:

■ Banks and building societies must tell them how much interest they have paid in the tax year to each customer.
■ Businesses can be asked to give details of all payments made to non-employees for services rendered.

You may also need to give information to your tax office. For example, if you do not get a tax return:

■ You should notify your tax office within six months of the end of the tax year in question if you have a new source of taxable income or have made taxable capital gains, unless all your income is taxed under

PAYE or has tax taken off at source (e.g. savings interest), and you are not a higher-rate taxpayer.

■ If you have allowances or income in your tax code which vary in amount (such as property income or untaxed interest), you may receive a Tax Review form (P810) every so often, asking the questions necessary to adjust your code.

■ If you want to claim tax relief on work expenses, ask your tax office. You may be sent a claim form P87 or a Tax Review form (P810).

■ If you need to claim tax back (because too much tax has been deducted from investments), fill in a Tax Repayment form (R40). You can get this from your tax office, or contact the relevant HMRC helpline (see the Fact file). If you claim tax back in one year, you are likely to receive a Tax Repayment form (form R40) automatically in future years. Alternatively, you may be able to register to get your interest paid before tax (on form R85, see Chapter 10).

■ If you want to tell your tax office about changes in your circumstances which won't be notified by your employer, see below.

Things to tell your tax office

■ Change of address, or leaving the UK to live abroad.

■ Being widowed, getting married or divorced, or registering as a civil partner, if this affects your tax.

■ If you are claiming tax credits, there are some changes you must tell HMRC about – see page 45.

■ Starting to work for yourself; you must notify HMRC within three months.

■ New sources of untaxed income, e.g. from letting out a property.

■ Savings or investments that produce taxable income paid out without tax deducted.

■ If you are a higher-rate taxpayer and need to claim higher-rate tax relief on regular pension contributions or gifts to charity. Even if you get a tax return, if the amounts are substantial and you are on PAYE you might want to notify your tax office earlier so that they can be incorporated in your tax code as soon as possible.

■ Capital gains above a certain limit – see page 272.

Filling in a Tax Repayment form (R40)

The Tax Repayment form (R40) is a simple four-page form that collects the information necessary to assess whether you are entitled to a tax repayment. From April 2007 the form has been redesigned although it covers the same ground as the old version.

You do not need to wait until the end of the tax year to make your claim. You can either send it in as soon as you have received all your income for the year, or send in an interim claim, ticking box 1.6 on the front page. If you make an interim claim you should enclose an estimate of how much income of each type you expect to receive over the whole year, and you may be asked for the actual figures after the end of the tax year.

Note that you should not send your dividend vouchers, interest certificates or other documents with the form.

Claiming on behalf of someone else

Repayment claims may be signed on behalf of a child or an adult who is incapable of doing so. However, you must have legal authority to do this, as the parent or guardian of a child, the person authorised by the courts to look after the affairs of a mentally incapacitated adult, or the executor or administrator of the estate of someone who has died.

Example 2.4: Claiming back tax

Arnold is 72. His main income consists of pensions worth £7,500 a year. However, he also has savings interest of £1,000, which takes his total income for 2006–07 to £8,500. This exceeds his personal allowance by £1,220, but all his taxable income falls in the 10% band.

Because Arnold is liable to pay some tax, he cannot register to have his interest paid gross. However, the tax on his savings income is deducted at 20% (£200), although he is only liable to pay tax at 10% (£122). He gets a Tax Repayment form to claim back the £200 − £122 = £78 overpaid tax. See Figure 2.5 overleaf for how he fills it in.

Figure 2.5: Tax Repayment form (see Example 2.4)

HM Revenue & Customs

Tax Repayment Form

OUI

LONDON PROVINCIAL 99
POLAR HOUSE
SHACKLETON
TYNE & WEAR
SR1 RQ3

Tax reference 12345 67890

Date of issue 30 April 2007

MR A RIDLEY
FIRST COTTAGE
2 SECOND STREET
ANYTOWN
X12 2SZ

UK employment income, pensions and state benefits

2.1 Total pay from all employments, before tax taken off (from P60/P45)

£

2.2 Tax taken off box 2.1 income

£

2.3 State pension - enter the amount for the year (not the weekly, or 4 weekly, amount). *Do not include Attendance Allowance, Disability Living Allowance or Pension credits*

£ 7 5 0 0 . 0 0

2.4 Total of other taxable state benefits

£

2.5 Tax taken off any Taxable Incapacity Benefit included in box 2.4

£

2.6 Total of other pensions and retirement annuities, before tax was taken off

£

2.7 Tax taken off box 2.6

£

UK interest and dividends

With joint accounts, only enter **your share**.

3.1 Net interest paid by banks or building societies etc. - after tax taken off

£ 8 0 0 . 0 0

3.2 Tax taken off

£ 2 0 0 . 0 0

3.3 Gross amount - the amount before it was taxed

£ 1 0 0 0 . 0 0

3.4 If you get interest that has not been taxed at all, put the ... in this box, not in box 3.3

3.5 UK company dividends (but do not add on the tax credit)

£

3.6 Dividends from authorised unit trusts and open-ended investment companies (but do not add on the tax credit)

£

3.7 Stock dividends - enter the appropriate amount in cash/cash equivalent of the share capital - without any tax

£

Record-keeping

Make sure you keep your coding notices, payslips and P60s and (if you get one) your P11D or P9D, P45 or P160. Your employer can give you a duplicate of your P60 if you lose it, but is not allowed to give you a duplicate P45, though your tax office should have the information from the employer's regular returns. Also keep a copy of any completed forms you send your tax office, copies of any correspondence, and notes of any phone calls.

➡ For specific documents relating to employment, pensions, state benefits or savings and investments, see Chapters 6, 8 and 11.
➡ For how long to keep your records, see Chapter 1.

Tax-planning hints

Checking your PAYE coding notice
1 Check that all the allowances and reliefs you are claiming are shown.
2 Check any estimated amounts.
3 Check that the amount of any taxable benefit included in your tax code is consistent with the taxable value shown on the form P11D or P9D your employer gives you (see Chapter 6).
4 Check the figures for any state pension or other taxable state benefits in your tax code.
5 If your circumstances have changed, keep your tax office informed so that your code can be changed if necessary.
6 Remember that if you have more than one source of income taxed under PAYE, you can ask to have your allowances set against your income in any way you choose.
7 If your tax code is used to collect tax on other income, such as untaxed interest or rent, you can ask your tax office to collect it through your tax return instead. This may give you a bit longer to pay the tax, but is less convenient than PAYE.
8 Don't assume that the right amount of tax has been deducted under PAYE. After the end of the tax year, check the total deducted and contact your tax office if this is more or less than expected.

9 Any claims for a repayment should be processed within four weeks of reaching HMRC. If not, chase up your claim.

Checking up on your employer (or pension company)

10 Is your employer (or pension company) using the right tax code? The code will usually be shown on your payslip.

11 At the end of the tax year, make sure your P60 (or P45 when you leave) is consistent with your payslips.

12 If you suspect that your employer is failing to deduct PAYE or National Insurance correctly, or to hand it over to HMRC, contact your tax office, or ring the HMRC tax evasion hotline (see the Fact file).

13 HMRC are also responsible for enforcing some aspects of the National Minimum Wage, and have a special helpline (see the Fact file).

Minimising National Insurance

14 It is possible to pay too much National Insurance, if you have two jobs, or a job as well as your own business, or if you have paid contributions even though you are over state pension age (see page 6). If you think you might have paid too much, contact HMRC's National Insurance Contributions Office (whose address is in the Fact file) and ask for a refund.

15 Remember that National Insurance is not worked out on a cumulative basis – if your earnings dip below one of the contribution thresholds in one earnings period, you cannot carry the unused amount forward. Try to avoid irregular earnings if this is likely to affect you.

16 Married women paying a reduced contribution should check whether paying the standard amount would make sense. (See page 25.)

17 Check whether you can defer some National Insurance contributions if you have more than one job or are self-employed as well. (See page 30.)

Keeping things simple

18 To ensure that you pay the right amount of tax when you change jobs, give your P45 to any new employer straight away.

19 If you are a student with a holiday job, ask your employer if you are eligible to complete form P38(S) to get your payments made without tax deducted.

20 If you employ someone in your home, such as a nanny, you are liable to operate PAYE provided they earn more than the earnings threshold, but there is a simplified deduction scheme. Contact HMRC's helpline for new employers (see the Fact file).

21 If you are a non-taxpayer, check if you can receive interest without having tax deducted, by completing form R85 – see Chapter 11.

22 If you are claiming tax back, write 'Repayment' on the front of your tax return. HMRC should give it priority.

3

Tax credits

Child Tax Credit and Working Tax Credit are state benefits administered by HM Revenue & Customs (HMRC). They do not affect your tax bill, but they are means-tested and you may have to fill out and return an annual form. Tax credits had a difficult birth, with many people being overpaid and having to pay money back. But families with an annual income of as much as £70,000, or even more, can benefit from them.

An old credit you may still be able to claim

You cannot usually claim Child Tax Credit and Working Tax Credit more than three months in arrears. But in 2001–02 and 2002–03 there was a different type of tax credit, the Children's Tax Credit, which worked like an extra tax allowance. You can still claim this credit for those tax years if you had a child under 16 living with you but failed to claim, but for the 2001–02 tax year you must claim by 31 January 2008.

Does this affect you?

You can claim Child Tax Credit if you are responsible for a child aged under 16, or under 20 and completing a course of full-time non-advanced education or an approved training scheme. Working Tax Credit is for people who work at least 16 hours a week, and who either have a child, or are disabled, or are over 50 and returning to work after claiming benefits. Even if none of these apply, you can still claim if you are aged at least 25 and work at least 30 hours a week.

Note that if you are married, or living with someone as husband and wife (including same-sex couples), you have to claim jointly. If you have a child who lives with an ex-partner for some of the time, you must either decide between you who will claim tax credit for the child, or HMRC will decide which of you has 'main responsibility'.

Contact HMRC's tax credits helpline or see the HMRC website, which includes further information and a calculator. A useful leaflet is WTC2 *Child Tax Credit and Working Tax Credit – a guide.*

How the credit is calculated

The maximum credit depends on how many 'elements' you can claim (listed in Table 3.1 on page 41). The basic element of Working Tax Credit in 2007–08 is £1,730 for a full tax year, and the basic (or 'family') element of Child Tax Credit is £545, plus a further £1,845 for each child. You may also qualify for extra elements: for example, a further £1,700 if you have a partner or are a lone parent. Note, though, that these are the maximum *yearly* amounts:

■ Tax credits are awarded on a daily basis, so if your award starts one day before the end of the tax year, say, the maximum amount is divided by 365

■ Your award is reduced if your income is above a limit (see page 40).

If you qualify for Working Tax Credit and pay for childcare, you also get the childcare element of 80 per cent of your eligible costs. The maximum eligible cost is £175 per week for one child, £300 for more than one – so, the maximum weekly amount is £300 × 80% = £240. The care must be provided by a 'registered' or 'approved' person, such as a childminder or a nanny registered with the Childcare Approval Scheme. A relative does not usually qualify. See HMRC leaflet WTC5 *Help with the costs of childcare.* Nor can you claim if your employer pays – see page 97.

Means-testing and income limits

Your total credit is reduced, depending on your income – or, if you are married, or living with someone as husband and wife, on your *joint* income. This is broadly the same as your income for tax purposes, but excluding:

- Most taxable perks from your job, except the taxable value of some share-related benefits, a company car and car fuel, mileage allowances above set limits (see page 121), vouchers and cheap or free goods.
- The first £300 of the total of your pension income, investment income, property income and foreign income.

If your annual income is above £5,220, you lose first your Working Tax Credit, then the childcare element of Working Tax Credit, and finally the child element of the Child Tax Credit. If your circumstances do not entitle you to Working Tax Credit, and you can only claim Child Tax Credit, you start to lose credit once your income rises above £14,495 in 2007–08 (£14,155 in 2006–07). You only start to lose the family element once your income exceeds £50,000 (sometimes more – see Figure 3.1). You lose credits at the rate of 37 pence for each pound above the threshold (6.7 pence for each pound above £50,000 for the family element).

HMRC will send you an 'award notice' showing what you are due. But to get an idea, use the calculator on the HMRC website. Also see Figure 3.1 on page 42 and Example 3.1 on page 43. If you qualify, payment will be made directly into the account you have nominated.

How to keep your income low

You can increase your tax credits by making a pension contribution or Gift Aid donation, as these are deducted from your income for tax credit purposes. Remember to deduct the gross amount, not the net (after tax relief) amount you paid! But beware of making a taxable insurance gain as this will increase your income (see page 243).

Table 3.1: Child and Working Tax Credits – maximum annual amounts

Working Tax Credit	2006–07	2007–08
■ Basic element for people with children or a disability, or 50+ and returning to work, who work at least 16 hours a week; other people aged 25 or over who work at least 30 hours a week	£1,665	£1,730
■ Extra for couples and lone parents	£1,640	£1,700
■ Extra for people who work at least 30 hours a week (including couples with children who work 30 hours between them, provided one works at least 16 hours)	£680	£705
■ Extra for disabled workers	£2,225	£2,310
■ Extra for workers with a severe disability	£945	£980
■ Extra for people aged 50+ who have moved into employment from benefits in the last 3 months		
– working 16+ hours a week	£1,140	£1,185
– working 30+ hours a week	£1,705	£1,770

Working Tax Credit childcare element		
■ People paying for childcare – see page 39		
Percentage of maximum eligible amount	80%	80%
Maximum eligible weekly amount for:		
– one child	£175	£175
– more than one child	£300	£300

Child Tax Credit	2006–07	2007–08
Child Tax Credit child element		
■ Amount for each child	£1,765	£1,845
■ Extra for each disabled child	£2,350	£2,440
■ Extra for each child with severe disability	£945	£980

Child Tax Credit family element		
■ Families with children	£545	£545
■ Extra in year of baby's birth (up to first birthday)	£545	£545

Figure 3.1: Working out your tax credits for 2007–08

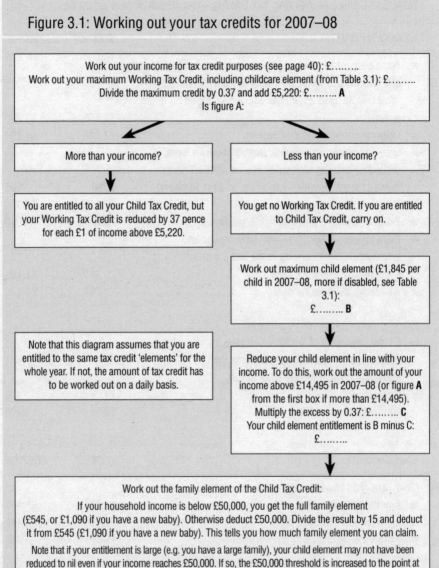

Work out your income for tax credit purposes (see page 40): £..........
Work out your maximum Working Tax Credit, including childcare element (from Table 3.1): £..........
Divide the maximum credit by 0.37 and add £5,220: £.......... **A**
Is figure A:

More than your income?

Less than your income?

You are entitled to all your Child Tax Credit, but your Working Tax Credit is reduced by 37 pence for each £1 of income above £5,220.

You get no Working Tax Credit. If you are entitled to Child Tax Credit, carry on.

Work out maximum child element (£1,845 per child in 2007–08, more if disabled, see Table 3.1):
£.......... **B**

Note that this diagram assumes that you are entitled to the same tax credit 'elements' for the whole year. If not, the amount of tax credit has to be worked out on a daily basis.

Reduce your child element in line with your income. To do this, work out the amount of your income above £14,495 in 2007–08 (or figure **A** from the first box if more than £14,495).
Multiply the excess by 0.37: £.......... **C**
Your child element entitlement is B minus C:
£..........

Work out the family element of the Child Tax Credit:

If your household income is below £50,000, you get the full family element (£545, or £1,090 if you have a new baby). Otherwise deduct £50,000. Divide the result by 15 and deduct it from £545 (£1,090 if you have a new baby). This tells you how much family element you can claim.

Note that if your entitlement is large (e.g. you have a large family), your child element may not have been reduced to nil even if your income reaches £50,000. If so, the £50,000 threshold is increased to the point at which all child element is lost.

Example 3.1: **Working out tax credits**

Susie and Simon have two children, aged two and four. They work full-time. For 2007–08 they get an initial tax credit award, based on their joint income for 2006–07 (£34,000). They pay £7,500 a year for childcare, well below the maximum eligible amount for two children (£300 a week). In 2007–08 they are initially entitled to Working Tax Credit of:

Basic element	£1,730
Extra for couples	£1,700
Extra for people working 30+ hours	£705
Childcare: £7,500 × 80%	£6,000
Total	£10,135

To work out their maximum income before their Working Tax Credit is reduced to zero, they divide this amount by 0.37, and add £5,220, to get £10,135 ÷ 0.37 = £27,391 + £5,220 = £32,611. As their 2006–07 income was more than this they get no Working Tax Credit in their initial award.

The maximum child element of their Child Tax Credit is £1,845 for each child, i.e. £3,690. But this is reduced by 37 pence for each pound of income above £32,611 or £14,495 (whichever is greater): £34,000 − £32,611 = £1,389 × 0.37 = £513.

This leaves them with child element of £3,690 − £513 = £3,177, but they qualify for the full family element, so their Child Tax Credit comes to £545 + £3,177 = £3,722.

How awards are decided

At the start of each tax year, your tax credits continue at the rate for the previous year on a provisional basis. In the summer you get a renewal pack to confirm your income for the previous year, which HMRC use to make an initial award based on the previous year's income – so your initial award for 2006–07 was based on 2006–07 tax credit rates, but your 2005–06 income. After the end of the tax year, when your actual income is known, your award may be recalculated. In previous years, you had to repay credits if your income increased by more than £2,500, but this led to hardship for many people. As a result the amount of extra income you can have without having to make a repayment was increased to £25,000 from 2006–07 (see Example 3.2 on page 45). So, if your actual 2006–07 income is:

■ less than your income for 2005–06 – your award will be recalculated using your actual income. You will get extra credit paid as a lump sum

■ not more than £25,000 higher than your 2005–06 income – your award is not recalculated (provided you have given HMRC the right information at the right time)

■ more than £25,000 higher than your 2005–06 income – your award is recalculated, using your actual income minus £25,000. You may have to repay tax credit. (See Example 3.2.)

Note that if you expect your income to fall, or rise by more than £25,000, you can ask during the year for the credit to be based on your estimated income.

During the tax year you may stop living with a partner or start living with a new one. If so, you must tell the Tax Credit office. Your award will stop and you will have to make a new claim. You must also tell the Tax Credit office about some other changes (see page 45), and if so, although your credits will not necessarily stop, the amount you get may change.

How overpayments are collected

You may receive too much tax credit either because your income rises, or because your circumstances changed, or because the Tax Credit office has made a mistake. Any overpayments that are identified during the tax year will reduce your tax credits for the rest of the year.

Overpayments from a previous tax year are usually collected by reducing future years' credit until the debt is paid off. Up to a quarter of your next year's credit can be lost in this way, or all of it if you are entitled to only the family element of Child Tax Credit. But people receiving the maximum award should lose no more than 10 per cent. From some point in 2007, these limits should also be applied automatically to overpayments identified during the tax year. But whenever an overpayment arises, you can ask for a top-up payment to help you budget.

Adjusting next year's credits is not possible if you are no longer entitled to credits, or if joint claimants have split up, or if single claimants have started living with someone. If so, you will have to make a payment direct to HMRC. You have 30 days to pay, although see below if you have problems paying.

Example 3.2: **Increases in your income**

Susie and Simon's tax credits for 2006–07 were initially calculated on the basis of the £30,000 they earned in 2005–06. In 2006–07 their income increased to £34,000. Because their income increased by less than £25,000, their award was not recalculated and they did not have to repay any credits. Their 2007–08 award was calculated on the basis of an income of £34,000 (see Example 3.1 on page 43), but they can have an income of up to £34,000 + £25,000 = £59,000 without having their award recalculated.

Problems with overpayments?

If you have to make repayments directly to HMRC, you can pay in 12 monthly instalments, or you might be able to negotiate longer. HMRC might write off the debt altogether if it was caused by their mistake and it was reasonable for you to think your award was right, or if repaying it would cause hardship, but it's up to you to ask. See form TC846 *Request to reconsider recovery of tax credits*, available from the tax credits helpline or the HMRC website, and HMRC Code of Practice COP26 *What happens if we have paid you too much tax credit?*. If the overpayment was due to an HMRC error, you should complain and claim compensation. See Code of Practice COP1 *Putting things right: how to complain.*

What to tell HMRC

To claim Working Tax Credit or Child Tax Credit, contact the tax credits helpline or get the forms from your tax office or Jobcentre Plus.

Changes will be picked up after the tax year through your annual review form, although HMRC plan to contact some groups of claimants sooner, and if your income goes up during the year it's best to tell HMRC at once so that they can get the next year's credits right to start with. You must tell the Tax Credit office during the tax year if:

- you reduce your hours of work to less than 30 hours a week, if you were working more than that, or to less than 16 hours if you were working between 16 and 30 hours a week
- you stop being responsible for a child – your child leaves home, say, or is over 16 and leaves full-time education, or goes to university
- you marry, start living with someone (including a same-sex partner), split up or your partner dies
- you go abroad for longer than eight weeks (or twelve weeks if you go abroad because of an illness, family illness or bereavement)
- you are claiming the childcare element and your childcare costs stop or go down by £10 a week or more for at least four weeks in a row.

There are penalties if you fail to notify a change within one month of being aware of it (three months before April 2007). And HMRC can open an enquiry into a tax credits claim up to one year and ten months after the end of the tax year (sometimes longer), so keep records of changes.

Tell HMRC promptly if things change

If a change in your circumstances increases your right to tax credits (e.g. you have a baby), the increase is backdated to the date of the change only if HMRC are told within three months. However, if you are not given the right amount because of an HMRC mistake, the increase can still be put into effect up to five years after the end of the tax year in question.

Changes that reduce your credit are always backdated, and you could end up having to repay a large sum if you don't notify HMRC as soon as possible.

Checking your annual review form

The annual review form that you receive after the end of the 2006–07 tax year has two purposes – to finalise your award for 2006–07, and to renew your claim for 2007–08. It will be pre-printed with the information the Tax Credit office has about you. If you received only the basic amount of tax credit (the 'family element') in 2006–07, all you need to do is to check that the information is still correct. If it is, you do not need to return the form and you will carry on getting tax credits. Otherwise, you should contact the tax credits helpline as soon as possible.

If you received more than the basic amount of tax credit, you will also get an Annual Declaration form asking about your income in 2006–07. You must provide details by 31 July 2007 (a month earlier than the return date in 2006). If you do not, your credits will stop and you may be penalised. If you do not have all the information you need, for example because you are self-employed and your accounts are not finalised, you can use estimates, but you must send the final figures in by 31 January 2008 at the latest, or the estimated figures will be used. And if you miss the 31 July deadline but have a good reason (such as ill-health), HMRC will renew your claim provided you get your forms in as soon as you can, and before 31 January.

When completing the forms, note that:

■ You must return one Annual Declaration for each 'award period'. (You may have had more than one award period in 2006–07 if, say, you split up with your partner and had to make a new claim as a single person.)
■ You should enter your income for the whole of the 2006–07 tax year on each Annual Declaration, even if the 'award period' is shorter.
■ Photocopied forms are not accepted. If necessary, ask for a new form. Alternatively, you can renew your claim over the phone.

Record-keeping

There are no formal rules on keeping records, but a reassessment of your income for tax purposes may also affect a tax credits award, so you should keep the following for the length of time described on page 13:

■ Records of any changes in circumstances (see page 45).
■ Full records of childcare costs (see page 39).

- All correspondence relating to any tax credits claim.
- Records of your (and your partner's) income for each year of claim.
- A record of any conversation with the tax credits helpline, including the date and time. Calls are recorded and it may be possible to trace them in case of disputes later on.
- A copy of any claim and all your tax credit award notices.
- Records of tax credit payments you have received.

Tax-planning hints

1   If your income is just at the level where you lose tax credits, paying a pension contribution or Gift Aid donation could reduce your income enough to qualify.

2   If you are not sure whether your income will entitle you to tax credits, claim anyway. You may not get anything now, but the credit depends on your annual income and you cannot backdate your claim beyond three months. However, once you have claimed you must tell the Tax Credit office about certain changes (see page 45).

3   Another reason for claiming Child Tax Credit is that children will get a higher Child Trust Fund payment (see page 234) if their parents are eligible for, and claiming, the full rate of Child Tax Credit.

4   If you are asked to repay tax credits, remember that HMRC may give you time to pay, provide top-up payments or (in a few cases) waive repayments (see page 45).

5   Joint claimants are both liable for overpayments – if one partner cannot or will not pay, the other may have to repay the whole amount. Couples who split up should make arrangements to cover potential overpayments.

6   Information that you give in a tax credits claim can be used to cross-check your income tax. Be consistent.

7   If you do not understand your tax credits award notice, ask the tax credits helpline for an explanation. More detailed calculations than those on the award notice should be available – but only if you ask.

8   Act promptly. The timescales for giving information are much shorter than for tax, and HMRC can charge penalties for delay of up to £300, plus a possible £60 a day for further delay.

4

If you get a tax return

A self-assessment tax return is not just a form to fill in: it brings you within a system of paying tax, with its own strict timetables, record-keeping requirements and penalties for non-compliance. 'Self-assessment' shifts the responsibility for working out your tax on to you, although Her Majesty's Revenue & Customs (HMRC) will do the sums for you if you send your return in on time.

Even if you get a tax return, your income may still be taxed largely under PAYE, so you may find it helpful to read Chapter 2 first. However, if you have income that is not taxed under PAYE, you may have to make 'payments on account'. These are twice-yearly payments of your tax, due at the end of each January and July, estimated on the basis of the previous year's tax bill. You will have to manage your financial affairs so that you are able to make these payments.

Does self-assessment affect you?

Not everyone gets a self-assessment tax return. You should always get one if you are a director of a limited company, self-employed or in partnership, or if you are an employee or pensioner with an annual income of £100,000 or more, or investment income of £10,000 or more (before tax).

You usually also have to submit a tax return if you have untaxed income, e.g. from investments, land or property or from overseas, although it is sometimes possible to collect the tax by adjusting your tax code, if you have one. Even if you are not sent a tax return, you must tell your tax office by 5 October 2007 if, in the 2006–07 tax year, you had any new source of taxable income that they do not already know about, or if you became liable to higher-rate tax on taxed investment income, or if you made a taxable capital gain.

You may also find yourself having to deal with a tax return if you are aged 65 and over and get a reduced age-related allowance (see Chapter 5). However, you may get the short tax return or a P810 Tax Review form (see page 32) or, if you are claiming back tax, you may be sent a Tax Repayment form (R40) instead – this is covered in Chapter 2.

The short tax return

There is a simplified four-page return for people with relatively straightforward affairs, such as some employees and pensioners and self-employed people with turnover under £15,000. If you are sent one, exactly the same deadlines apply as for the full tax return, except that the form does not expect you to work out the tax, and so it is best to file it by 30 September so that your tax office can do it for you. You cannot file it over the internet. If you prefer, you can opt to complete the full tax return, either on paper or online.

How the tax is worked out

Submitting your return

As well as your income tax, the full tax return covers capital gains tax, Class 4 National Insurance contributions (payable by the self-employed) and student loan repayments.

There are two steps to submitting your return:

■ *Enter the necessary information on the return itself.* There is a 'Filling in your tax return' section at the end of this and later chapters.
■ *Work out the amount of tax due.* You can delegate this to HMRC or do

the calculation yourself, for which you can use either HMRC's tax calculation guide that is sent out with the return, or one of the computer-based returns now available. If you file your tax return using the internet, the calculation is done automatically.

Note that you do not always get a paper tax return. If you use a computerised return or HMRC's Filing by internet service (see overleaf), or your tax adviser has done so on your behalf, you may get a *Notice to Complete a Tax Return* (SA316) instead of a full return the following tax year.

You must normally send in your return for the 2006–07 tax year by 31 January 2008 (see Table 4.1 on page 53). But it is worth getting it in early:

■ HMRC will work out the tax for you, provided you get your return in by 30 September (or within two months if the return was issued after 31 July). If you send it in later, they will still do it, but not necessarily before you have to pay any tax due, in which case you would have to estimate the amount.

■ If you owe tax of less than £2,000 and you are taxed under PAYE, you can ask HMRC to collect this through your tax code over the next tax year, rather than paying it in one go. You should get your return in by 30 September (if you use a paper return) to give them time to organise this. After this date it may still be possible, provided you get your return in by 30 December, but cannot be guaranteed. If you make your return using the internet, the deadline is 30 December.

■ From the 2007–08 tax year, the government plans to bring forward the final date for sending in a paper tax return to 31 October 2008. If you file online, the deadline will remain 31 January 2009.

Can you stop returns being sent?

Tax offices review taxpayers' records in January or February each year to decide whether to send a return in April. If your circumstances have changed, send back your previous year's return (or notify your tax office) early so that the information is logged before the review. You should get a letter from your tax office if you no longer need to complete a return.

Filing by internet

Most people can complete their returns using HMRC's free internet service. This doesn't save you any tax, but your return – and any tax repayment – should be processed more quickly and accurately, your tax will be worked out automatically, and if you have made an obvious mistake your return will be rejected immediately. You can also view your statements of account online. There are full details on the HMRC website.

Penalties, surcharges and interest

Penalties are charged if you get your return in late – usually £100, but possibly more. Surcharges are extra amounts you have to pay if you fail to pay your tax on time. And interest is charged on any amount paid late, including surcharges and penalties, so you may prefer to pay the amount demanded even if you are appealing against it. See Table 4.1 opposite.

You have 30 days in which to appeal against a penalty or surcharge if you think it is incorrect or if you have a reasonable excuse (see below). If your return was submitted late but the amount of tax outstanding on 31 January was less than the £100 penalty, the penalty should be reduced to the amount of the tax. However, this does not apply to the penalty of up to £60 a day which may be charged for very late returns (even if no tax is due), or to the penalty charged if your return is over a year late.

Acceptable and unacceptable excuses

HMRC will not accept the following as an excuse for late returns or late payment of tax: pressure of work, a failure by your tax adviser, lack of information (you can send provisional figures if necessary), difficulty with the tax return, or inability to pay (ask about 'time to pay' arrangements). An acceptable excuse might be an unforeseen postal strike, loss of your records by fire, flood or theft, or serious illness (if you can show that you would otherwise have met the deadline).

Table 4.1: Self-assessment timetable for 2006–07 tax year

31 January 2007	If you are liable to make payments on account, your first instalment of tax for 2006–07 is due. If you don't pay, interest starts to clock up on the outstanding amount.
April 2007	Tax returns for the 2006–07 tax year are issued.
31 May 2007	Your employer must give you your end-of-year statement (P60) by now. You need this to complete your return.
6 July 2007	Your employer must give you your statement of taxable expenses and benefits (P11D or P9D) by now.
31 July 2007	Second instalment of tax for 2006–07 due. If you don't pay, interest is charged on the outstanding amount.
30 September 2007	Get your return in by this date if you are not filing by internet and you want HMRC to work out the tax for you or you want tax of under £2,000 collected through PAYE.
5 October 2007	If you do not get a tax return you must tell HMRC by this date if you had taxable income in 2006–07 on which tax was not collected at source, or taxable capital gains.
30 December 2007	Latest date for filing your return if you are filing by internet and you want tax of under £2,000 collected through PAYE.
31 January 2008 (filing date)	You must return your 2006–07 tax return by this date (or within three months of the date of issue if the return was issued after the end of October), or pay a £100 penalty. There is a further £100 penalty if the return is still outstanding on 31 July 2008, but HMRC can apply to charge a daily penalty of up to £60 instead. You must pay any tax still outstanding for 2006–07 by this date, or pay a surcharge of 5 per cent of the tax outstanding on 28 February 2008, and a further 5 per cent of any tax still owed on 31 July 2008 (plus interest).
31 January 2009	Latest date for amending your return, if necessary. Your tax office must tell you by now if they intend to open an 'enquiry'. They have longer to do so if you sent your return in late or amended it, if further information comes to light, or if you have been negligent or fraudulent. If your return for 2006–07 is still not in, you can be penalised an amount equal to the tax payable.

After your tax office gets your return

HMRC do not acknowledge receipt of a return, although they will let you know when it has been processed. However, if you have made a very basic mistake, such as failing to sign and date it, your return may be rejected altogether. You will have to correct and resubmit it by the 31 January filing date, unless it is rejected after 17 January, in which case you have 14 days to resubmit it.

Once your tax return has been logged, an initial check is run for obvious mistakes, such as inconsistencies, faulty arithmetic and so on:

■ *If HMRC find a mistake,* they have nine months to correct any obvious mistakes and inform you. If you disagree with a correction, you have the right to reject it.

■ *If you find a mistake on your return* you can correct it without explaining why, if you write to your tax office within 12 months of the filing date (i.e. by 31 January 2009 for the 2006–07 tax year). But this won't protect you from HMRC action if they think you have been fraudulent or negligent. If you have overpaid tax due to a mistake or omission, you can claim relief up to five years after the filing date.

In addition to the initial check, your return may be one of around 75,000 selected for further checking. This is called an 'enquiry'. An enquiry may be instigated because something looks odd, or entirely at random. You aren't told why HMRC have chosen your return, although the questions they ask might identify particular areas of interest.

You need to keep all the documentation backing up the information in your return in case you are involved in an enquiry (and you have a legal duty to do so in any case, see Chapter 1). HMRC have a code of practice for how enquiries are run, COP11 *Self Assessment. Local office enquiries,* and leaflet IR160 *Enquiries under self assessment* explains what happens at the end of an enquiry. However, you should consider getting professional help in responding to the enquiry. (Tips on choosing a tax adviser are given in Chapter 1.) You can claim reasonable professional costs as a business expense, unless the enquiry uncovers fraudulent or negligent behaviour on your part.

Don't count your chickens

HMRC have 12 months from the filing date to notify you if they are going to open an enquiry into your return – that is, by 31 January 2009 for returns for the 2006–07 tax year. They have longer if they suspect fraud or negligence. So even if your return passed through the initial check without problems, don't assume that everything has been settled, and don't throw away any supporting paperwork.

Agreeing your tax liability

HMRC will only send their tax calculation (on form SA302) to you if you have asked them to work out your tax, or if they disagree with your calculation.

If you have problems reconciling the calculation with your tax return, contact your tax office without delay. If your query is not resolved by the payment deadline pay the tax bill anyway – you will get a refund if one turns out to be due, whereas if you don't pay you could find yourself faced with interest and possibly a surcharge.

Check HMRC's calculation notice

Even if you ask HMRC to work out your tax for you, it is worth checking any calculation they send you on form SA302. Although computers have largely taken over, your information is transferred to the computer manually (unless you file by internet or receive the short tax return). Check that all your information has been carried across correctly. The SA302 may also reveal a mistake you have made.

How the tax is paid (or repaid)

A tax account is opened for everyone who is sent a tax return. You will get a statement of your account when there are changes to the items on it, or when a tax payment is due.

- *If HMRC owe you money,* you will be sent a refund (plus interest) if you have ticked Question 19 on page 8 of the main tax return, or if you write to your tax office asking for one. Otherwise, the money is credited to your account, plus interest.
- *If you owe HMRC money,* it will be collected by adjusting your tax code, if you have income taxed under PAYE and you owe less than £2,000. If you want this to happen, make sure you do not tick box 23.1 on page 9, and get your tax return in by 30 September, or 30 December if filing by internet. Otherwise, the tax is due for payment on the same day as the latest date for sending back your return – that is, by 31 January 2008 for the 2006–07 tax year.

Payments on account

Unless the bulk of your income tax can be collected at source through PAYE, you have to pay tax in instalments, called 'payments on account'. Note that these apply only to income tax and Class 4 National Insurance contributions – capital gains tax is paid in one lump sum on 31 January following the end of the tax year.

Each payment on account is half of your previous year's income tax bill (excluding tax deducted at source). However, you do not have to make payments on account if more than 80 per cent of your tax bill for the previous tax year was met from tax paid at source, or if the tax *not* deducted at source was less than £500. So you are unlikely to have to make payments on account if you are an employee or pensioner, and your pay or pension is your main source of income.

You can claim to reduce your payments on account if you expect your tax bill to fall (see page 60).

Payments on account are made on 31 January during the tax year, and 31 July just after the end of the tax year, with a final 'balancing' payment on 31 January following the end of the tax year (by which time your tax return should be in and your final tax bill calculated). If your return is issued after 31 October, you have three months from the date of issue to make your final payment.

If you are registered to file your tax return over the internet, you can also view your self-assessment statements online.

Payments on account – a summary

If you are liable to make payments on account for the 2006–07 tax year:

■ The first payment on account was due on 31 January 2007 (half your tax bill for 2005–06 not met at source).

■ The second payment on account is due on 31 July 2007 (half your tax bill for 2005–06 not met at source).

■ If these two payments come to *less* than your total tax bill for 2006–07, a final, balancing payment will be due on 31 January 2008 (unless it is under £2,000 and can be collected through your tax code). If they come to *more* than your tax bill for 2006–07, you will be due a repayment instead, which can either be paid out to you or set against your first payment on account for the 2007–08 tax year.

Example 4.1: Calculating payments on account

Sam is a self-employed plumber. His tax bill for 2005–06 was £8,000, including his Class 4 National Insurance contributions. He made no taxable capital gains. Sam's payments on account for 2006–07 are £8,000 ÷ 2 = £4,000 each, which he pays in January 2007 and July 2007. However, 2006–07 turns out to be a good year and Sam's tax bill comes to £10,000. He has a further £10,000 − £8,000 = £2,000 to pay by 31 January 2008.

On 31 January 2008 Sam must also make his first payment on account for 2007–08. This is half his tax bill for 2006–07, that is £10,000 ÷ 2 = £5,000. The total tax due on 31 January is therefore £2,000 + £5,000 = £7,000.

Planning your tax payments

The final payment for one year overlaps with the first payment on account for the next. If your income is rising, year on year (or if you pay less tax at source, or expect to pay capital gains tax), you need to be careful to put enough cash aside to meet the January payment.

Understanding your self-assessment statement

A simpler version of the statement of account, now called a 'self-assessment statement', has been introduced (see Example 4.2). The new version only shows the transactions on your account over the period of the statement, and the balance at the beginning and end of the period, like a credit card statement. However, it follows the same principles as the full statement, and you can opt for the full statement if you wish. This is what some of the entries on the simple statement mean.

1 *Brought forward.* This is the balance shown at the end of your previous statement.
2 *Payment.* What you have paid, and when.
3 *Interest/repayment supplement.* If you have been late paying your tax, the amount of interest incurred will appear. If you have overpaid, you might see a 'repayment supplement' instead – HMRC-speak for the interest you get if you have overpaid tax.
4 *Balancing payment/overpayment.* A balancing payment will be shown in your January statement if you still owe tax for the previous tax year (after deducting payments on account). If you paid too much, it will appear as an overpayment.
5 *Payments on account/Claims to reduce.* The full amount of each payment on account is shown even if you have made a claim to reduce your payments – but the amount of the reduction will appear as a credit.
6 *Amount to pay/You have overpaid.* If you have outstanding tax that cannot be collected through PAYE, a payslip will be attached. If you have paid too much, the money usually stays in your account, to be set against any future tax, unless you ask for it to be paid to you. To claim a repayment, either tick Question 19 on the tax return or contact your tax office.
7 *Adjustment.* An adjustment made to your return after it is sent in may change your balancing payment (if one is due). It may also affect your payments on account for the following year, in which case the amount of the adjustment is split equally between your January and July payments.

Example 4.2: **Understanding your self-assessment statement**

In December 2006 Steven received the statement below, showing that he owed HMRC £5,524.91 (6). This is how the amount was calculated.

The amount brought forward (1) is Steven's second payment of account for 2005–06. This was due at the end of July, but Steven paid it late, in August (2) and as a result he is charged interest for the period between 31 July and 27 August (3).

Steven's payments of account for 2005–06 came to less than the tax owed, and as a result he has a balancing payment to make in January 2007 of £1,478.54 (4). At the same time he must make his first payment on account for the 2006–07 tax year, which is £4,544.18 (5). However, because he expects his income to fall slightly in 2006–07, in his tax return he made a claim to reduce his payment on account by £500 (5). So in total he is liable to pay the balancing payment and payment on account, plus late payment interest, but minus the reduction in his payment on account – £5,524.91 in total (6).

HM Revenue & Customs

Self Assessment Statement

Date	Description	Tax Due	Credits	Balance
	Brought forward from previous statement ❶			3,804.91
26 Aug 06	Payment - thank you ❷		3,804.91	0.00
26 Aug 07	Interest ❸	2.19		
31 Jan 07	Balancing payment due for year 05/06	1,478.54 ❹		
31 Jan 07	1st payment on account due for year 06/07 ❺	4,544.18		
		6,024.91		6,024.91
31 Jan 07	Claim to reduce 1st payment on account for 2006-07 ❺		500.00	5,524.91
	Amount to pay			**5,524.91**
	Amount due by 31 Jan 07			**5,524.91** ❻

HMRC 06/06

SA300 (Shipley)

Please make sure that your payment reaches us by the date it becomes due. You will be charged interest if you pay late.

▼   Please detach payslip here when making payment direct to the Accounts Office or by Girobank   ▼

Reducing your payments on account

If your taxable income is falling, you can claim to reduce each payment on account to half of your anticipated tax bill (ignoring capital gains tax). You can claim either in Question 18 of your tax return, or by completing form SA303 that should come with your statement of account.

Your tax office will not 'approve' your claim – you simply go ahead and pay the reduced amount – but your claim may be rejected if you have not given a valid reason for reducing your payment. Note also that:

- If your tax bill turns out to be more than you anticipate, you will have to pay interest on the difference between the full payment and the amount you actually paid, from the date the payment was due – and at a higher rate than you receive if you have overpaid tax.
- If you make a fraudulent or negligent claim to reduce your payments on account to less than they realistically should be, HMRC can charge you a penalty equal to the extra tax that should have been paid.

Example 4.3: Claiming to reduce your payments on account

Sam had an unusually good year in 2006–07 (see Example 4.1 on page 57) and his tax bill of £10,000 means that he should make payments of account for 2007–08 of £10,000 ÷ 2 = £5,000 in January and July 2008. However, he was off work in September 2007 after an accident. He thinks this will bring his tax bill for 2007–08 down to about £7,000. In his tax return for the 2006–07 tax year he makes a claim to reduce his payments on account to £7,000 ÷ 2 = £3,500.

Accounting for interest

If you receive a self-assessment statement and you know your payment is overdue, you might want to pay a bit extra to cover any interest clocked up from the date of the statement to the date you pay. Your tax office should be able to give you an idea of how much.

What to tell HMRC

Once you are within the self-assessment system, HMRC send you the forms they think you need, with notes to help you fill them in. The full tax return is ten pages long, plus supplementary pages to cover such matters as capital gains, employment, self-employment and rental income. HMRC are planning to redesign the return, but currently this is only at the pilot stage.

Check that you have all the supplementary pages you need, by looking at the questions on page 2 of the main return. You can get extra pages from the HMRC Orderline or website (see the Fact file), or you can use a computerised tax return.

If you get the short tax return (see page 50), remember that this does not cover every type of income you might get, or deduction you can claim, and it remains your responsibility to tell HMRC about anything that it does not cover, and to complete the full return if necessary. Read the notes carefully and if in doubt contact your tax office.

> Tips for completing your tax return

- The hard part of completing your tax return is collecting the necessary information. It helps to gather it together as it comes in, in a separate file for each tax year.
- Work on a rough copy first and check it before completing the real thing.
- Forget the pennies – you are allowed to round to the nearest £ in your favour. This means rounding income down and deductions up.
- Use HMRC's help sheets. Many include work sheets to help with calculations.
- Use the 'additional information' boxes to explain anything that might look odd or any major changes from last year.
- When calculating your tax, take into account amounts already paid or included in your tax code. When taking information from your statements of account be careful to use figures for the right tax year (excluding balancing payments for an earlier tax year).
- Give yourself plenty of time. Avoid a last-minute panic in late January.
- Consider filing by internet to get the calculation done automatically – but you will need to allow time to register for the service before you can use it.

Calculating your own tax

Unless you have asked HMRC to work out your tax, you will have to tell them how much you think you owe. This includes income tax, capital gains tax, Class 4 National Insurance (the type payable on business profits – you do not need to calculate any other type of National Insurance), and student loan repayments.

HMRC send a tax calculation guide with tax returns to help you, but this will not help people with capital gains and some types of income (listed on the front of the guide). A comprehensive tax calculation guide is available from the HMRC Orderline and website, but filing online (see page 52) is much easier.

Filling in your tax return

Start by filling in page 2 – a checklist of the kinds of income you have, and the supplementary pages you need. Then go on to:

- ⇒ Questions 10 and 12, for savings and investments – see Chapter 11.
- ⇒ Question 11, dealing with pensions and benefits – see Chapter 8.
- ⇒ Question 13, covering any other income that doesn't fit in elsewhere.
- ⇒ Questions 14, 15 and 16, for tax reliefs and allowances you can claim – see Chapter 5, and Chapter 8 for pension contributions.
- ⇒ Questions 17 to 24, covering other information needed – see below.

Question 13 – Other taxable income

See the notes to the return for what to enter here. This includes some dividends from a UK Real Estate Investment Trust (see Chapter 9), odd bits of freelance income that do not amount to a trade and income received after a business has ceased. You may be able to deduct allowable expenses and losses, but first read HMRC help sheet IR325 *Other taxable income* as expenses and losses can only be deducted from some types of income.

You may also have to enter something here if you are caught by the 'pre-owned assets' rules. These stop people avoiding inheritance tax by giving something away, but continuing to benefit from it (see page 283).

Question 17 – Student loan repayments

Tick the 'Yes' box in this question only if you were liable to make *income-contingent* student loan repayments during the 2006–07 tax year. However, if your loan is likely to be repaid in full before 31 January 2008 see the notes to the tax return. (See pages 6 and 25 for more on these loans.)

■ Enter repayments deducted from your salary on your employment supplementary pages, if you are an employee (see Chapter 6).
■ Enter the overall amount of repayments due in box 18.2A, if you are calculating your own tax. Use HMRC Help Sheet IR235 *Calculation of student loan repayments on an income-contingent student loan.*

Question 18 – Do you want to calculate your tax?

Tick the 'Yes' box if you want to calculate your own tax, Class 4 National Insurance contributions and student loan repayment. If you send in your return after 30 September, you can still tick 'Yes', but HMRC may not be able to tell you how much tax you owe by the date you must pay it (31 January). If so, you should make an estimate of tax owed and pay it by the deadline in order to avoid being penalised. You must tick 'Yes' if you are filing by internet, but the programme will work out the tax for you.

The other boxes in this question need to be completed only if you tick 'Yes'. HMRC's tax calculation guide will help you work out the tax to enter in boxes 18.2A, 18.2B, 18.3 and 18.7, so go through that first. Box 18.2C (pension charges) applies only if you have exceeded the limits for pension savings (see page 185).

Boxes 18.1 and 18.2 Underpaid tax included in your tax code
If you are taxed under PAYE, any tax outstanding from one tax year may be collected by adjusting your tax code for a future year. Amounts to go in box 18.1 will be shown as 'Unpaid tax' on your most recent coding notice for 2006–07 (P2). (See Example 4.4 overleaf.)

Box 18.2 applies only if your tax code for 2006–07 was reduced during the year, for example because you got a new taxable employment benefit. This may result in an underpayment, but this will normally be collected by adjusting your final tax bill. If so, no entry needs to be made here. You only

Figure 4.1: Completing Question 18 (see Example 4.4)

Q18 Do you want to calculate your tax and, if appropriate, Class 4 National Insurance contributions and Student Loan Repayment? **YES** ✓	Use your Tax Calculation Guide then fill in boxes 18.1 to 18.8 as appropriate.
• Underpaid tax for earlier years included in your tax code for 2006-07	**18.1** £ *340*
• Underpaid tax for 2006–07 included in your tax code for 2007–08	**18.2** £
• Student Loan Repayment due	**18.2A** £
• Class 4 NICs due	**18.2B** £
• Pension charges due - enter the amount from box 32 of the Pensions supplementary Page	**18.2C** £
• Total tax, Class 4 NICs and Student Loan Repayment due for 2006–07 **before** you made any payments on account (put the amount in brackets if an overpayment.)	**18.3** £ *780*
• Tax due calculated by reference to earlier years - see the notes on page 10 of your Tax Calculation Guide (SA151W).	**18.4** £
• Reduction in tax due calculated by reference to earlier years - see the notes on page 10 of your Tax Calculation Guide (SA151W).	**18.5** £
• Tick box 18.6 if you are claiming to reduce your 2007–08 payments on account. Make sure you enter the **reduced** amount of your first payment in box 18.7. Then, in the 'Additional information' box, box 23.9 on page 10, say why you are making a claim	**18.6**
• Your first payment on account for 2007–08 (please include the pence.)	**18.7** £
• Any 2007–08 tax you are reclaiming now	**18.8** £

Example 4.4: Completing Question 18

George underpaid £340 tax in 2004–05. This affected his tax return for several years.

September 2005	Sends in 2004–05 return, showing £340 underpayment in box 18.3.
January 2006	Receives 2006–07 coding notice, showing adjustment to his tax code to collect £340 underpaid tax.
2006–07 tax year	£340 tax deducted from George's salary under PAYE.
September 2007	Sends in 2006–07 tax return, showing £340 in box 18.1 (see Figure 4.1). Because part of his 2006–07 PAYE has gone to pay tax from an earlier year, the amount in box 18.1 has to be added to the £440 tax he owes for 2006–07 and the result – £780 – shown in box 18.3.
January 2008	Receives 2008–09 coding notice, showing adjustment to collect £780 underpaid tax.

need to make an entry here if your 2007–08 tax code has been adjusted to collect the estimated underpayment. (HMRC help sheet IR208 *Payslips and coding notices* tells you what to look for.)

Boxes 18.4 and 18.5 Tax calculated by reference to earlier years

You will have something to enter here if you want income or expenditure for the 2006–07 tax year treated as if earned or incurred in an earlier year, thus affecting that year's tax bill. This applies if you have received a refund of foreign tax for which you have already claimed tax credit relief (see page 221), if you are carrying back business losses or receipts (see page 155) or if you are a farmer, writer or artist claiming to average your income over several years (see HMRC help sheets IR224 and IR234). Enter the difference that the amount carried back has made to your tax bill for the earlier year, in box 18.4 if you owe extra tax, in box 18.5 if it is a tax saving.

Boxes 18.6 and 18.7 Claiming to reduce a payment on account

Tick box 18.6 if you are claiming to reduce your payments on account due in January and July 2008. Write the reasons for your claim in the 'Additional information' box on page 10 (e.g. your income has fallen), and write the reduced amount of your first payment in box 18.7.

Box 18.8 2007–08 tax you are reclaiming now

You may have something to enter here if you make a trading loss after 5 April 2007, but you want to claim tax relief for it in your 2006–07 tax return. You need to work out the difference this makes to your tax for the 2006–07 tax year and enter the saving here. In some circumstances, you can also treat a loss you make on some types of shares in the same way, in which case you should have an entry at box 8.13B of the Capital Gains pages (see page 277).

Question 19 – Do you want to claim a repayment?

If you don't tick this, any tax overpaid will be set against a future tax liability on your statement of account. This may be a problem if your tax stops being collected through self-assessment. Use section 19B to say whether you want a repayment to be credited to your bank or building society account, or a payment to be sent to your nominee (such as a tax adviser).

HMRC do not send repayments of less than £10, unless requested.

You can also ask HMRC to give your repayment directly to a charity, by ticking box 19A. If it turns out that you made a mistake and are not due a repayment, HMRC can reclaim the donation from you, so it is sensible to enter a maximum donation in box 19A.2. Your details will not be given to the charity unless you tick box 19A.5. The charity must have a code number – available from the HMRC helpline or website, from tax offices or from the charity itself – which you enter in box 19A.3. Also tick box 19A.4 if you are a taxpayer and want to claim Gift Aid (see page 81).

Common mistakes on tax returns

- Failing to sign and date your tax return, if you are sending in a paper return
- Ticking one of the 'Yes' boxes on page 2, suggesting that you need supplementary pages, but failing to send in the correct pages
- Entering notes such as 'see accounts' in boxes, rather than giving figures
- Failing to sign box 19B.14 if you want a repayment to be sent to a nominee
- Ticking box 18.6 to reduce your payments on account, but failing to give a reason
- Entering underpaid tax for the wrong period in Box 18.1 or 18.2 – if in doubt, check with your tax office.

Question 20 – Have you already had any 2006–07 tax refunded?

You may have received a tax refund part way through the tax year, for example if you are a non-taxpayer and reclaimed tax deducted from a savings account, or if you became unemployed. Enter any such refunds here, including amounts that have not actually been paid to you, but set against tax you owe. However, only include tax which has been refunded directly by HMRC or by your Jobcentre Plus – tax refunds from other sources (such as your employer) will be taken into account in your P60 or other end-of-year statement.

Questions 21 and 22 – Personal details

This information keeps your tax record up to date.

Question 23 – Additional information

Box 23.1 – Tick if you do not want 2006–07 tax collected through PAYE

If you pay tax under PAYE, you submit your tax return by 30 September (30 December if you file by internet) and you owe less than £2,000, your tax office will collect it by adjusting your 2008–09 tax code, unless you tick here to say that you would prefer to pay it in a lump sum. See page 51.

Box 23.1A – Tick if you do not want 2007–08 tax collected through PAYE

If your return includes income that was paid out without tax deducted (such as untaxed interest, rental income, or casual earnings), HMRC will assume that it will continue in 2007–08 and adjust your 2007–08 tax code accordingly, if you have a job or private pension taxed under PAYE. But if you don't want them to do this tick box 23.1A. Note that HMRC will not include untaxed income of more than £10,000 in your code, unless you have agreed to this.

Box 23.2 – Tick if this tax return contains provisional figures

HMRC accept provisional amounts only if you have taken 'all reasonable steps' to get the final figures. You need to explain under 'Additional information' on page 10 why the figures are provisional, the box numbers for the figures affected, and the date by which you expect to supply the final ones. If HMRC do not accept your reasons and you do not supply the figures as soon as you can, the return is incomplete and will attract a late filing penalty. HMRC may open an enquiry and you may be penalised if they believe you have been negligent or fraudulent.

Box 23.3 – Tick if you are claiming relief now for 2007–08 losses

This applies if you want to carry back business losses (see page 155) or losses entered in box 8.13B of the capital gains tax pages (see page 277).

Box 23.4 – Tick if you are claiming to have post-cessation etc. receipts taxed as income of an earlier year

This may apply if you have closed a business. If you want income received after closure to be taxed as if received on the date you closed down, tick this box and write in the details under 'Additional information'.

Boxes 23.5 and 23.6 – Disclosure of tax avoidance schemes

Professionals who devise or market certain tax avoidance schemes are required to notify HMRC (see page 68). Ordinary taxpayers are unlikely to be affected, but if you are, your adviser will normally give you a reference number to enter in box 23.5. In some cases it's up to you to tell HMRC, so if in doubt, contact HMRC's Anti Avoidance Group (see the Fact file).

Boxes 23.7 and 23.8 – Business Premises Renovation Allowance

This scheme did not come into effect before the end of the 2006–07 tax year (see page 146), so you will have nothing to enter here.

Question 24 – Declaration and signatures

Sign and date the return, or it will be rejected. If you are signing someone else's return – because they have died and you are their executor, or they are incapable of signing and you have been legally appointed to act for them – enter the capacity in which you are signing in box 24.2.

A letter from HMRC?

HMRC analyse tax returns for common features that suggest potential inaccuracies. If one of these features crops up in your return, you may get a letter explaining how to avoid common errors. This does not mean that HMRC are opening a formal enquiry, or that there is necessarily something wrong. But you should check that your records support the figures in your return, and that you have completed it correctly. If there is anything unusual (see page 169), explain it in the 'Additional information' section of your return.

Record-keeping

You must keep adequate records to support your tax return. Chapter 1 explains the general rules and other chapters list documents to keep. Also keep all your statements of account, a photocopy of everything you send HMRC and notes of phone calls.

Tax-planning hints

1 If your financial circumstances changed in 2006–07, send back your return (or tell your tax office) early so that the change is logged before your tax office decides what extra pages to send you next year, or whether to send you a tax return at all.

2 Don't leave submitting your return until the last minute, particularly if you also have to make a tax payment. It gets very confusing if your tax office doesn't have time to update your records before they issue your next statement of account.

3 HMRC only accept very good excuses for being late with your return or your tax. Get proof of posting if you are sending in a paper return (tax offices no longer give receipts for hand-delivered returns).

4 Information on a full tax return sent in by post is transferred to the HMRC's computers manually. Check everything HMRC send you about your calculation. Consider filing by internet instead.

5 If your tax office issues a formal decision or a penalty you disagree with, act fast – you usually have only 30 days in which to appeal.

6 HMRC have until 31 January 2009 to notify you if they are going to open an enquiry into your return for the 2006–07 tax year. Hang on to your records until at least that date, or until 31 January 2013 if you are self-employed or have letting income.

7 If you pay tax through PAYE, tax you owe up to £2,000 can be collected by adjusting your tax code. To be sure of this, send your return in by 30 September (or 30 December if filing by internet).

8 If you have to make payments on account, and your income is rising, be careful to put enough cash aside to meet the January payment.

9 You may get a short tax return. It should be much easier to complete, but you cannot use it if you have income or reliefs not covered by the form. You can either complete the full tax return or file by internet if you prefer.

10 Keep a copy of your completed tax return – though if you forget your tax office should be able to give you one.

5

Allowances and reliefs

Allowances and reliefs both save you tax, but some are more valuable than others. The most valuable – such as the personal allowance and blind person's allowance, and relief for pension contributions – are deducted from your overall income at the start of the calculation. This reduces your taxable income and the likelihood of paying higher-rate tax. Other allowances and reliefs give limited relief – for example, married couple's allowance gives you only 10 per cent relief.

This chapter covers the main allowances and reliefs. Other forms of tax relief are covered in chapters dealing with specific areas of tax (such as pensions). Use Table 5.1 to see what you might be able to claim, and for how to claim see page 84.

Old allowances you may still be able to claim

You must claim a relief within six years of 31 January in the tax year to which it relates (or later if you did not get the relief because of an HMRC mistake). So as long as you claim by 31 January 2008, you can claim reliefs to which you were entitled for tax years back to 2001–02. This includes an allowance that has since been abolished, Children's Tax Credit, the precursor of the current tax credits. See page 38.

Does this affect you?

Table 5.1: Allowances, credits and reliefs

Who can claim?	*Which relief?*
Anybody (except some non-residents)	Personal allowance (see this chapter)
People who were born before 6 April 1935 (or whose spouse, ex-spouse or civil partner was)	Married couple's allowance and relief for maintenance or alimony payments (see this chapter)
People looking after a child	Child Tax Credit (see Chapter 3)
Blind people	Blind person's allowance (see page 75)
Contributors to a pension scheme	Relief for pension contributions (see Chapter 7)
Contributors to some (rare) types of life insurance	See page 84
Employees	Relief for some expenses (see Chapter 6)
Investors in Venture Capital Trusts, Enterprise Investment Schemes and Community Investment Schemes	Income tax relief for money invested (see page 81 and Chapter 11)
People giving to charity (whether cash, investments or land)	Gift Aid and covenants to charity (see page 81)
People with some types of loan	Business loans (see page 143 and Chapter 7)
	Loans to buy property to rent out (see Chapter 9)
People with overseas income	Foreign tax credit relief (see Chapter 10)
	10% deduction for foreign pensions (see page 212)
Sole traders, partners	Relief for some business expenditure (see Chapter 7)
	Relief for business losses (see page 155)
Working people on modest incomes	Working Tax Credit (see Chapter 3)

How tax relief is worked out

Personal allowance

Everybody gets a basic personal allowance, except some non-residents (see page 220). This makes the first slice of your income free of income tax. For the 2006–07 tax year the minimum personal allowance was £5,035, rising to £5,225 for 2007–08.

If you are aged at least 65 at any point in the tax year you are eligible for an increased personal allowance of £7,280 in 2006–07, £7,550 in 2007–08. See Table 5.2 opposite. A further increase applies if you are at least 75, giving an allowance of £7,420 in 2006–07, £7,690 in 2007–08.

However, the extra age-related amount is gradually withdrawn, once your total income rises above a certain level known as the 'income limit' (£20,100 in 2006–07 and £20,900 in 2007–08). It is withdrawn at the rate of £1 for every £2 of income above the income limit, until it is reduced to the minimum personal allowance (£5,225 in 2007–08).

Example 5.1 shows how the allowance is worked out, but Table 5.2 also shows the levels of income at which all age-related allowance is lost – so, for example, you lose all age-related allowance in 2007–08 if you are between 65 and 74 and your income rises above £25,550.

What is 'income'?

When you are working out whether you are above the income limit for age-related allowances, you can deduct the following from your income:

- tax-free income
- a lump sum from deferring your state pension (see page 184)
- pension contributions
- charitable donations and loan interest that qualify for tax relief
- relief for business losses.

If your income is too high for you to get the maximum age-related allowance, see page 74 for some ways of saving your allowance. Note that from April 2008 the value of age-related allowances will go up, to compensate for losing the 10 per cent starting rate of tax (see page 3).

Example 5.1: **Calculating age-related allowance**

Harry is 80, so the maximum personal allowance he could claim in 2006–07 was £7,420. However, Harry's taxable income was £21,500, which is above the income limit of £20,100 (in 2006–07), so his personal allowance was reduced. To find the reduced allowance, he checks to see whether he can deduct anything from his income. He can claim tax relief on charitable donations of £156 (£200 after adding back basic-rate relief), so his total income was £21,500 − £200 = £21,300.

His income was still above the income limit, by £21,300 − £20,100 = £1,200. His allowance was reduced by half of this: £1,200 ÷ 2 = £600. So his personal allowance for 2006–07 was £7,420 − £600 = £6,820.

Table 5.2: Personal allowances for people aged 65 and over

2006–07	Your income	Allowance
Aged under 65	Any income level	£5,035
Aged 65–74	Below £20,100	£7,280
	£20,100–£24,590	£7,280, minus half of income above £20,100
	Above £24,590	£5,035
Aged 75+	Below £20,100	£7,420
	£20,100–£24,870	£7,420, minus half of income above £20,100
	Above £24,870	£5,035
2007–08	**Your income**	**Allowance**
Aged under 65	Any income level	£5,225
Aged 65–74	Below £20,900	£7,550
	£20,900–£25,550	£7,550, minus half of income above £20,900
	Above £25,550	£5,225
Aged 75+	Below £20,900	£7,690
	£20,900–£25,830	£7,690, minus half of income above £20,900
	Above £25,830	£5,225

Making the most of your personal allowance

If your taxable income is below your personal allowance, part of your allowance is wasted – you cannot transfer it to anybody else. You may be able to make better use of your allowances as a family by transferring income from higher-income family members to those with lower income, e.g. by putting investments in the name of a non-working partner (see page 244 for how to do this). But watch out for the following:

- Transferring income to your children does not work if the child is under 18. Although children have their own allowances from birth, any taxable income arising from gifts from a parent counts as the parent's if it amounts to more than £100 a year. This does not apply to gifts from a grandparent or other relative.
- The transfer has to be a genuine gift, with no strings attached.
- The transfer may be liable to capital gains tax, or inheritance tax on your death, if the recipient is not your spouse or registered civil partner.
- Get advice before transferring shares in your own business.

Changes for same-sex couples

The Civil Partnership Act 2004 gives same-sex couples the right to register as civil partners. From 5 December 2005 registered civil partners have been treated as married couples for tax purposes:

- They can claim married couple's allowance, if either partner was born before April 1935, and transfer unused married couple's and blind person's allowance between them.
- Gifts between civil partners are exempt from inheritance tax, and there is no capital gains tax at the time of the gift. But they can claim capital gains tax relief on only one home between them (see page 268).
- See page 39 for tax credits and page 244 for jointly owned investments.

Saving age-related allowances

These are some ways of hanging on to your age-related allowance if you are aged 65 or more and your income pushes you above the income limit (£20,900 in 2007–08):

■ Investing in tax-free investments (see Chapter 11), or those which produce capital rather than income.
■ If you are close to the income limit, but expect your income to drop, consider deferring any further income until it does – your state pension, say (see the Pension Service booklet SPD1 *Your guide to State Pension Deferral*, from social security offices).
■ Donations to charity through Gift Aid or pension contributions reduce your taxable income and so can increase your age-related allowances.
■ Beware of making a taxable gain on insurance bonds (see page 243). Even though basic-rate tax on the payout is settled by the insurance company, the gain counts as income for age-related allowances.
■ Married couples and civil partners should consider splitting income-producing assets between themselves.

Blind person's allowance

This is worth £1,660 in the 2006–07 tax year (£1,730 in 2007–08) and you can claim it if you are so blind that you cannot perform any work for which eyesight is essential. You automatically qualify if you are registered as blind (but not partially sighted) with the local authority. You must register in order to claim unless your local authority does not keep a register. You can claim for the year before you were registered, provided that you had evidence of blindness, such as an ophthalmologist's certificate.

The tax relief is worked out in the same way as for the personal allowance – an extra £1,660 of your income (£1,730 in 2007–08) is tax-free. If your income is too low for you to use up all your allowances, you can transfer any unused allowance to your husband or wife or civil partner, even if they are not blind. To do this, either tick box 16.14 or 16.15 on your tax return, or contact your tax office. If you are unlikely to use your allowance in future tax years and your partner could benefit from it, your tax office may adjust your partner's tax code to allow for the expected transfer.

Married couple's allowance

You can claim this relief only if either you or your spouse was born before 6 April 1935 – that is, aged at least 72 on 5 April 2007. You must be living with your spouse, or, if not, neither of you must intend to make the separation permanent. Registered civil partners can also claim if they meet these conditions.

The amount of the allowance depends on the older partner's age, and the income of the claimant. For people who were married before 5 December 2005, the claimant is the husband. For civil partners and people who meet the age conditions but get married on or after that date, it is the partner with the higher income. The maximum amounts are shown in Table 5.3 opposite.

Unlike the personal allowance, you get relief at only 10 per cent of the full allowance, knocked off your tax bill at the end of the calculation. So an allowance of £6,065, say, is actually worth only £6,065 × 10% = £606.50.

Once the claimant's total income rises above the income limit (£20,100 in 2006–07, £20,900 in 2007–08), his or her age-related personal allowance is reduced. Then, when the personal allowance has been reduced to the minimum level (or if the claimant is under 65 and gets only the minimum allowance anyway), the married couple's allowance is reduced, by £1 for every £2 of excess income remaining, until it reaches the minimum of £2,350 in 2006–07 (£2,440 in 2007–08). This is why, in Table 5.3, the income level at which married couple's allowance is reduced depends on the age of the claimant. Example 5.2 on page 79 shows how it works.

Note, though, that you get the full allowance for a tax year only if you were married before 6 May in that year. In the year of marriage, you get one-twelfth of the full allowance for each full tax month of marriage (a tax month runs from the 6th of one month to the 5th of the next). So if you got married after 5 December 2006 but before 6 January 2007, say, you will be able to claim three-twelfths of the full allowance.

The married couple's allowance is normally given to the claimant, but it can be allocated to the other partner. You can allocate half or all of the minimum allowance (i.e. half or all of £2,440 in 2007–08), provided that you do so before the start of the tax year (in the year of marriage, you have until the end of the tax year). But whoever gets the allowance, if it turns out

Table 5.3: Married couple's allowance if born before 6 April 1935

2006–07 tax year	Claimant's income	Allowance:
Claimant under 65, older partner aged 72 to 74*	Below £20,100 £20,100–£27,530 Above £27,530	£6,065 £6,065 minus half of income above £20,100 £2,350
Claimant under 65, older partner aged 75+*	Below £20,100 £20,100–£27,670 Above £27,670	£6,135 £6,135 minus half of income above £20,100 £2,350
Claimant aged 65–74, older partner aged 72 to 74*	Below £24,590 £24,590–£32,020 Above £32,020	£6,065 £6,065 minus half of income above £24,590 £2,350
Claimant aged 65–74, older partner aged 75+*	Below £24,590 £24,590–£32,160 Above £32,160	£6,135 £6,135 minus half of income above £24,590 £2,350
Both partners aged 75+*	Below £24,870 £24,870–£32,440 Above £32,440	£6,135 £6,135 minus half of income above £24,870 £2,350

2007–08 tax year	Claimant's income	Allowance
Claimant under 65, older partner aged 73 or 74*	Below £20,900 £20,900–£28,590 Above £28,590	£6,285 £6,285 minus half of income above £20,900 £2,440
Claimant under 65, older partner aged 75+*	Below £20,900 £20,900–£28,750 Above £28,750	£6,365 £6,365 minus half of income above £20,900 £2,440
Claimant aged 65–74, older partner aged 73 or 74*	Below £25,550 £25,550–£33,240 Above £33,240	£6,285 £6,285 minus half of income above £25,550 £2,440
Claimant aged 65–74, older partner aged 75+*	Below £25,550 £25,550–£33,400 Above £33,400	£6,365 £6,365 minus half of income above £25,550 £2,440
Both partners aged 75 +*	Below £25,830 £25,830–£33,680 Above £33,680	£6,365 £6,365 minus half of income above £25,830 £2,440

*At any point in the tax year. 'Age' means your maximum age in the tax year. 'Partner' means either your spouse or your civil partner (see opposite).

that his or her income was too low to make full use of it, the unused part can be transferred to the other partner after the end of the tax year (see Example 5.7 on page 92), and this applies to all of the available married couple's allowance, not just the minimum.

Married before 5 December 2005?

You can elect to be treated in the same way as people married on or after 5 December 2005 – so that the allowance always goes to the higher-income partner rather than the husband. This might be convenient if a husband's income is so low that he regularly transfers unused allowance to his higher-income wife, but don't make the election if her income is above the income limit (£20,900 in 2007–08), because the allowance will be reduced. And, once you have made the election, you can't change your mind.

Allowances if you are widowed or divorced

On death, any married couple's or blind person's (but not personal) allowance still unused is transferred to the surviving partner for the rest of the tax year.

On divorce, or the dissolution of a civil partnership, the partner claiming the married couple's allowance continues to get it for the remainder of the tax year, plus – if either partner was born before 6 April 1935 – tax relief on maintenance paid under a legally binding agreement (see page 80).

From the start of the next tax year after being divorced or widowed, you are taxed as a single person. If you remarry in the same tax year as being divorced or widowed, and you were already getting married couple's allowance, you can continue to get it at the current rate for the remainder of the tax year. Alternatively, you can put in a new claim based on your new spouse's age, but you will only get one-twelfth of the allowance for each month of the new marriage.

Example 5.2: **Calculating married couple's allowance**

Janet and John are both 72. They use Table 5.3 on page 77 to check the married couple's allowance they can claim for 2006–07. This shows that the allowance would be £6,065 if John's total income was below £24,590, and £2,350 if his income exceeded £32,020. However, John's total income was £25,000.

Once John's income rises above the income limit, his age-related personal allowance is reduced by £1 for each £2 of income above £20,100. However, his personal allowance cannot be reduced to less than £5,035. This point is reached at an income of £24,590. John's remaining income above £24,590 reduces his married couple's allowance.

John loses £1 of his married couple's allowance for each £2 of income above £24,590. This comes to £25,000 − £24,590 = £410 ÷ 2 = £205 of his allowance. The full allowance is £6,065, so he gets £6,065 − £205 = £5,860.

Tax reliefs

Relief for loan interest

You can claim tax relief for interest on some types of loan, and on some 'alternative finance' arrangements which do not involve the payment of interest (e.g. to comply with Shari'a law, see page 235). You cannot claim tax relief on a loan to buy a home (unless you let it out). However, you can claim relief at your top rate of tax on a loan or alternative finance deal to:

■ *Buy shares in (or fund) a 'close' company.* A close company is one controlled either by its directors or by fewer than six shareholders (or other key 'participators').
■ *Buy shares in an employee-controlled company for which you work.*
■ *Buy shares in a co-operative.*
■ *Buy into (or fund) a trading or professional partnership.*
■ *Buy equipment or machinery you need for your work as an employee.* Note, though, that you cannot claim relief on a loan or arrangement to buy a car or motorbike. If the equipment is used partly privately, you can claim relief only on the business part of the interest.

■ *Buy equipment or machinery to be used by a partnership of which you are a member* (unless the partnership has already claimed it as a business expense, see Chapter 7).

You cannot claim relief for interest on credit cards or bank overdrafts (unless it is a business expense that can be claimed against profits). And you can claim only the interest or alternative payment, not any capital repayments. (See HMRC help sheet IR340 *Interest and alternative finance payments eligible for relief.*)

Any tax relief of this sort will be given through your self-assessment return, or by adjusting your tax code. The lender should give you a certificate showing how much you have paid. Keep this to back up your claim.

You can also claim relief for loans or alternative finance arrangements for business purposes (including buying a property to rent out). However, you get the relief by deducting an amount from your business profits (see Chapter 7 or Chapter 9).

Relief for maintenance or alimony

Provided that either you, your former spouse or former civil partner were born before 6 April 1935, you can get tax relief on the alimony or maintenance you pay, up to £2,350 in 2006–07 (£2,440 in 2007–08). The maximum is the same however many ex-partners you support. The rate of relief is 10 per cent, so the maximum tax saving in 2007–08 is £2,440 × 10% = £244.

You must make the payments under a legally binding agreement, such as a written agreement, a court order or a Child Support Agency assessment – voluntary payments do not count. Legally binding agreements made in most European countries (listed in the notes to the tax return) also count. But be careful about the wording: to claim relief the payments must be for the maintenance of your ex-partner or any children aged under 21. Payments directly to a child do not qualify.

Note that tax relief stops on the date an ex-partner remarries.

Relief for some investments

These forms of investment give you tax relief on the money you invest:

■ Registered pension schemes (such as most occupational pension schemes, personal pensions and stakeholder pensions – see Chapter 8)
■ Venture Capital Trusts (VCTs)
■ Enterprise Investment Schemes (EIS)
■ Community Investment schemes

Both VCTs and EIS are designed to encourage investment in unquoted companies. They are covered in more detail on page 246. You get tax relief at 20 per cent on EIS investments and at 30 per cent on VCT investments.

Community Investment schemes are a way of encouraging investment in accredited schemes such as social banks. Investors can claim a community investment tax credit of 5 per cent of the amount invested for up to five years, i.e. 25 per cent in total.

Relief for gifts to charity

There are three main ways of getting tax relief on gifts to charity:

■ payroll giving, for donations deducted regularly from your pay
■ Gift Aid, for most other donations
■ gifts of investments and land.

If you get a tax return, you can also ask HMRC to give any tax repayment direct to a charity by ticking box 19A, and you can specify that the gift is made under Gift Aid (see page 81). But take care unless you have a good idea of the rebate due. You can specify a maximum donation, but if, after it has been made, you find a mistake in your return which means that the repayment is *less* than the gift, HMRC can claim the excess from you.

Before 6 April 2000, you could get tax relief on donations paid under a deed of covenant. Payments under a covenant taken out before then now fall within Gift Aid. Payments under later deeds of covenant do not qualify – but Gift Aid is easier and more flexible. Gifts to charity also qualify for capital gains tax and inheritance tax relief (Chapters 11 and

12). For more information, see HMRC help sheet IR342 *Charitable giving* or go to the 'Charities' section of the HMRC website.

Payroll giving

This route is open to employees or pensioners of an employer who runs a payroll giving scheme. You ask your employer to deduct a set amount from your pay packet, which is then passed on to one or more charities through an approved agency. You get tax relief at your highest rate of tax.

Gift Aid

You can increase the value of your gifts to charity – whether these are one-off or regular cash donations, or donations of tax repayments – by using Gift Aid. You can also give to amateur sports clubs by this route, if they are registered with HMRC. The charity or club can reclaim basic-rate tax from HMRC. With the basic rate of tax set at 22 per cent, this is $^{22}/_{78}$ of your gift. So, for every £10 you give, the charity benefits by £12.82.

If you are a higher-rate taxpayer, you benefit further – you can claim higher-rate relief either through your tax return or by asking your tax office to change your tax code. The higher-rate relief works out at 18 per cent of the value of the gift to the charity – the 40 per cent higher rate of tax, minus the 22 per cent relief the charity has reclaimed. So, for every £10 you give, you get tax relief of £12.82 × 18% = £2.31.

You can claim on your tax return to have charitable donations treated as if made in the previous tax year, providing that you claim by the following 31 January. This is helpful if your top rate of tax has fallen since the previous year, and means that you get tax relief more quickly. But you cannot claim to have donations of tax repayments treated in this way.

There are no limits on the amount of donations for which you can claim tax relief, but you must make a 'Gift Aid' declaration for each charity you give to. Usually, the charity provides a form, but telephone, email or even text message declarations are also possible. Declarations do not have to be made for every gift; they can be worded to cover a number of gifts, and they can be made after the date of the gift.

Note that from April 2008, when the basic rate of tax falls from 22 per cent to 20 per cent, the basic-rate tax relief on charitable donations will also fall.

Non-taxpayers beware

If you pay little or no tax do not give to charity via Gift Aid. HMRC can claw back the basic-rate tax claimed by the charity from you – unless your tax bill for the year is at least as much as the amount the charity will claim. Your tax bill for this purpose includes income tax, capital gains tax and tax credits on dividends. If you have made a Gift Aid declaration, you can cancel it by notifying the charity.

If HMRC find that a charity has claimed Gift Aid on a non-taxpayer's donation, they may ask the charity to repay the tax. But if you get a tax return, the tax will automatically be added to your tax bill.

Gifts of investments and land

If you give shares and securities, unit trusts, OEICs or land and buildings (freehold or leasehold) to a charity, or sell them to a charity at a discount, you are likely to qualify for Gift Aid relief. (See the 'Charities' section of the HMRC website.)

Example 5.3: **Gift Aid and your tax rate**

Andrew decides to donate to his favourite charity by monthly direct debit, and makes a Gift Aid declaration. He pays £15 a month, £180 a year, and the charity reclaims tax of the amount paid, divided by the basic rate of tax, that is £180 $\times$ 22 $\div$ 78 = £51. However, as a higher-rate taxpayer, Andrew also claims higher-rate tax relief at 18% of the gift plus the tax: £180 + £51 $\times$ 18% = £42. If Andrew's tax bill for the year wasn't at least £51, HMRC would adjust his tax to recover the £51 the charity had already received.

Relief for business expenses

Business expenses are usually deducted from the profits of the business. But in a few cases (covered on page 79) you can deduct them from other income. You can also claim to set some *losses* against your total income, rather than carrying them forward to set against future business profits (see Chapter 7).

Relief on insurance premiums

The only types of life insurance that now qualify for relief are:

- Compulsory insurance bought through an employer's pension scheme.
- Half of any part of a trade union subscription that provides pension, life insurance or funeral cover.
- Half of any premiums of under £25 a month you pay to some (now unusual) friendly society insurance policies.

It used to be possible to get tax relief at your highest rate on 'pension term insurance' policies bought through a pension plan (see Chapter 8). The government has ended this relief, although policies applied for before 14 December 2006 and taken out before 6 April 2007 are not affected.

What to tell HMRC

Your basic personal allowance should be given automatically through either your tax return or, if you have income taxed under PAYE, your tax code. Check that 'personal allowance' appears on your coding notice (see page 17). All other reliefs can be claimed on your tax return or, if you do not get one, by contacting your tax office. Your tax office may adjust your tax code or send you a tax return or form R40 (see page 33).

If you are approaching 65 you should make sure HMRC know so that you receive the higher age-related allowances. There is space to give your age in Question 22 of the tax return. If you don't get a tax return, you may be asked to complete a form P161 (see page 30).

Filling in your tax return

Allowances and reliefs that are deducted from your total income or overall tax bill are claimed on pages 5, 6 and 7 of the basic tax return. These are covered in this chapter. Other tax reliefs are claimed on the supplementary pages dealing with that income – e.g. the Self-employment pages for business expenses. (See relevant chapters.)

Some questions in the 'Reliefs' section of the tax return ask you to enter the amount paid, others ask for the amount paid up to a maximum and one asks for half the amount paid. Check that you are giving the figures requested.

Question 15 – Do you want to claim any of the following reliefs?

Box 15.1 Interest and alternative finance payments

Not many loans now qualify for relief, but if you have one, or an alternative finance arrangement (see page 79), enter in box 15.1 the amount that qualifies for relief in the 2006–07 tax year. If you haven't already got the information, ask your lender. Remember that you claim relief only on the interest or alternative finance payment – not on the cost of paying off the capital itself.

Boxes 15.2, 15.2A Maintenance or alimony payments

This applies only if you, your former spouse or former civil partner were born before 6 April 1935, and the payments are made under a legally binding order or agreement. If so, enter the total maintenance paid in 2006–07 up to a maximum of £2,350. If your ex-partner has remarried, enter only payments up to the date of marriage.

If you are able to claim the relief because your ex-partner was born before 6 April 1935 but you were born after that date, enter your ex-partner's date of birth in box 15.2A. In the 'Additional information' box (23.9) at the end of the tax return you must give the dates of the court order or other agreement under which you are making the payments.

> Example 5.4: **Claiming reliefs**

Andrew has tax relief to claim in Question 15 of his tax return (see Figure 5.1). He pays maintenance to his ex-wife under a court order, and as she is 72 he can claim tax relief. He pays her £4,000 a year, but he enters £2,350, as this is the most he can claim in 2006–07.

Figure 5.1: Question 15 (see Example 5.4)

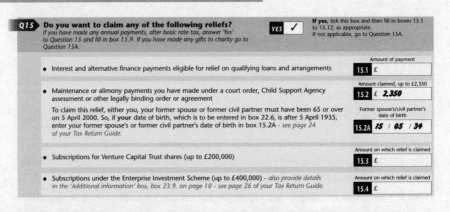

Boxes 15.3 to 15.7 Subscriptions for Venture Capital Trust shares, the Enterprise Investment Scheme and Community Investment Tax relief

Enter in box 15.3 the amount you invested in VCT shares in 2006–07, up to a maximum of £200,000.

Enter in box 15.4 the amount of any EIS investment in 2006–07, up to a maximum of £400,000. Quite a bit of 'Additional information' needs to be given in box 23.9 (see the guide sent with the tax return). You also need to complete and return the claim form included in the form EIS3 or EIS5 that you should have received from the scheme.

You can claim to have up to half of EIS shares issued before 6 October in one year (with a maximum cost of £50,000) carried back to get tax relief in the previous year. Remember to adjust the figure you enter in box 15.4:

- by deducting any amounts you are claiming to 'carry back' to 2005–06
- by adding any amounts you are carrying back from 2007–08.

If you have put money into a Community Investment scheme and received the necessary certificate, enter the amount invested in 2006–07 in box 15.6 and the total amount invested in previous years in box 15.5. Add these two boxes up and enter the total in box 15.7.

Box 15.8 Post-cessation expenses etc.; Box 15.9 Trade annuities and patent royalties

These two boxes cover tax relief arising from a business or job which is set against your income as a whole.

■ You can claim post-cessation expenses for up to seven years after you stop trading, for example the costs of collecting debts of your former business. And if you are transferring your business to a limited company, you may be able to claim some pre-incorporation losses. Enter the total in box 15.8, but see the conditions in the tax return guide first. Do not enter any other business losses – they are claimed on the Self-employment or Partnership pages.
■ If you were an employee, costs and liabilities arising from problems with your work can be claimed in box 15.8 (unless you have already claimed in the Employment supplementary pages).
■ Payments made under some annuities or covenants for business purposes (e.g. to buy out a retiring partner) can be claimed in box 15.9, as well as royalties for the use of a patent.

You can also use box 15.8 to claim tax relief if you made a loss on some listed discounted securities held since 26 March 2003 (see page 238).

Box 15.10 Payments to a trade union or friendly society for death benefit

Enter half of your payments to a trade union or friendly society that qualify for relief. Check first that your policy qualifies.

Box 15.11 Payments to your employer's compulsory benefit scheme

Only enter here any payments where (unusually) tax relief has not been given through PAYE. You can get relief at 22 per cent on up to £100, so the most you can enter here is £22.

Box 15.12 Relief on the redemption of bonus shares or securities

This box applies only if you have entered in box 10.17 on page 3 an amount received when you redeemed bonus shares and securities, and you are a higher-rate taxpayer. If so, see HMRC's tax return guide.

Question 15A – Do you want to claim relief on gifts to charity?

Enter in box 15A.1 the total amount you actually handed over to charities under the Gift Aid scheme (ignoring any basic-rate tax reclaimed by the charity), or under a deed of covenant made before 6 April 2000. Also include any amount given to community amateur sports clubs under Gift Aid.

Include in box 15A.1 any 2005–06 tax repayment that was donated direct to charity, if you ticked box 19.4A in your 2005–06 tax return to claim Gift Aid. (You cannot claim Gift Aid on repayments donated in your 2006–07 return until you send in your 2007–08 return.)

Then, work out how much of the payments already entered in box 15A.1 were one-off gifts rather than regular donations, and enter the amount of one-off gifts in box 15A.2. Your tax office will adjust your tax code if necessary, to give you any higher-rate tax relief on the regular donations at source.

If you are claiming to have any donations made between 6 April 2006 and 5 April 2007 treated as if paid in 2005–06, enter the amount in box 15A.3. If you want any amounts paid after 5 April 2007 treated as if paid in 2006–07, enter them in box 15A.4. (Remember that you cannot do this for a tax repayment donated through your tax return.)

Finally, enter in box 15A.5 the total amounts on which you want to claim tax relief in 2006–07, that is the total of boxes 15A.1 and 15A.4, minus the amount in box 15A.3. Remember, the figure to enter is the amount you actually paid – do not add on the basic-rate tax.

Boxes 15A.6, 15A.7 Gifts of qualifying investments, land or buildings to charities

If you have given shares or securities, unit trusts or OEICs, or land (real property) to charity, enter in boxes 15A.6 and 15A.7 the amount of relief that you are claiming. If you are giving real property, you will need a certificate from the charity. (For more information, see the 'Charities' section of the HMRC website.)

Example 5.5: **Charitable donations**

Andrew makes regular Gift Aid donations of £15 a month (see Figure 5.2), but in 2006–07 he also made a lump sum donation of £150. He enters in box 15A.1 the total paid in 2006–07 (£330), not including the basic-rate tax relief, with the one-off donation in box 15A.2.

In June 2007 Andrew made another lump sum donation of £500 to a disaster relief fund. He claims to carry this back to the 2006–07 tax year by entering it in box 15A.4 (he should make a note to enter it in box 15A.3 in next year's return as well).

The advantage of carrying back the payment is that it will increase the amount of personal allowance Andrew gets in 2006–07. Because he is over 65, he is eligible for the higher rate of personal allowance, but the amount is reduced because his income was over £20,100. The donation, plus the basic-rate tax relief on it, can be deducted from his income when working out the allowance. By carrying the donation back to 2006–07 he will bring his income for the year below £20,100 and qualify for the full allowance.

In box 15A.5 Andrew claims a total of £330 + £500 = £830.

Figure 5.2: Question 15A (see Example 5.5)

Q15A	Have you made any gifts to charity?	YES ✓	If yes, tick this box and then read page 25 of your Tax Return Guide. Fill in boxes 15A.1 to 15A.7 as appropriate. If not applicable, go to Question 16.

- Gift Aid payments, including covenanted payments to charities, made between 6 April 2006 and 5 April 2007 — 15A.1 £ *330*

- The total of any 'one-off' payments included in box 15A.1 — 15A.2 £ *150*

- Gift Aid payments made after 5 April 2006 but treated as if made in the tax year 2005–06 — 15A.3 £

- Gift Aid payments made after 5 April 2007 but to be treated as if made in the tax year 2006–07 — 15A.4 £ *500*

- Total relief claimed in 2006–07 — box 15A.1 + box 15A.4 minus box 15A.3 — 15A.5 £ *830*

- Gifts of qualifying investments to charities – shares and securities — 15A.6 £

- Gifts of qualifying investments to charities – real property — 15A.7 £

Question 16 – Do you want to claim blind person's allowance or married couple's allowance?

You do not need to claim personal allowance – this is given automatically.

Boxes 16.1, 16.2 Blind person's allowance

Enter the name of the authority with which you are registered as blind in box 16.2, or 'Scotland claim' or 'Northern Ireland claim' (where there are no registers) as appropriate. If 2006–07 was the first year in which you were registered as blind, enter the date of registration.

Boxes 16.3 to 16.13 Married couple's allowance

This applies only if either you, your spouse or your civil partner were born before 6 April 1935. It falls into two parts:

- A husband (or higher-income partner, if married or registered as a civil partner after 4 December 2005) completes boxes 16.3 to 16.9.
- A wife (or lower-income partner, if married or registered as a civil partner after 4 December 2005) completes boxes 16.10 to 16.13 – but only if all or half the minimum allowance was allocated to them. This had to be agreed before 6 April 2006 (or before 6 April 2007 if married or registered as a civil partner during the year).

If you are responsible for completing boxes 16.3 to 16.9, you need to show that the age condition for claiming the allowance is met:

- enter your date of birth in box 16.3 (if it is before 6 April 1935)
- enter your partner's date of birth in box 16.4, if you are claiming on the basis of his or her age
- if you separated and remarried during 2006–07, and your previous partner was born before 6 April 1935, enter his or her date of birth in box 16.9.

HMRC will use whichever date of birth saves you most tax. Also enter your current partner's full name in box 16.5. If you married or registered as a civil partner between 6 April 2006 and 5 April 2007, enter the date of marriage or registration in box 16.6 so that your tax office can work

Figure 5.3: Boxes 16.1 to 16.8 (see Example 5.6)

Q16 **Do you want to claim blind person's allowance, or married couple's allowance?**
If you are resident in the UK you get your personal allowance of £5,035 automatically.
If you were born before 6 April 1942, enter your date of birth in box 22.6 - you may get a higher age-related personal allowance.

YES ✓

If yes, tick this box and then read pages 26 to 28 of your Tax Return Guide. Fill in boxes 16.1 to 16.17 as appropriate.
If not applicable, go to Question 17.

▪ *Blind person's allowance*

If first year of claim, date of registration
16.1 / /

Local authority (or other register)
16.2

▪ *Married couple's allowance*

This allowance can only be claimed if either you or your spouse or civil partner were born before 6 April 1935, and:

• you are a man or woman who married before 5 December 2005, **or**
• you are a man, woman or civil partner who married or formed a civil partnership on or after 5 December 2005.

The allowance is made up of two amounts - a minimum amount (worth up to £235) and an age-related amount, dependent on the income of the husband (for marriages before 5 December 2005) or the person with the higher income (for marriages and civil partnerships formed on or after 5 December 2005). Special rules apply if you are a married woman or a civil partner who does not have the higher income. Further guidance is given, beginning on page 27 of the Tax Return Guide.

If both you and your spouse **or** civil partner were born after 5 April 1935 you cannot claim. Do not complete boxes 16.3 to 16.13.

If you can claim, fill in boxes 16.3 and 16.4.

● Enter your date of birth (if born before 6 April 1935)

16.3 *15 / 02 / 33*

● Enter your spouse or civil partner's date of birth (**only** if born before 6 April 1935 **and** if older than you)

16.4 *04 / 04 / 30*

ALLOWANCES AND OTHER INFORMATION *for the year ended 5 April 2007*

Then, if you are a married man, who married before 5 December 2005, or you married or formed a civil partnership on or after 5 December 2005 and you have the higher income, **fill in boxes 16.5 to 16.9.**

If you are a married woman, who married before 5 December 2005, or you married or formed a civil partnership on or after 5 December 2005 but you do not have the higher income, **fill in boxes 16.10 to 16.13** to claim half, or all, of the minimum amount of the married couple's allowance.

● Spouse or civil partner's full name
16.5 *ERNEST MACDONALD*

● Date of marriage or formation of civil partnership (if after 5 April 2006)
16.6 *02 / 05 / 06*

Example 5.6: **Claiming allowances**

Eric and Ernest registered their civil partnership in May 2006. They can claim the married couple's allowance because they were both born before 6 April 1935. Eric, aged 74, is the higher-income partner so he completes boxes 16.3 to 16.9 in his return, but they get the higher age-related allowance for those over 75 (£6,135 in 2006–07) because Ernest is 77. So in Eric's tax return (see Figure 5.3), he enters Ernest's date of birth as well as his name and the date of registration.

out how much of the full allowance to give you (one-twelfth for each tax month of marriage). Finally, if you allocated half or all of the allowance to your partner, tick box 16.7 or 16.8.

If you are responsible for completing boxes 16.10 to 16.13, simply tick box 16.10 or 16.11 to show how much of the allowance has been allocated to you, enter your partner's name, and give the date of marriage or registering as a civil partner if this took place after 5 April 2006.

Boxes 16.14 to 16.17 Transfer of surplus allowances

You can transfer blind person's allowance and married couple's allowance to your spouse or civil partner if your income is too low to use it all.

To transfer allowances, tick boxes 16.14 or 16.15 as relevant (and ask your partner to tick the equivalent boxes on his or her form). You cannot lose out by ticking these boxes – your tax office will transfer allowances only if it is in your interests. In 'Additional information' (box 23.9) you will need to give your partner's name, address, tax reference or National Insurance number and tax office. If you are claiming to transfer married couple's allowance, also enter your partner's date of birth.

If your spouse or civil partner is transferring allowances to you, and you are working out your own tax, the unused amount to be transferred should be entered in box 16.16 or 16.17 as appropriate. If you don't know the unused amount, ask your partner to contact their tax office or get your returns in by 30 September 2007 or file by internet.

Example 5.7: Transferring allowances

In 2006–07 Andrew, aged 72, can claim blind person's allowance as well as an age-related personal allowance and married couple's allowance. However, his £7,655 income is too low to use all of his allowances. He has £1,285 of his blind person's allowance left to transfer to his wife Anna (who is 75), and the whole of the married couple's allowance.

Andrew ticks box 16.14 on his tax return to transfer his allowances (see Figure 5.4) – he doesn't have to enter any figures. Anna ticks box 16.15 on her tax return (see Figure 5.5), and, because she is calculating her own tax, she enters the £1,285 unused blind person's allowance in box 16.16 and the £6,135 unused married couple's allowance in box 16.17.

Figure 5.4: Andrew's tax return (see Example 5.7)

■ *Transfer of surplus allowances* - read page 28 of your Tax Return Guide before you fill in boxes 16.14 to 16.17.

- Tick box 16.14 if you want your spouse or civil partner to have your unused allowances   **16.14** ✓
- Tick box 16.15 if you want to have your spouse's or civil partner's unused allowances   **16.15**

Please give details in the 'Additional information' box, box 23.9, on page 10

If you want to calculate your tax, enter the amount of the surplus allowances you can have

- Blind person's surplus allowance   **16.16** £
- Married couple's surplus allowance   **16.17** £

Figure 5.5: Anna's tax return (see Example 5.7)

■ *Transfer of surplus allowances* - read page 28 of your Tax Return Guide before you fill in boxes 16.14 to 16.17.

- Tick box 16.14 if you want your spouse or civil partner to have your unused allowances   **16.14**
- Tick box 16.15 if you want to have your spouse's or civil partner's unused allowances   **16.15** ✓

Please give details in the 'Additional information' box, box 23.9, on page 10

If you want to calculate your tax, enter the amount of the surplus allowances you can have

- Blind person's surplus allowance   **16.16** £ *1,285*
- Married couple's surplus allowance   **16.17** £ *6,135*

Record-keeping

Key records you should keep are listed below.

- Birth certificate, or other proof of age, if claiming age-related allowances.
- Marriage certificate or civil partnership registration certificate if claiming married couple's allowance.
- For blind person's allowance, notification that you are registered blind and/or an ophthalmologist's certificate.
- Certificate of amount paid on a loan or alternative finance arrangement which qualifies for relief.
- If claiming tax relief on maintenance payments, court orders or other legally binding agreements, and proof of amounts actually paid.

- Certificates issued by Venture Capital Trusts.
- Forms EIS3 or EIS5 for Enterprise Investment Scheme shares.
- Copies of Gift Aid declarations, charitable deeds of covenant and records of amounts actually paid. Valuations of shares or other property gifted to charity and related expenses.
- Details of any other payments on which you are claiming relief.

Tax-planning hints

1 If you've forgotten to claim a relief or allowance, you have five years and ten months from the end of the tax year in question to claim.

2 Remember that it is not too late to claim Children's Tax Credit for the 2001–02 and 2002–03 tax years, if you were eligible but have not yet claimed (see page 38). But the deadline for claiming for 2001–02 is 31 January 2008.

3 If you cannot use all your personal allowance in one year, it may make sense to transfer income to another family member (see page 75).

4 Transfer any unused blind person's and married couple's allowance to your husband or wife, or registered civil partner.

5 If you are losing age-related allowance because you are above the income limit, see page 74 for ways of minimising the loss.

6 Do not give money to charity via Gift Aid if you pay little or no tax. HMRC can claw back from you the basic-rate tax claimed by the charity.

7 Always make sure that your tax office knows the amount of any Gift Aid donations you have made, even if you are a basic-rate taxpayer and not entitled to any more relief. The donations may increase your entitlement to age-related allowances or tax credits.

8 If you are an employee, a gift to charity could cost you less if you pay by payroll giving. Ask your employer if they run a scheme.

9 You can claim blind person's allowance for any tax year in which you had evidence of blindness (e.g. an opthamologist's certificate), even if you weren't actually registered until after the end of the year.

6

Income from a job

If you are an employee, your employer deducts tax before paying you (see Chapter 2) and you usually get a tax return only if you are a director, have a high income or your tax is complex (see Chapter 4). Even if you don't get a tax return, you should still check your tax – there may be ways of saving tax and traps to avoid.

Does this affect you?

In most cases it is clear whether or not you are an employee, but there is often a grey area between being employed and being self-employed, as explained in Chapter 7. For tax purposes an 'employee' also includes:

- *Directors*, including people who are directors of a company they own. There are special rules for people who are 'controlling' directors.
- *Casual employees* (although whether or not your employer actually has to deduct PAYE depends on your income – see page 16).
- *Part-time workers*. If you have more than one job, you can be an employee for one, self-employed for the other – it is the nature of the work and your contract with the employer that count.
- *Agency staff* (in most cases – see page 29).
- *Ex-employees* receiving benefits from a former employer. The benefits are taxed in the same way as for employees (see page 103).

A director or partner of your own firm?

If you are a director of a service company that you control, you may have extra tax to pay, if HMRC think that you are effectively an employee of a client for whom you are working (see page 101). The same may apply to some partners in a partnership.

Tax-free income

You can start from the assumption that all your rewards for working are taxable – pay, expenses payments and employee benefits. However, you can claim tax relief on some 'allowable' expenses payments which you incur for work purposes and your employer may get a 'dispensation' from your tax office not to include them in your taxable pay (see page 117). Your employer may also agree with your tax office to pay the tax for you on some minor taxable benefits and expenses, under a 'PAYE settlement agreement'.

A few types of pay and perks, listed below, are completely tax-free, provided various conditions are met. Your employer should ensure that what is offered meets the necessary conditions. Also see HMRC help sheet IR207 *Non-taxable payments or benefits for employees,* or ask your employer or tax office if you can see the HMRC tome 480 *Expenses and benefits. A tax guide* (also available on the HMRC website).

Tax-free pay

- Your (and your employer's) contributions to a registered pension or life or sick pay insurance scheme (you still have to pay employee's National Insurance contributions). (See Chapter 8 for more on pensions.)
- Donations to a payroll giving scheme (often called 'Give As You Earn').
- The first £30,000 of some payments on leaving a job (see page 115).
- Some payments from your employer if you are a full-time student at a university or technical college.
- Injury awards to members of the Armed Forces.
- Armed Forces operational allowance.

Tax-free expenses and benefits

- Subsidised meals at a staff restaurant and free tea and coffee, if available to all employees; the first 15 pence a day of luncheon vouchers.
- Loans of computer equipment for private use are tax-free, within limits, if made before 6 April 2006; loans made on or after 6 April are taxable, but occasional private use of a work computer is tax-free.
- Loans of money, in some circumstances (see page 111).
- Some living accommodation (see page 112).
- Payments of up to £2 a week for extra household costs if you regularly work from home under a contractual arrangement with your employer (not if you simply take work home in the evenings). Higher payments can be tax-free if you have supporting evidence (see page 117).
- Most relocation costs paid by your employer, up to a maximum of £8,000 for the relocation as a whole, if you are moving for your job.
- A phone line at home, if your employer is the subscriber, you have a clear business need for it and any private calls are kept to a minimum.
- Mobile phones (one per employee). Line rental and calls paid directly by your employer are also tax-free.
- Eye tests and corrective glasses if you work at a computer screen.
- Medical check-ups (but not treatment) for you and your family.
- Treatment (or medical insurance) if you fall ill while working abroad.
- Workplace nurseries or playschemes, and the first £55 a week of free childcare or childcare vouchers. Care must be provided by an approved person, such as a registered childminder or a nanny approved under the Childcare Approval Scheme, not generally a relative. Note that this perk could leave you worse off if you lose tax credits as a result – there is more information on this in the 'Childcare' section of the HMRC website (see the Fact file).
- Work-related training, including (in some cases) retraining costs met by your employer on leaving your job.
- Welfare counselling or redundancy counselling.
- Pension information and advice worth up to £150 a year.
- Long service (20 years) gifts and suggestion scheme awards.
- Non-cash gifts, worth under £250, if not from your employer.
- Staff parties costing less than £150 per head per year.
- Special staff sports and leisure facilities.

Tax-free travel expenses and benefits

- Approved mileage allowance payments (see page 120).
- Parking provided at or near your work.
- Travel or overnight expenses if public transport is disrupted by strikes.
- Taxis home if you occasionally work after 9 p.m. and public transport has either shut down or it would be unreasonable to expect you to use it.
- The travel expenses of your husband or wife if they have to accompany you on a foreign trip because of your health.
- Personal expenses such as newspapers and laundry if away overnight for work, up to an average of £5 a night in the UK, £10 a night overseas (if they come to more, the whole lot is taxable).
- Subsidised bus travel from home to your place of work.
- The loan of a bicycle used mainly for travel to work and free meals provided on official 'cycle to work' days.
- Help for travel from home to work if you are disabled.
- Taking an emergency vehicle home, if an emergency worker on call.
- Travel expenses of some directors, such as unpaid directors of some clubs.

Tax-free share perks

If your employer has given you free shares in the company, or the right to buy shares on special terms, this counts as a tax-free perk *provided* that it is done through one of the schemes below. (For taxable schemes, see page 113.) Dividends received from the shares and capital gains when you eventually sell them are taxable in the normal way (see Chapters 11 and 12) unless otherwise stated.

Your employer will tell you what sort of scheme you are in and what the rules are. See also the 'share schemes' area of the HMRC website and HMRC help sheet IR287 *Employee share and security schemes and capital gains tax*.

- *Approved profit-sharing schemes* give you free shares, which are kept in a trust on your behalf. They are tax-free provided that they are kept in the trust for at least three years. New schemes are not possible, but you may still have shares in one.
- *Approved share incentive plans.* Your employer can give you free shares,

or you can buy them. They are free of income tax and National
Insurance provided that you keep them in the plan for at least five
years (in most cases). There is no capital gains tax on free shares if you
keep your shares in the plan until you sell them.

■ *Enterprise management incentives.* You have an 'option' to buy shares at
a particular price at some point within ten years. The option is free of
income tax and National Insurance provided that the price at which
you can buy the shares is not below their market value at the time the
option is granted, and provided that, if there is a 'disqualifying event'
such as you leaving the company, you buy the shares within 40 days of
the event.

■ *Approved savings-related share option schemes.* You have an 'option' to
buy shares at a fixed price at a particular time, free of income tax and
National Insurance. You can buy the shares only with amounts you
have saved under a special Save As You Earn (SAYE) savings scheme,
which pays a tax-free bonus at the end of the savings period.

■ *Approved discretionary share option schemes* (called company share
option plans) give you an 'option' to buy shares at a fixed price at a
particular time. The option is free of income tax and National
Insurance provided that (in most cases) you buy shares no earlier
than three years, or later than ten years, after receiving the option.

How the tax is worked out

This is how your taxable pay is worked out for income tax purposes (the
rules for National Insurance contributions differ slightly, see page 122).

■ *Step 1: add up taxable pay* (listed on page 100). You can ignore any tax-
free income (listed on page 96).

■ *Step 2: add extra taxable pay, for some directors and partners.* HMRC call
this a 'deemed employment payment' but it applies only if you are
affected by the 'IR35' rules (see page 101).

■ *Step 3: add the taxable value of employee benefits.* If you get a perk which
is not tax-free, there are special rules for working out the amount on
which you are taxed (see page 103).

- *Step 4: add any taxable amounts from share schemes* (see page 113).
- *Step 5: add any taxable lump sums.* This includes some payments when your job changes or ends (see page 115).
- *Step 6: deduct expenses on which you can claim tax relief.* HMRC call these 'allowable expenses' (see page 117).

The result is your taxable pay from employment. You pay tax on this at 10 per cent, if it is in the starting-rate band, 22 per cent if it is in the basic-rate band and 40 per cent if it is in the higher-rate band (see page 5).

Example 6.1: Working out taxable pay

Mindy is a personnel manager. In 2006–07 she receives a salary and expenses of £35,524 (after deducting pension contributions, which are tax-free) from her job (Step 1). Her company car and other benefits add £9,450 to her taxable pay at Step 3. At Step 6, she can deduct £936 of her expenses that qualify for tax relief.

Mindy's taxable pay is £35,524 + £9,450 − £936 = £44,038. She qualifies for the personal allowance of £5,035: £44,038 − £5,035 = £39,003. However, her benefits have pushed her into the higher-rate tax band, which starts (in 2006–07) at £33,300.

Taxable cash payments

- Payments from your employer, such as salary, wages, fees, bonuses, commission and overtime – you are taxed on these when you receive them or become entitled to them, whichever is earlier.
- If you are a director, amounts credited to your account in the company's books (normally taxable from the date they are credited).
- Expenses payments, whether these are reimbursing you for amounts you have laid out, flat-rate expense allowances, or tickets etc. bought for you (don't worry – any expenses for which you can claim tax relief are taken away at Step 6.). This excludes any expenses covered by a 'dispensation' (see page 117). Expenses payments are shown on the form P11D or P9D you get from your employer.

- 'Honoraria' from any posts that count as employment rather than self-employment (this can be a grey area – see Chapter 7).
- 'Golden hellos'.
- Sick pay, maternity, paternity or adoption pay (including any statutory amounts). However, if you contribute to the cost of a sick-pay scheme, any benefits arising from your own contributions are tax-free.
- Loans that have been written off by the lender.
- Taxable amounts from a profit-sharing scheme.
- Payments from someone other than your employer, received because of your job, for example tips. You can exclude goodwill entertainment and gifts (other than cash) costing less than £250 a year.
- One-off payments to compensate you for agreeing to changes in your terms and conditions of employment.
- In most cases, income from working abroad, if you are resident in the UK for tax purposes – but see Chapter 10 for special rules.

Documents that make life easier

Your employer should send you two helpful forms after the end of the tax year: the P60 by 31 May, and a P11D (or P9D) by 6 July. The P60 tells you the taxable amount of pay you received, and the P11D or P9D tells you the taxable value of your perks and expenses (if you receive any).

Extra taxable pay, for some directors and partners

You may be affected by rules designed to counter tax avoidance if you are an employee of your own company, or of a 'managed service company' (see page 134).

In addition, you may have extra tax to pay if you are providing services through your own company and you are caught by the 'IR35' rules (named after the press release in which they were announced). HMRC can apply these rules if they think that you are effectively an employee of a client. Guidelines for deciding whether you are an employee are in Chapter 7.

These rules even apply to domestic workers, e.g. nannies, who set themselves up as companies.

The IR35 rules mean that instead of paying tax on the pay or dividends you receive, you will be taxed on the total payment received by the company or partnership for your services, *minus* an allowance of 5 per cent of the contract value (to cover the costs of running a company).

HMRC call the result a 'deemed employment' payment and add it to your taxable income. Your company or partnership must pay any extra PAYE and National Insurance due on this by 19 April after the end of the tax year in question. (See Example 6.2 opposite.)

Are you affected?

The rules may affect you if you provide services to a client through:

- *either* a company in which you (or your family) control more than 5 per cent of the ordinary share capital, or are entitled to more than 5 per cent of the dividends
- *or* a partnership in which you (or your family) are entitled to at least 60 per cent of the profits, or where most of the partnership's income comes from a single client.

Even if neither of these applies, you may be caught if you are entitled to receive an income from any payments made to the company or partnership for your services.

If you think you may be affected, there is an HMRC helpline and a special area on the HMRC website (see the Fact file). You can ask HMRC to give an 'opinion' on whether you are affected, but they will do this only for existing contracts.

Contracts – part, but not all, of the IR35 solution

You cannot sidestep the tests for being self-employed by stating in a contract that you are not an employee – it is the nature of the work that counts. On the other hand, it is sensible to ensure that your contract helps rather than hinders. Take professional advice.

Example 6.2: **What IR35 means**

Hannibal is the only employee of his own company. In 2006–07 he worked on an engineering contract, for which his client paid him £50,000. Hannibal took a salary of only £25,000. If he is caught by the IR35 rules, he is taxed roughly as if he received the whole £50,000 minus a 5% allowance, that is £47,500, and minus the tax and National Insurance he has already paid on £25,000.

Employee benefits

Some perks are tax-free – see page 97. Others are taxable whatever your income. The tax on non-cash benefits is collected by adjusting your tax code (see Chapter 2). However, if you are lower-paid some perks may be tax-free, or favourably taxed (see page 106). Note that any perks your family gets as a result of your job count as yours.

Are you 'lower-paid'?

Employee benefits are tax-free for lower-paid employees, except for mileage allowances above certain limits (see page 120), living accommodation, free or cheap goods, vouchers, company credit cards and tokens (see rule 5 on page 105).

You are lower-paid if your total gross pay is under £8,500 a year, including any expenses and taxable perks (valued as if you earned £8,500 or more), but minus pension contributions and payroll-giving donations. If you are in a job for only part of the year, the annual equivalent of your pay is used – so if you earn £5,000 for six months, the annual equivalent is £10,000. And if you have more than one job in a year, the £8,500 limit applies to each job separately.

Directors count as lower-paid only if they earn less than £8,500 and:

■ they (and others associated with them) control 5 per cent or less of the shares in the company *and*
■ *either* they are full-time working directors, *or* the company is a charity or non-profit-making.

How employee benefits are valued – eight general rules

When it comes to working out the taxable value of your perks, there are special rules for some types. Otherwise, there is a set of general rules that apply in all other circumstances. There is a quick guide to the most common taxable perks in Table 6.1 on page 106, which will tell you where to find more detail. Your employer should give you a form P11D or P9D after the end of the tax year, telling you the taxable value of your perks. Tax-free perks are listed on page 97.

Rule 1: Cheap or free use of something. Tax-free if you are lower-paid, otherwise you pay tax on 20 per cent of the market value of the item (such as a television or motorbike) at the time when it was first provided as a perk, or on the rent or hire charge paid by your employer if greater, plus any running costs or other expenses met by your employer as a result. (See HMRC help sheet IR210 *Assets provided for private use*.) However, there are special rules for cars, vans and living accommodation.

Rule 2: Gifts of things previously used as a perk. For example, being given a television you have previously borrowed. You are taxed on the market value of the asset at the time of the gift, or (if higher) the initial market value minus any amounts on which tax has already been paid under the rule above (see Example 6.3 opposite). However, if the item is a bike or computer the market value is always used. (See HMRC help sheet IR213 *Payments in kind – assets transferred*.)

Rule 3: Cheap or free services. Tax-free if you are lower-paid, otherwise you are taxed on the extra cost to your employer of providing the services (e.g. hairdressing at work). However, if the services are those your employer provides in their business the extra cost may be nil (e.g. free travel for rail company employees).

Rule 4: Cheap or free goods. If you are lower-paid, you are taxed on the second-hand value of the goods. If you are not lower-paid, you are taxed on either the second-hand value or, if higher, the cost to your employer. If you are given goods your employer makes, you are taxed on the materials and manufacturing costs, not the retail price.

Rule 5: Credit cards, tokens and vouchers. Spending on these is taxed as cash, unless the item is tax-free (see the list on page 98), or counts as an allowable business expense. You can exclude payments for a company car or van – you are taxed on these separately. Note, too, that for non-cash vouchers you are taxed on the cost to your employer, not the face value, and you are not taxed on any interest or subscription fee on a company credit card. (See HMRC help sheet IR201 *Vouchers, credit cards and tokens.*)

Rule 6: If you pay for something. You can deduct from the taxable value of a perk anything you pay for it.

Rule 7: Restricted use. The taxable value is reduced if you have the benefit for only part of a tax year, or if it is shared with another employee.

Rule 8: If you use a perk partly privately, partly for work. You can claim a deduction from the taxable value for the work use of a perk.

Example 6.3: **How the general rules fit together**

Ian's employer lends him a plasma television. Each year, Ian is taxed on 20% of the television's market value at the time he first got it. This was £2,000, so the annual taxable amount is £400 (rule 1).

Eighteen months later, the company gives Ian the television for a token payment of £500. As he had it for only half of the second year, he is taxed only on half of the annual value: £200 (rule 7). The gift itself is taxed at either the current market value (£1,200) or, if higher, the initial market value minus any amounts on which Ian has already been taxed, i.e. £2,000 − £400 − £200 = £1,400 (rule 2). He is taxed on £1,400 minus the £500 he is paying, i.e. £900 (rule 6).

Company cars and free fuel

The taxable value of your company car is a percentage of its list price (even if it is second-hand or leased), with reductions if you have the car for only part of the year or pay something for it. The percentage on which you are

Table 6.1: A quick guide to taxable employee benefits

	Taxable value	Taxable value if lower-paid
Chauffeur	Cost to employer (rule 3)	Tax-free
Company cars	Taxed on up to 35% of car's price, and on up to £5,040 for free fuel – see opposite	Tax-free
Company motorbike	20% of value, or rent if higher (rule 1)	Tax-free
Company vans	From 2007–08, taxed on a flat £3,000, plus £500 for free fuel (see page 110)	Tax-free
Educational assistance for your children	Rule 3 applies, unless help is 'fortuitous'	Tax-free
Free or cheap goods	See rule 4	Second-hand value
Free or cheap services	Cost to employer (rule 3)	Tax-free
Gifts of things previously borrowed	See rule 2	Second-hand value
Living accommodation, unless tax-free (see page 112)	Basic charge of rental/rateable value	Taxable
Loans of goods	20% of value, or rent if higher (rule 1)	Tax-free
Loans of money	Taxed on interest saved, but only if total loans are over £5,000 – lower amounts are tax-free	Tax-free
Mileage allowances	Covered under 'Expenses', see page 120	See page 120
Private medical or dental insurance for UK treatment	Cost to employer (rule 3)	Tax-free
Relocation expenses	The first £8,000 is tax-free (see page 97) – anything else is taxed in the same way as other perks of the same kind	See previous column
Vouchers, tokens and credit cards	Taxed on most spending on these	Taxable

taxed is between 15 and 35 per cent, depending on your car's carbon dioxide (CO_2) emissions. As shown in Table 6.2 on page 109, the lowest percentage applies if your car's emissions are below 145 grams per kilometre (g/km). These percentages will be frozen until 2008, when emissions must be below 140g/km to qualify for the 15 per cent charge, and a new rate of 10 per cent will apply to cars with emissions below 125 g/km. A discount will also be introduced for cars running on E85 fuel.

If you get free fuel for private use, its taxable value is the same percentage (i.e. up to 35 per cent) of £14,400. Note that the taxable value is not reduced if you reimburse your employer for some of your private fuel – you can avoid it only if you repay the full cost of all fuel used for private journeys. The charge is reduced if you have free fuel for only part of the year – but not if you receive free fuel again in the tax year. (For more information, see HMRC help sheet IR203 *Car benefits and car fuel benefits* and the 'Cars' section of the HMRC website.)

The price of a car – the whole price

You cannot reduce a car's taxable value by excluding the cost of accessories if they were fitted before you got the car (except for disability equipment and mobile phones). Accessories fitted afterwards will also be added to the taxable value if they are worth more than £100 per accessory or set of accessories (e.g. alloy wheels).

Working out the taxable value of a company car

1 *Find its 'price'.* This is usually its list price when registered, including delivery charges, taxes, VAT and accessories, but not road tax or the car registration fee. You can deduct anything up to £5,000 you paid towards the cost of the car – and the maximum 'price' is £80,000. The price of a classic car (at least 15 years old, worth at least £15,000 and worth more now than when first registered) is its market value.

2 *Find the approved CO_2 emissions figure.* Use this to find the relevant percentage in Table 6.2 on page 109. CO_2 emissions appear on your car registration document, if registered after 1 March 2001; if not, try

the manufacturer, or the Car Fuel Data website of the Vehicle Certification Agency (see the Fact file). There are discounts for electric or gas-powered cars, listed in Table 6.2.

3   *Multiply the car's price by the percentage charge.* This gives its annual taxable value.

4   *Adjust if the car was unavailable for part of the year.* Multiply the annual taxable value by the number of days it was available, and divide the result by 365 (366 in a leap year). Gaps of under 30 days are ignored.

5   *Deduct anything you paid towards your private use of the car.* The result is your car's taxable value.

6   *Find the taxable value of any free fuel.* The taxable value is worked out using the same percentage as for the car itself (from Table 6.2), but using a set 'price' for the fuel of £14,400. If the car was unavailable for part of the year, multiply the charge by the same percentage used in step 4 above. (See Example 6.4.)

Example 6.4: How much tax on your company car?

Graeme's company car has a price of £18,000, and a CO_2 emissions figure of 220. Table 6.2 shows that he is taxed on 31% of the price in 2006–07. The taxable value of his car if he has it for the whole tax year is £18,000 × 31% = £5,580.

Graeme changed his car in July 2006 for one with CO_2 emissions of 175 and a list price of £20,000 – an annual taxable value of £20,000 × 22% = £4,400.

The taxable value of the free fuel Graeme gets for his company car is worked out at the same percentage as charged on the car itself but using a set 'price' for the fuel of £14,400. So, Graeme would pay tax on £14,400 × 31% = £4,464 on his old car if he had it for the whole of 2006–07, and £14,400 × 22% = £3,168 on his new car.

Graeme has had his first car for 122 out of the 365 days in 2006–07, his second car for 243 days. The annual taxable values are adjusted as follows:

Car		Fuel	
£5,580 × $^{122}/_{365}$ =	£1,865	£4,464 × $^{122}/_{365}$ =	£1,492
£4,400 × $^{243}/_{365}$ =	£2,929	£3,168 × $^{243}/_{365}$ =	£2,109
Total for 2006–07 =	£4,794	Total for 2006–07 =	£3,601

Table 6.2: Taxable percentage of car's price 2006–07 and 2007–08

Approved CO_2 emissions g/km*	Petrol car %	Diesel car†%
Below 145	15	18
145–149	16	19
150–154	17	20
155–159	18	21
160–164	19	22
165–169	20	23
170–174	21	24
175–179	22	25
180–184	23	26
185–189	24	27
190–194	25	28
195–199	26	29
200–204	27	30
205–209	28	31
210–214	29	32
215–219	30	33
220–224	31	34
225–229	32	35
230–234	33	35
235–239	34	35
240 or more	35	35

Discounts for electric or gas-powered cars in 2006–07 and 2007–08

Fuel type	Appropriate percentage	Discount on percentage %
Electricity only	15%	6
Gas only	see Table 6.2	2
Hybrid electricity and petrol	depends on cyclinder capacity	3
Manufactured to run on bi-fuel gas/petrol	see Table 6.2	2

Cars with no approved CO_2 emissions figure

	0–1400cc	1401–2000cc	Over 2000cc
Cars registered before 1 January 1998	15	22	32
Petrol cars registered later	15	25	35
Diesel† cars registered later	18	28	35

*Grams per kilometre.

†Diesel cars approved to Euro IV standards and registered before 1 January 2006 are treated as petrol cars.

Free fuel – is it worth it?

You will cover the cost of the tax only if you spend more on fuel for private use than the amount of tax you will be charged. If you don't do much private mileage, consider paying for all your private fuel yourself, and negotiating a pay rise instead.

Alternatives to a company car

A company motorbike might be a cheaper alternative, or even (in spite of a recent tax increase) a van. Pool cars – used by more than one person, and not usually left overnight at your home – are completely tax-free, as are bicycles used mainly for travel from home to work or between workplaces. Some employers provide an increased salary instead of a car, but HMRC are reviewing 'employee car ownership schemes' set up to avoid tax and National Insurance, and the government may take action to stop these.

Company vans

A company van you use for private travel is always tax-free if you are lower-paid (see page 103). It is also tax-free if the only private use of it that you are allowed is to commute between home and work, and any other private use is insignificant. If you can use it for any other private travel, it counts as a taxable benefit.

If the van does count as a taxable benefit, the taxable value for the 2006–07 tax year was £500, or £350 if the van was four or more years old, counted from when it was first registered to 5 April 2007. You can deduct anything you paid for its use. The taxable value is also reduced if the van was not available for the whole tax year. If several employees share a van or vans the taxable value is split between them.

However, from 6 April 2007, a van's taxable value is £3,000, plus £500 if you get free fuel for private use (previously, there was no tax on any free fuel). The taxable value is reduced if the van is not available for the whole year, or if it is shared.

Free or cheap loans

A free or cheap loan is tax-free if:

- your employer is in the loan or credit business, and you get your loan on the same terms and conditions as members of the public
- *or* you could claim full tax relief on the loan (see page 79), with no deduction for personal use
- *or* the total amount you owe throughout the tax year in question comes to £5,000 or less, excluding loans on which you can claim full tax relief. This exemption would normally cover season-ticket loans. If you go over the £5,000, the whole lot is taxable, not just the amount over £5,000.

The taxable amount, if any, is the difference between the interest you actually paid in the tax year (if any), and the interest you would have paid at the 'official' rate of interest set by HMRC (currently 5 per cent).

The taxable amount is usually worked out using the average of the official rate for the year, and the average loan outstanding. The current and average rates of interest are listed on the HMRC website (see the Fact file). However, if the average figures would give an unrealistic answer (because you paid off most of the loan at the start of the year, say) either you or your tax office can opt to use the real figures worked out on a daily basis.

Low-cost alternative finance arrangements (see page 79) are now taxed in the same way as free or cheap loans.

Example 6.5: the value of a cheap loan

Alberta works for a bank and gets a mortgage on preferential terms. She wants to know roughly how much this will cost her in tax in the coming year. She assumes an average 'official' interest rate of 5%, and an average actual rate of 3.5%, so the perk has saved her interest of 5% − 3.5% = 1.5%.

She finds the average loan outstanding by adding the amount outstanding at the beginning of the tax year (£31,000) to the amount outstanding at the end of the tax year (£29,500) and dividing by two. This gives an average loan of £31,000 + £29,500 = £60,500 ÷ 2 = £30,250. The taxable amount is £30,250 × 1.5% = £454.

Figure 6.1: Tax on free or cheap living accommodation

You are taxed on whichever of the following is higher:

- the yearly rent, if the property is rented
- *or* the gross rateable value of the property (or an estimate agreed with your tax office if there is no rateable value); the rateable value is multiplied by $^{100}\!/_{27}$ if the property is in Scotland to account for differences in rating revaluations
- *minus* any rent you pay

plus (if the property cost over £75,000)

- the cost (or market value, if whoever provides the property has owned it for at least six years before you moved in)
- *minus* £75,000
- *multiplied by* the 'official' rate of interest, set from time to time by HMRC

plus (unless you are 'lower-paid')

- any expenses of the property paid by your employer, such as heating (tax-free for the lower-paid if the supplier's contract is with your employer)
- loans of furniture – see page 104. If the accommodation is tax-free (needed for your job, say), the maximum taxable amount is 10% of your taxable pay.

Free or cheap accommodation

Free or cheap housing is tax-free if it is necessary for you to live there to do your job properly, or it is customary for people doing your type of job (e.g. newsagents running paper rounds) and helps you do your work better. (See HMRC help sheet IR202 *Living accommodation*.) This does not apply to company directors, unless they are 'lower-paid' and they are full-time working directors or they work for a charity or a not-for-profit company. But housing is tax-free for all employees if there is a security threat and they are living there as part of special security measures.

Otherwise you are taxed on any accommodation provided by your employer, however much or little you earn. You are taxed on a basic amount, plus an extra amount if the property cost over £75,000, minus anything you pay for the accommodation. Figure 6.1 shows how this works. If part of the property is used for business, or it was available to you for only part of the year, you can also deduct a proportion to account for this.

Note that if you could choose higher pay instead of free accommodation, you are taxed on the extra pay if this is more than the taxable value of the accommodation.

Share schemes

Various governments have tried to encourage employee share ownership. As a result, there are now several broad categories of 'approved' scheme (see page 98). Benefits from approved schemes are taxable only if you breach the conditions in some way (e.g. by withdrawing benefits early).

Because of the restrictions laid down for approval, employers may prefer to give their directors and employees 'unapproved' shares or share options (an 'option' is the right to buy shares at a set price at some point in the future). Below we explain how unapproved share schemes are taxed. However, the government is on the lookout for tax avoidance using shares or other securities, and you may be affected by the requirement to tell HMRC about some tax avoidance schemes in advance – see page 68.

Free or cheap shares or other securities

The normal rule, if you receive free or cheap shares from an unapproved share scheme, is that you are liable for income tax and National Insurance contributions on the difference between what the shares are worth and the price you paid for them. The rules apply to a wide range of securities, such as loan stock, bonds, unit trusts and futures. (See HMRC help sheet IR219 *Securities acquired from your employment*.)

To prevent employers reducing the taxable value of the shares by artificial schemes, you may also have a further tax bill (a 'post-acquisition charge') on benefits such as perks not available to other shareholders. A charge will also apply if schemes are constructed with restrictions or conversion options which can be used to increase their value later.

There is also special treatment for shares that were issued partly-paid or paid for in instalments. And, in a few circumstances, shares are taxed as if they were employee benefits, rather than pay. If so, they may be taxed as if you had received an interest-free loan to buy them. (See HMRC help sheet IR216 *Securities as benefits* and page 111.)

Share options or securities options

You might have to pay income tax and National Insurance contributions on an option to buy shares or securities:

- When you use the option to buy shares ('exercise' it) through an unapproved scheme.
- If you receive anything in return for cancelling the option – that is, agreeing not to exercise the option, or transferring it to someone else. You are taxed on the amount you receive, whether the scheme is approved or unapproved.

You are unlikely to have to pay tax at the time you are granted an option in an unapproved scheme.

With all taxable options, you are taxed on the difference between the market value of the shares and what you would pay for them using the option. You can deduct anything you paid for the option itself, plus any employers' National Insurance contributions which you may have agreed to pay on your employer's behalf.

How the tax is collected

Your employer must generally deduct income tax and National Insurance from any taxable amount you have received, as described in HMRC help sheet IR218 *Employees' shares: operation of PAYE and National Insurance contributions*. Even if tax has been deducted, you must complete the Share Schemes supplementary pages of the tax return. Make sure that you enter in box 2.41 any amounts on which you have already paid tax under PAYE, or you might end up being taxed twice.

Sheltering your shares

If you are likely to make a taxable capital gain when you sell your shares, check whether you can transfer them into an Individual Savings Account (ISA). In some cases, transfers are free of capital gains tax, and shares in the ISA are tax-free when you eventually sell them. You may also be able to transfer shares into a personal pension fund. See HMRC help sheet IR287 *Employee share and security schemes and capital gains tax.*

Taxable lump sums when you leave a job

These payments fall into three categories: always tax-free, always taxable and sometimes taxable. (See HMRC help sheet IR204 *Lump sums and compensation payments.*)

Negotiate before you leave

Lump sums are a difficult area, and much depends on the circumstances. Before leaving, do your best to make sure that the deal is set up to produce the smallest tax bill for you. If the sum involved is large, or if you are a director, get professional advice.

Always tax-free
- Payments from a registered pension scheme or a foreign government pension scheme.
- Special contributions from your employer to a registered pension plan for you, within limits (see Chapter 8).
- Lump sums paid on account of medical unfitness caused or aggravated by service in the Armed Forces.
- Statutory redundancy pay; Armed Forces redundancy pay.

Always taxable
- Any payment under your terms of employment – e.g. holiday pay, bonuses or outstanding salary paid out in a lump sum – except

those specifically referred to as redundancy pay or benefits.

■ Pay in lieu of notice (but this may be in the 'sometimes taxable' category if you were not entitled to this in your contract, and there was no custom of your employer making such payments), and pay where notice is given but not worked.

■ A non-contractual payment that your employer is accustomed to make or that you could reasonably have expected to receive.

■ Compensation for changes in the terms and conditions of your job.

■ Payment in return for agreeing to restrict your behaviour, e.g. not poaching your ex-employer's staff.

■ Lump sums from a non-registered pension scheme (see page 175), unless you paid the contributions, or your employer paid them but you paid tax on them at the time, or (in some cases) they come from an overseas scheme. Payments paid because of an accident are also tax-free.

■ Contributions paid by your employer into a non-registered overseas pension scheme for you (with some exceptions, listed in the Notes to the employment pages). Before 6 April 2006, contributions to UK non-registered schemes were also taxable.

These payments will usually have tax and National Insurance deducted through PAYE like your ordinary pay.

Sometimes taxable

Other payments and benefits, including non-statutory redundancy pay, compensation for loss of your job and genuine ex gratia payments, are potentially liable to income tax, but not usually National Insurance. When working out the taxable amount, you can deduct:

■ Payments if your job ends because of injury or disability.

■ Some or all payments if your job involved 'foreign service' (help sheet IR204 will help you work this out).

■ The first £30,000 in total of any 'sometimes taxable' payments. Note that statutory redundancy pay, while tax-free itself, must be included when working out how much of the payment is over £30,000.

Any taxable amount is treated separately from your earnings, and taxed after your investment income. This means that a one-off lump sum does not push your investment income (which is favourably taxed in the lower- and basic-rate bands) into a higher tax bracket.

Example 6.6: **Leaving a job**

Alphonso is made redundant, with redundancy pay of £40,000 and pay in lieu of notice. He is taxed on the pay in lieu of notice because this was in his contract. The first £30,000 of his redundancy pay is tax-free, and the remaining £10,000 is taxable at his highest rate of tax.

Tax reliefs you can claim

Expenses

You can deduct from your employment income expenses you incur for work, whether or not your employer reimbursed you. The reimbursements are taxable, so it is important to claim any possible deductions. But some reimbursements are tax-free or your employer may have a 'dispensation' from your tax office to ignore them (see page 96). If so, the reimbursements are not included in your taxable pay and you cannot claim a deduction for them.

Any expenses you claim must meet quite stringent tests. To qualify for tax relief on non-travel expenses, you must incur them 'wholly, exclusively and necessarily' in carrying out your work. Table 6.3 overleaf lists the main expenses that you might be able to claim.

Working at home

You can claim expenses for working at home only if you have to carry out all or part of the key duties of the job there, and have no choice about doing so, and if appropriate facilities are not available at your employer's premises or it is too far away. If these conditions are met, you can claim the extra cost of gas, electricity, metered water, business phone calls and 'dial up'

Table 6.3: Non-travel expenses you might be able to claim

Books	If needed to do your job, not just to keep up to date. May have to claim capital allowances instead if costly and expected life of over two years.
Business entertaining	You can claim only if you work for: ■ a non-trading organisation *or* ■ a trading organisation which has not itself claimed tax relief on the payments (look for a tick in section O of your form P11D), and which has reimbursed you or provided a special entertaining allowance.
Capital allowances for cost of buying equipment and machinery necessary for your work, e.g. office equipment	Percentage of the cost of things such as office equipment, but not cars, motorbikes or bikes. If you make a profit when you sell things on which you have claimed an allowance, there is a taxable 'balancing charge'. (See HMRC help sheet IR206 *Capital allowances for employees and office holders*.)
Employee liabilities and indemnities	Cost of meeting claims for your errors or omissions as an employee, or insurance to cover such costs.
Guide dog if blind	Cost of keeping and replacing a dog.
Home phone and internet access	May be tax-free, see page 97. If not, you can claim work-related share of call charges if a phone is necessary (e.g. for a health worker on call or if you are required to work at home). You cannot claim line rental costs, or the cost of an 'unlimited access' internet package, so get your employer to pay direct.
Loan interest	Only if you can also claim capital allowances on the item you are buying, and the loan is repaid within three years.
Professional fees and subscriptions	Payments that are relevant to your work, or a condition of working (e.g. as a solicitor). Ask your professional body or tax office which fees qualify.
Special security measures	If they are necessary because of your job.
Cost of maintaining or replacing tools, special clothing (but not ordinary clothing worn at work)	Fixed expense deductions have been agreed for workers in some industries, e.g. £100 for plumbers. You can claim more if you spend more. Ask your trade union or other similar body what you can claim.
Working at home	See page 117.

internet access. You can claim £2 a week without having to show what you spent, but you can claim more if you have records to back up your claim. Alternatively, your employer can pay you £2 a week, tax-free, or more if you can give your employer supporting evidence (see page 97).

Travel expenses

If you have to travel for work, whether or not you are reimbursed, you can claim tax relief on travel expenses, such as fares, and the cost of 'subsistence', e.g. accommodation and meals arising from business travel.

There are two types of journey for which you can claim relief (in both cases, the travel must be 'necessary', not just for personal convenience):

■ Travel 'on the job', e.g. between two workplaces, or between appointments if you work at your clients' premises.
■ Travel to or from a place that you go to in order to do your job – but not ordinary commuting, or private travel to a place you do not have to attend for work purposes.

It is usually quite clear when the first type of journey applies, but the second can be tricky. Start by ruling out ordinary commuting, defined as any travel between a permanent workplace and home, or any place that is not a workplace. 'Permanent' can apply to an area, if you have no single permanent workplace and your work is defined by reference to a particular area that you visit regularly – as area representative for Essex, say.

You *can* claim tax relief for travel between your home and a temporary workplace – somewhere you go to for a limited time or for a temporary purpose. But you cannot claim if you carry out, or expect to carry out, a significant part of your duties there over a period of 24 months, or as long as your job lasts if less than 24 months. HMRC interpret 'significant' as more than 40 per cent of your working time. See Example 6.7 overleaf. There are more examples in HMRC guide 490 *Employee travel. A tax and NICs guide for employers.*

More generous rules for foreign travel

If you travel abroad for your work – and providing your employer pays the expenses or re-imburses you – you can claim the cost of all journeys from anywhere in the UK and for a spouse and children who accompany you, if your work keeps you abroad for 60 days or more. See Chapter 10 for the rules if you do all your work abroad.

Example 6.7: Is it business travel?

Annie, Betty and Charlie are all full-time engineers based at head office in Reading. They are all sent to work on a contract in Norwich:

■ Annie is sent to work full-time on a particular phase of the work expected to last about 14 months. Norwich counts as a temporary workplace, and she can claim tax relief on the cost of getting there, hotel bills and meals.
■ Betty spends only three days a week in Norwich, but as this is more than 40% of her working week and her work there is expected to last for three years, Norwich is not a temporary workplace and she cannot claim tax relief.
■ Charlie is also expected to be in Norwich for three years, but he spends only one day a week there. This is not a significant part of his duties so he can claim relief.

Using your own car, van or bike for work

Whichever way your employer reimburses you – flat-rate allowance, mileage allowance, or not at all – you are entitled to the same amount of tax relief, worked out using HMRC-approved mileage rates. These 'approved mileage allowance payments' (AMAP) are shown in Table 6.4.

■ If your employer pays you more than the approved rates, any excess is taxable pay – even if you count as lower-paid (see page 103) – and will be shown on your P11D or P9D.
■ If your employer pays you the approved rates the amount will not appear on your P11D or P9D, but you cannot claim any tax relief.

■ If your employer pays you less than the approved rates, you can claim tax relief on the difference (see Example 6.8). You need to keep a log of business mileage.
■ If you carry other employees on business travel your employer can also pay you a tax-free allowance of up to 5p per passenger per mile, but you cannot claim tax relief if you are paid less than 5p a mile.

The AMAP rates are designed to take account of the capital cost of buying a car. You cannot claim any additional tax relief to cover the cost of buying or renting the car, or for depreciation.

Note that if you have a company car but no free fuel, and your employer reimburses you for your business mileage, this is tax-free. But you cannot claim tax relief if your employer pays you less than the AMAP rates.

Table 6.4: Approved mileage rates for 2006–07 and 2007–08

	First 10,000 business miles — in tax year —	Each mile over 10,000 miles — in tax year —
Cars and vans	40p	25p
Motorcycles	24p	24p
Bicycles	20p	20p

Example 6.8: Tax relief if you use your own car

Amina works as an educational adviser. In 2006–07, she drove 12,000 business miles in her own car. Her employer paid her 35p a mile, £4,200 in total. This is less than the approved rates, so nothing is shown on the form P11D provided by her employer, and she does not have to enter the amounts received on her tax return. Amina works out that she has received £300 less than the approved rates, so she can claim tax relief on this amount.

Using approved rates

First 10,000 miles at 40p a mile	£4,000
Next 2,000 miles at 25p a mile	£500
Total approved mileage payments	£4,500

National Insurance contributions (NICs)

You have to pay NICs on your earnings, unless you are over state pension age. Your earnings for National Insurance purposes are different from your taxable pay for income tax purposes, although the rules are gradually being aligned. Here are the main differences:

- You do not have to pay NICs on most employee benefits, but your employer does.
- The NIC-free mileage allowance for business journeys in your own car or van is also 40p per mile, but it is not reduced if you do more than 10,000 business miles (see page 121).
- Contributions you make to a pension scheme or payroll-giving scheme are included in your pay when working out your NICs. You get income tax relief on these payments, but no relief from your NICs.

The contributions payable are shown in Table 6.5, and see page 24 for information on how they are collected and how to check the deductions.

Saving tax on pension contributions

You pay National Insurance on your own contributions to a pension, but not on your employer's contributions. You may save money by giving up some of your salary in return for a higher employer's pension contribution. This won't work if you pay and your employer reimburses you – if your employer is paying into a personal pension for you, the pension application form should state that these are your employer's contributions.

Table 6.5: Class 1 National Insurance contributions 2006–07 (2007–08)

Earnings	Employee	Employer
First £97 (£100) weekly, £420 (£435) monthly, £5,035 (£5,225) annually	**Nil**	**Nil**
Next £548 (£570) weekly, £2,375 (£2,468) monthly, £28,505 (£29,615) annually	**11%** or **9.4%** if a member of an occupational pension scheme 'contracted out' of the State Second Pension. Some married women may pay less, see page 25	**12.8%** reduced if employer offers a 'contracted-out' pension scheme
Anything above £645 (£670) weekly, £2,795 (£2,903) monthly, £33,540 (£34,840) annually	**1%**	**12.8%**

National Insurance contributions on perks

Employees do not generally have to pay National Insurance on employee benefits, except in the case of:

- fuel for private use in your company car, unless supplied from a company fuel pump, or bought on a company credit card or garage account and the garage is told that the fuel is being bought on behalf of the employer
- other things you buy on a company credit card for your own use, unless the supplier is told that you are buying them on behalf of the employer
- things that are easily convertible into cash, such as shares (unless provided through an approved scheme), fine wine or gold bullion.
- non-cash vouchers, such as gift vouchers, unless they provide one of the tax-free benefits listed on pages 97 and 98.

What to tell HMRC

As an employee, you are unlikely to get a tax return unless you are a director or a minister of religion (of any faith), or if your income is high or you have untaxed income (see Chapter 4). Your employer should give your tax office the information that it needs. But you should tell your tax office if things change (see pages 32 and 46) or if you have a new source of taxable income, or if you want to claim tax relief on work expenses and do not get a tax return – ask for form P87.

If you get a tax return and receive any income or benefit from employment, tick Question 1 in the main tax return and fill in the Employment supplementary pages *unless:*

■ all your employment income is from overseas and you are claiming that you were not resident in the UK (see Chapter 10)
■ *or* you are a director who received no payment in any form, or held a position such as honorary secretary and received only expenses.

Even in the two cases above, you need to tick Question 1 and write an explanation in 'Additional information' at the end of the return.

You will also have to tick Question 2 in the main return and fill in the Share Schemes supplementary pages if you have received taxable benefits from an unapproved employee share scheme in 2006–07, or breached the conditions of an approved share scheme (see pages 98 and 113).

You may have left your job but received sickness or disability benefit paid for by your ex-employer (benefits you pay for yourself are tax-free), or a taxable lump sum from a non-registered pension scheme (see page 175). If so, enter the taxable amounts in Question 13 in the main tax return.

Filling in the Employment supplementary pages

If you had more than one job during the tax year, you will need to fill in one copy of these pages for each employer. Usually, you can just carry information across from the P60 your employer gives you after the tax year (or P45 if you left a job), and from your P11D *Expenses and benefits* form, or the equivalent form P9D if you are 'lower-paid'. (See HMRC help sheet IR208 *Payslips and coding notices*.)

If you had two jobs, or are unemployed at the end of the tax year, note that your P60 may include figures for both jobs and any taxable Jobseeker's Allowance. If so, you will need to separate the figures to put them on separate pages, using your payslips, P45 or other records.

Boxes 1.1 to 1.7 Details of employer

This will allow your tax office to check and update your file. Note that you have to tick box 1.6 if you are a director, and box 1.7 if a director of a 'close' company (one controlled either by its directors or by less than six shareholders or other key 'participators'). This is because special rules often apply to directors, for example when taxing employee benefits.

Boxes 1.8 to 1.11 Money

You should enter in boxes 1.8 to 1.10 any of the following income received in the 2006–07 tax year:

■ all the taxable income listed on page 100, excluding expenses payments (these go in box 1.23); don't include pension contributions and payroll-giving donations (your P60 will already have excluded these)
■ any extra taxable pay, if you are a director or partner affected by the IR35 rules (see page 101)
■ all tips – employers must notify HMRC if they know that a tip-sharing scheme (tronc) is in existence. (See HMRC leaflet E24 *Tips, gratuities, service charges and troncs*.)
■ any taxable income from share schemes that has already been taxed under PAYE (this should be included in the figure on your P60).

It is not always clear what your employer has included in the P60 figure – if you have received a taxed lump sum on leaving a job, say – so you may need to ask your employer what has been included.

Box 1.11 is for any tax deductions shown on your P60 (or P45). Do not include non-UK tax – either enter this on page 2 or claim a separate relief for it in the Foreign supplementary pages (see Chapter 10). Remember to enter figures for the 2006–07 tax year.

Boxes 1.12 to 1.23 Benefits and expenses

Enter here any taxable benefits and expenses you have received. You should be able to take all the figures straight from your P11D or P9D. See page 103 onwards for how these figures are arrived at, but note that:

- you need to enter a figure in box 1.15 (mileage allowance) only if your employer pays you *more* than the HMRC approved mileage rates shown in Table 6.4
- the 'balancing charges' referred to in box 1.23 apply only if you have disposed of (e.g. sold) something on which you previously claimed capital allowances.

Example 6.9: **Filling in the Employment pages**

Mindy is a personnel manager (see Example 6.1 on page 100). In her Employment pages (shown in Figures 6.2 and 6.3), she enters the 'Pay' figure (£34,500) from her P60 in box 1.8, and the 'Tax' figure (£9,213) in box 1.11. (She contributes to the company pension scheme, but the 'pay' figure in her P60 has taken account of this.)

Mindy takes the figures for her benefits and expenses from her P11D. These add £10,474 to her pay, but on page 2 she can claim tax relief for some expenses – £840 for travel expenses and £96 for her subscription to her professional institute. Her taxable pay is £34,500 + £10,474 – £936 = £44,038.

Boxes 1.24 to 1.30A Lump sums

If you received a redundancy payment in 2006–07, the first £30,000 is tax-free. Put the tax-free amount in box 1.24 and anything else in box 1.29.

However, it is not always clear whether a payment counts as 'redundancy', and amounts such as pay in lieu of notice are often taxable (for an overview, see page 115). If you are unsure, or receive any payments within the 'always taxable' category on page 115, or are claiming deductions other than the £30,000 exemption, read HMRC help sheet IR204 *Lump sums and compensation payments* to help you work out the taxable amount. To sum up:

Figure 6.2: Employment page 1 (see Example 6.9)

HM Revenue & Customs

EMPLOYMENT

Fill in these boxes first

Name
MINDY MALONE

Tax reference
12345 67890

If you want help, look up the box numbers in the Notes.

Details of employer

Employer's PAYE reference - the 'HM Revenue & Customs office number and reference' on your P60 or 'PAYE reference' on your P45

1.1 A1111234

Employer's name
1.2 DUSTY MILLER BAKERIES

Date employment started
(only if between 6 April 2006 and 5 April 2007)
1.3 / /

Date employment finished
(only if between 6 April 2006 and 5 April 2007)
1.4 / /

Employer's address
1.5 CRUSTY HOUSE
FRIARY ROAD
CRUNCHESTER

Tick box 1.6 if you were a director of the company
1.6

and, if so, tick box 1.7 if it was a close company
1.7

Postcode CR1 2AB

Income from employment

■ *Money* - see Notes, page EN3.

● Payments from P60 (or P45)

Before tax
1.8 £ 34,500

● Payments not on P60, etc. - tips
1.9 £

- other payments (excluding expenses entered below and lump sums and compensation payments or benefits entered overleaf)
1.10 £

● UK tax taken off payments in boxes 1.8 to 1.10

Tax taken off
1.11 £ 9,213

■ *Benefits and expenses* - see Notes, pages EN3 to EN6. If any benefits connected with termination of employment were received, or enjoyed, after that termination and were from a *former* employer you need Help Sheet IR204, available from the Orderline. Do not enter such benefits here.

● Assets transferred/ payments made for you
Amount
1.12 £

● Vans
Amount
1.18 £

● Vouchers, credit cards and tokens
Amount
1.13 £

● Interest-free and low-interest loans see Notes, page EN5.
Amount
1.19 £

● Living accommodation
Amount
1.14 £

box 1.20 is not used.

● Excess mileage allowance and passenger payments
Amount
1.15 £

● Private medical or dental insurance
Amount
1.21 £ 1,200

● Company cars
Amount
1.16 £ 5,400

● Other benefits
Amount
1.22 £

● Fuel for company cars
Amount
1.17 £ 2,850

● Expenses payments received and balancing charges
Amount
1.23 £ 1,024

101 v7

Figure 6.3: Employment page 2 (see Example 6.9)

Income from employment continued

■ *Lump sums and compensation payments or benefits including such payments and benefits from a former employer*

You must read pages EN6 and EN7 of the Notes **before** filling in boxes 1.24 to 1.30.
Reliefs

- £30,000 exception `1.24` £
- Foreign service and disability `1.25` £
- Retirement and death lump sums `1.26` £
- Exempt employer's contributions to an overseas pension scheme `1.26A` £

Taxable lump sums

- From box B of *Help Sheet IR204* `1.27` £
- From box K of *Help Sheet IR204* `1.28` £
- From box L of *Help Sheet IR204* `1.29` £

- Tax taken off payments in boxes 1.27 to 1.29 - *leave blank if this tax is included in the box 1.11 figure but tick box 1.30A.*   Tax taken off `1.30` £

- Tick this box if you have left box 1.30 blank because the tax is included in the box 1.11 figure `1.30A`

■ *Foreign earnings not taxable in the UK in the year ended 5 April 2007* `1.31` £
  - see Notes, page EN7.

■ *Expenses you incurred in doing your job* - see Notes, pages EN7 and EN8.

- Travel and subsistence costs `1.32` £ *840*
- Fixed deductions for expenses `1.33` £
- Professional fees and subscriptions `1.34` £ *96*
- Other expenses and capital allowances `1.35` £
- Tick box 1.36 if the figure in box 1.32 includes travel between your home and a permanent workplace `1.36`

■ *Seafarers' Earnings Deduction*
  - enter the amount of the earnings that attract the deduction, not the tax
  - enter ship names in box 1.40 (see Notes, page EN8 and Help Sheet IR205) `1.37` £

■ *Foreign tax for which tax credit relief not claimed* `1.38` £

Student Loans

■ *Student Loans repaid by deduction by employer* - see Notes, page EN8. `1.39` £

- Tick box 1.39A if your income is under Repayment of Teachers' Loans Scheme `1.39A`

`1.40` *Additional information*

Now fill in any other supplementary Pages that apply to you.
Otherwise, go back to page 2 in your Tax Return and finish filling it in.

- Box 1.27 is for payments received under the terms of your employment – the 'always taxable' category on page 115.
- Box 1.28 is for lump sums from non-registered retirement schemes, minus any tax-free amounts (which should be entered in box 1.26 or 1.26A).
- Box 1.29 is for other payments in the 'sometimes taxable' category on page 116, including redundancy, minus deductions for foreign service or disability (box 1.25) and minus the £30,000 exemption (box 1.24).

Note, though, that the £30,000 exemption is per job, so if you received payments relating to one job in more than one tax year you may already have used part of the exemption. If so, you should use help sheet IR204.

Your employer may deduct tax on your lump sum. If the tax is included in your P60 or P45 (you may need to check this with your employer), you will have entered it in box 1.11. If so, make sure you leave box 1.30 empty and tick 1.30A. Only enter in box 1.30 tax deducted by your employer that you have not already entered in box 1.11.

Boxes 1.32 to 1.36 Expenses

Enter here work expenses for which you are claiming tax relief (see Table 6.3 on page 118). Note that box 1.36 ('includes travel between your home and a permanent workplace') is a bit of a trap. You cannot usually claim tax relief for home-to-work travel, and if you tick box 1.36 prepare to justify your claim to your tax office.

Boxes 1.31, 1.37, 1.38 and 1.40 Foreign earnings and foreign tax

If you have included income from working abroad in boxes 1.8 to 1.10 you may be able to claim deductions:

- in box 1.31 depending on whether or not you are a UK resident for tax purposes, and where the job was done (see HMRC help sheet IR211 *Employment – residence and domicile issues*)
- in box 1.37 if you were a seafarer working outside the UK (see HMRC help sheet IR205 *Seafarers' earnings deduction*). Also enter in box 1.40 the names of the ships you worked in
- in box 1.38 to account for any foreign tax you have paid. Note,

though, that 'tax credit relief' may be a better option – if so, you will need to complete the Foreign supplementary pages (see page 223).

Boxes 1.39 and 1.39A Student loans and Teachers' Loan Scheme

If you have an 'income-contingent' student loan (see page 6) and your employer has deducted loan repayments from your pay, enter the total deductions here. The amount will be shown on your P60, but if you change jobs you should also check the amounts shown on your payslips. Tick box 1.39A if you have a loan, but the government is paying it for you under the Repayment of Teachers' Loans Scheme and your employer has been notified of this.

Common mistakes

- Failure to complete a separate supplementary page for each job.
- Entering your pay in box 1.8 but not entering any tax deducted in box 1.11.
- Entering your gross pay in box 1.8, before deducting pension contributions and payroll giving.
- Entering tax deductions more than once – e.g. tax on a lump sum should go in either box 1.11 or box 1.30, not both.
- If you have a cheap or free loan, entering in box 1.19 the amount borrowed instead of the taxable amount.

Record-keeping

Here are some of the key records you should keep.

Your pay

- Your P60 or P45 as evidence of your taxable pay, and your P11D or P9D showing taxable benefits and expenses.
- A note of any tips or gratuities, or any other taxable pay. Record these as soon as you get them, rather than estimating them later.
- Correspondence relating to any lump sum payment.

Your expenses

- Copies of expense claims and foreign travel itineraries.
- Records of business mileage; VAT receipts for motoring expenses.
- Receipts, credit statements and other purchase records. If you have to give these to your employer, keep copies of your expense claims.
- Notes of cash payments for which you have not got a receipt.

If you are in a share scheme or receive share-related benefits

- Any related correspondence from your employer.
- The price you paid for your shares or options, and the relevant dates.
- The market value of the shares at relevant dates, such as when you received them (or options to buy them) or exercised your option to buy.
- A copy of each share option certificate or exercise notice.
- Notes of any benefits received, or alteration in the rights or restrictions attached to your shares.
- A note of any tax you have already paid on the benefit.

Tax-planning hints

1 Beware of the IR35 rules if you are a director or partner in your own business providing services (see page 101).
2 Make life easy – keep your P60, P45 and P11D carefully. And keep your own records of expenses, particularly business mileage.
3 If you use your own car for work, you can claim tax relief at the approved mileage rates even if your employer pays less (see page 120).
4 You can claim tax relief on home-to-work travel if you are working at a temporary but not a permanent workplace (see page 119).
5 Free fuel for your company car is now heavily taxed, particularly if you end up paying National Insurance on fuel bills reimbursed by your employer (see page 122). Consider paying for your private fuel yourself (but you have to pay for the whole cost of private use, not just part).
6 A more fuel-efficient company car will save you tax (and see page 110 for cheaper alternatives).

7 Beware – the tax payable on private use of a company van has risen sharply from April 2007. You can avoid this if the only private use you are allowed is ordinary home-to-work commuting.

8 Tax relief going begging? You may be able to claim a fixed expense deduction for things like tools or special clothing (see page 118).

9 If you regularly work from home, your employer can pay you £2 a week tax-free, to cover extra household costs (see page 117). If you are not reimbursed, you may be able to claim a £2 a week expense deduction.

10 If your employer offers you free childcare or childcare vouchers, check the effect on your tax credits. You cannot claim tax credits for childcare costs met by your employer, so you could end up worse off, particularly if you give up salary in return for the perk.

11 If you are in an approved share scheme, check the rules – you may have to pay tax if you breach the conditions.

12 Capital gains tax may be payable when you sell shares from some share schemes. You may avoid this if you transfer the shares to an ISA first.

13 If you get a pay-off on leaving a job, negotiate with your employer to make sure it is paid in a way that minimises your tax bill (see page 115).

14 Your own contributions to a pension scheme are liable to National Insurance, but your employer's are not. You save National Insurance if you sacrifice salary for higher employer's pension contributions.

15 Don't forget to enter on your Employment supplementary pages *all* the tax you have paid or had deducted.

16 Even if you don't have to fill in a tax return, and your tax is deducted under PAYE, don't assume that it's right. Check your tax position after the end of the tax year.

7

Income from your business

As the 'job for life' moves towards extinction, more people are experiencing self-employment for at least part of their working lives. However, becoming self-employed also means taking responsibility for sorting out your own tax, and organising your cashflow so that you can pay your tax in two instalments, on 31 January and 31 July each year.

When you are starting up on your own, sorting out your tax may be a less immediate concern than meeting your first orders. However, it cannot be ignored. You must notify Her Majesty's Revenue & Customs (HMRC) within three months of starting up, or risk a £100 penalty.

Does this affect you?

This chapter affects you if you are self-employed, either as a sole trader or in a partnership. If you are a director of your own company, you are also 'in business', but strictly speaking you are an employee of the company and your tax is covered in Chapter 6. The company has its own tax return and is subject to corporation tax – not covered in this book.

This chapter does not affect you if receive odd bits of freelance income but have not set up in business to do this. Income of this type is taxed separately and should be reported under 'All other income' in Question 13 of the tax return (see page 62). However, if you regularly receive such income – from frequent eBay trading, say – or the amount is substantial, you might be regarded as trading. If in doubt, contact your tax office.

Sole traders

A 'sole trader' is what you are if you simply start up on your own, without creating (or buying into) a partnership or setting up a company (a separate legal entity). The whole of any profits or losses counts as your income, on which you are liable to pay income tax and Class 2 and Class 4 NICs. You may also have to pay capital gains tax (see Chapter 12) on profits from disposing of or transferring business equipment or property, although there are special tax reliefs for businesses.

Partners

As a partner, you have a share in the partnership's profits or losses, and any capital gains, as set out in the partnership agreement. The partnership has its own tax return, but is not itself taxed – you pay income tax and National Insurance on your share of profits as if you were a sole trader. And you can make your own choices about how you use your share of any losses – your choices may be different from those of other partners.

Sole trader, partner or company?

Many people working for themselves do so as a company or partnership. A key reason is that you can pay yourself in the form of either a salary or dividends (with a company), or alter the profit-sharing agreement (with a partnership), to benefit from differing tax and National Insurance rules.

However, the attraction of doing this has been reduced:

- The small company rate of corporation tax is rising from 1 April 2007.
- If you provide services through a company or partnership that you control and HMRC think that you are effectively an employee of your client, you may be treated as if you received extra pay (see page 101).
- From 6 April 2007 'managed service companies' – umbrella companies through which workers supply services on a self-employed basis – must deduct PAYE and Class 1 National Insurance.
- In some situations, if you pay dividends to a family shareholder who is taxed at a lower rate than you, HMRC may seek to tax the dividends as your income. There is guidance to the 'settlements legislation', as

this is known, on the HMRC website, but HMRC's views are being challenged, so get professional advice.

Even if you are a sole trader, your tax office may decide that you are not self-employed, but an employee of your client, liable to PAYE and employee's National Insurance. Note that you can be employed for one piece of work and self-employed for another.

There is no simple definition of self-employment, but there have been many court cases, and a number of 'tests' have developed. (See Table 7.1 overleaf, but note that it is the overall picture that counts, and each test cannot be looked at in isolation.) You can ask your tax office for a written decision about your 'employment status', but you can appeal if you disagree. (See HMRC leaflet IR56 *Employed or self-employed?*.) There is also an interactive 'employment status indicator' on the HMRC website, and a guide for people who sell items online or at car boot sales.

Sole trader, partner or company?

The legal form your business should take depends on your individual situation and the nature and needs of your business. Get specialist advice, but do not be driven by tax considerations alone – companies have to meet many more legal requirements than sole traders.

Should you register for VAT?

You have to register if your turnover over the previous 12 months (excluding exempt sales) rises above a threshold, or you expect it to do so in the next 30 days. The threshold was £61,000 in 2006–07, £64,000 from 1 April 2007. The rate of VAT is currently 17.5 per cent, although a few goods and services are exempt, zero-rated, or chargeable at 5 per cent.

Even if you do not have to register, you may choose to do so voluntarily, because it allows you to reclaim the VAT on things you buy for the business. However, it will put up your prices for private customers (business customers will be able to reclaim the VAT you charge). Note that if your products are exempt (e.g. health services) you cannot reclaim VAT.

Table 7.1: Tests for self-employment

These suggest employment	*These suggest self-employment*
Control Your client has the right to tell you at any time what to do, or when, and where and how to do it	**Right to subcontract** You can choose whether to do the work yourself or hire (and pay) someone else to do it for you
Location You work at your client's premises, or at a place or places he or she decides	**Providing your own equipment** You supply the main items needed to do your job
Payment You are paid by the hour, week or month, receive overtime pay and benefits (e.g. sick pay or expenses) and work set hours or a given number of hours a week or month	**Risking your own money** You bear the cost of overheads, for example by working on a fixed price, or paying for your own skills training for use in future work
Part and parcel of the organisation You have staff management responsibilities, for example	**Risk of losses** You have to correct unsatisfactory work in your own time and at your own expense
Right of termination Either you or your client can end the contract by giving a set period of notice, even if there is no breach of contract	**Personal factors** You may be, for example, a skilled worker working for several clients in a year
Long periods working for one client	**No right to work and pay** Your client has no obligation to provide work or pay when no work is available

There is also the paperwork to consider. If you register you must complete a VAT return each quarter, showing the VAT you have charged your customers ('output tax') and the VAT you have paid on your business purchases ('input tax'). Your input tax is deducted from your output tax and you pay the balance over to HMRC (who administer VAT). If your input tax comes to more than your output tax, you get a refund.

If the record-keeping puts you off, remember that you are required to keep similar records for income tax purposes. There are also several schemes to simplify the record-keeping for small businesses and retailers.

Contact the VAT National Advice Service (see the Fact file) and see leaflet 700/1 *Should I be registered for VAT?*.

Flat rate VAT – a simpler way

This scheme allows small businesses (with turnover up to £150,000) to charge the full 17.5% rate of VAT but pay over to HMRC a smaller percentage, ranging from 2% to 13.5% of turnover depending on your trade, with a further 1% reduction in the first year of VAT registration. If you do this, you cannot reclaim VAT on the things you buy. Ask the VAT National Advice Service (see the Fact file) whether you qualify.

Many businesses will save VAT by using the Flat Rate Scheme (see the ready reckoner on the HMRC website) and, if you keep your books on a VAT-inclusive basis, it is simpler.

How income tax on your business is worked out

You are taxed on your business profits (or losses) for a 'basis period'. Normally, your basis period is the accounting period ending in the tax year in question. So if you make up your accounts to the end of December each year, say, in the 2006–07 tax year you pay tax on your profits for the period for 1 January 2006 to 31 December 2006. HMRC help sheet IR222 *How to calculate your taxable profits* explains basis periods, and see page 149.

Working out your taxable profits

You must work out your profits on an 'earnings' basis – i.e. income is included in your accounts from the date it is earned, not when you receive it, and expenses on the date you incur them, not the date paid.

■ *Step 1: add up your business income,* i.e. the turnover from your trade or profession. There is no tax-free income to ignore, but exclude sales of capital items. If you take things from stock for your own or your family's use, this counts as a sale.

- *Step 2: deduct your business expenses,* adjusted to take account of any expenses in your accounts not allowed for tax, such as depreciation on cars and business equipment (see page 140).
- *Step 3: deduct capital allowances* – you can claim these instead of depreciation (see page 144).

Work in progress for service businesses

Businesses providing services used to be able to include income in their turnover only when invoiced. However, changes in accounting rules – known as the UITF40 rules – mean that you should now include in your profits an amount for unbilled work, valued at its full selling price. This applies to accounting periods ending after 21 June 2005.

Say you are working on a job for which you will charge £12,000 and at your year end, you have spent half the time you expect to spend on it overall. Under the new rules, you must add £6,000 to your profits for the year just ending.

In the first tax year you do this – which, if your year end is between 22 June and 5 April, would have been 2005–06 – extra income may be taxable. This is treated as a one-off adjustment, not part of your normal profits for that year, but you can spread it over three to six years. For what to enter in your tax return, see page 166 and HMRC help sheet IR238 *Revenue recognition in service contracts.*

The result of steps 1 to 3 is your net business profit (or loss) for an accounting period for tax purposes. But you may need to adjust this:

- *Step 4: adjustments if your basis period is not the same as your accounting period.* This usually affects you in the first year or so you are in business or in your final year of trading (see page 149 for how it works).
- *Step 5: deduct losses from previous years* – the result is your taxable profit for a basis period. See page 155 for more about losses.
- *Step 6: add on any other taxable business income.* This includes business start-up allowances and incentives received if you take a lease on business property. You cannot deduct anything for expenses.

The result gives you your taxable income from self-employment, which is taxed at 10 per cent, 22 per cent or 40 per cent, according to what falls into the lower-, basic- and higher-rate bands (see page 5).

A partner in a partnership? Steps 1 to 3 all take place in the partnership's tax return. The business profits (or losses) are then shared out according to the partnership agreement, and the adjustments covered in steps 4 to 6 are made in your own tax return. Joining a partnership counts as starting in business, and leaving counts as closing down.

What expenses can you deduct?

The law concentrates on what you *cannot* do rather than what you can – in particular, you cannot deduct expenses which are not 'wholly and exclusively' for your trade. However, there are many expenses that HMRC commonly accept. There is useful guidance on HMRC practice in the *Business Income Manual* in the practitioners' area of their website.

If an expense is partly for business, partly private, you can usually claim a proportion in line with the business use. For example, you can claim some expenses for using your car or home for work. Table 7.2 overleaf summarises the main items, but there is more detail in the notes to the Self-employment or Partnership pages of the tax return.

The main expenses you cannot deduct
- The cost of buying or improving fixed assets, or depreciation (you can claim capital allowances instead).
- Costs and fines for breaking the law (parking fines, say).
- Business hospitality – you can claim the cost of entertaining staff, but not if this arises as part of business hospitality (e.g. if an employee takes a customer out to lunch, the whole cost is business hospitality).
- The non-business part of any expense.
- Tax (but you can deduct employer's NICs and, if you are not VAT-registered, VAT).
- Your own pay, benefits, pension contributions and NICs.

Table 7.2: Summary of business expenses you can claim

Advertising and promotion	Newspaper advertisements, mailshots, non-consumable gifts with a prominent advertisement worth £50 or less per person
Bad debts	Amount of money included in turnover but written off at end of accounting period (not a general bad debts reserve)
Employee costs	See opposite
General administrative costs	Phone bills, postage, stationery, printing, office expenses, insurance, and publications if necessary for work
Interest and other finance	See page 143
Legal and professional costs	Fees of accountant, solicitor, surveyor, stocktaker etc., professional indemnity insurance, costs of debt recovery (but not costs of buying or selling fixed assets)
Premises costs	See page 142
Raw materials and goods bought for resale	See opposite
Business costs of cars and other vehicles	See page 143
Other business travel costs	Rail, air and taxi fares, hotels, meals when away overnight on business. Lunches only if away overnight, or if you habitually travel on business, or on occasional trips outside your normal pattern of travel
Pre-trading expenditure	Allowable expenses are treated as if incurred on the date you start trading
Research and development costs related to a trade (not a profession)	Excludes costs of acquiring rights to research – you may be able to claim capital allowances instead
Trade and professional subscriptions	Subscriptions to relevant associations. Also contributions to local enterprise agencies and other such bodies

Raw materials and goods bought for resale

If you make or sell things, you will need to carry out a stock-take at the end of each accounting period. You should value your stocks (including your work in progress) at their cost to you or, if lower, the amount they would fetch. Include things that you have received but not yet paid for.

To work out what you have used during the period:

■ take the value of your stock and work in progress at the start of the period
■ *add* anything you bought during the period
■ *deduct* what you have left at the end of the period.

Employee costs

You can deduct all the costs of hiring other people, whether they are permanent, temporary or casual staff, or subcontractors. This includes pay, pension contributions, employer's NICs and all other staff-related costs, such as employee benefits and training.

However, you cannot deduct your own pay, National Insurance, benefits or pension contributions. You can claim the cost of your own training if this is to update your existing skills, but you are likely to have difficulty justifying your claim if the result is a completely new skill.

If you take on an employee, you will have to comply with the requirements for operating PAYE (see Chapter 2). HMRC have a new employer's helpline which you can use to register or get advice (see the Fact file).

Employing family members

You can claim tax relief on the pay and National Insurance of a family member you employ, but you must be able to show that the work is needed for the business, the family member actually does it and is formally paid for doing it, and that you are paying a reasonable rate for the job. There is no National Insurance on earnings below £5,225 in 2007–08 (see Chapter 2), but if you pay at least £87 a week your employee will become entitled to contributory state benefits such as the retirement pension. You should also pay at least the National Minimum Wage (see page 28).

Premises

If you have business premises, you can claim rent, business rates, water rates, light, heat, power, maintenance and repairs (but not improvements), property insurance, security costs and so on. For leases of 50 years or less, you can claim part of any premium you pay. You cannot claim the cost of buying property, although you may be able to claim capital allowances for fixtures and fittings if they are 'plant' (see page 144), or for some industrial buildings or hotels, or for renovating vacant premises in Enterprise Areas.

If you work from home, you can claim the same types of expense (including mortgage interest and council tax), in line with the proportion of your home used for business. But HMRC say that when part of the home is being used for business then that must be the sole use for that part at that time. The basis for any claim should be explained – and records kept to support it. Alternatively, you can claim a flat £2 a week without having to keep records. HMRC have a section on working from home in the Business Income Manual on their website.

Example 7.1: **Using your home for work**

Paul runs a software business from home. He has one of the eight rooms set aside as an office, and he claims one-eighth of his mortgage interest as a business expense. At the end of the tax year he asks his lender for a 'certificate of interest paid' and claims one-eighth of the interest shown (he can't claim capital repayments). He also claims the same proportion of his heating, lighting and council tax bills.

Using part of your home exclusively for work

If part of your home is used for business alone, with no private use, part of any gain when you sell the house is liable to capital gains tax (see Chapter 12). However, even if part of your home does become liable to capital gains tax, the gain would be reduced by taper relief for business assets, and possibly roll-over relief (see page 271).

Interest and other finance costs

You can claim bank charges, credit card charges and overdraft interest. You can also claim interest on a loan to buy something you use in your business (or a proportion of the interest if you use it partly for business, partly privately). This includes hire purchase interest (but not capital repayments), finance lease rentals and alternative finance payments (see page 79).

However, if you lease a car (but not a van) worth more than £12,000 when new, you can claim only part of the hire charge. The percentage you can claim is the car's price plus £12,000, divided by twice the car's price.

Cars and other vehicles

You can claim running costs of a car or other vehicle you use for work, including fuel, servicing, repairs, road tax, insurance, parking charges (but not fines) and the cost of rescue services.

If you use the car for private purposes as well as for business, there are two methods of claiming vehicle costs, but you can only change between methods when you acquire a car. Whichever method you use, you can claim interest on a loan to buy the car, or other finance costs. The two methods are:

■ you can claim a proportion of the costs, in line with the amount of business mileage you do, plus capital allowances (see page 144)

■ *or* if your turnover is below the level at which you need to register for VAT (see page 135), whether or not you have registered, you can claim a set figure per business mile, using the mileage rates shown in Table 6.4 on page 121. If so, you cannot claim capital allowances.

Example 7.2: **Claiming your car as an expense**

About 20% of Leah's mileage is for business. She can either claim 20% of the running costs of her car, plus a £600 capital allowance for the cost of buying it (see Example 7.4 on page 148), or, because her turnover is below the VAT registration limit, she can claim just the HMRC-approved mileage rate (40p per mile in Leah's case). In either case, she can also claim 20% of the interest on her car loan.

VAT

Unless you sell only exempt goods or services, you can deduct the VAT you pay on most things you buy for your business.

If you are not VAT-registered you get your tax relief by deducting the VAT-inclusive cost of expenses and capital allowances from your turnover. If you are VAT-registered, your profits are usually worked out excluding VAT on both your income and your expenses. If you have opted for the Flat Rate Scheme, you can keep your books either way. But if your accounts exclude VAT, then any VAT you save by being on the scheme must be declared as taxable income on your tax return, otherwise you will get income tax relief on more VAT than you have paid – see page 162.

Capital allowances

If you buy plant and machinery (capital assets) for use in your business, such as cars, vans, tools, computers and office equipment, you can claim capital allowances to be deducted from your profits. Only part of the allowance can be claimed if an asset is used partly for private purposes.

You can also claim capital allowances on some industrial or agricultural buildings and hotels, and on things like patents and scientific 'know-how'. However, here we concentrate on plant and machinery. You cannot claim capital allowances on houses or (except in an enterprise zone) on shops or offices, but you can claim them on some fixtures and fittings and the costs of converting flats over shops (see Chapter 9).

The basic principle of capital allowances on plant and machinery is that you claim 25 per cent of the cost of an item in the first year, and 25 per cent of the remaining cost in each later year. However, in the accounting period of purchase, you may be able to claim a higher 'first-year allowance', and see page 148 for changes on the way.

Capital allowances don't always save tax

If you don't claim allowances in full one year, you have more value remaining in your pool to claim in future. Don't claim if you wouldn't have to pay tax on your profits anyway.

Figure 7.1: What happens in the year you buy a new item

1 Can you claim a 100% first-year allowance (see overleaf)? **YES** → Claim the whole of the cost. The item is still added to your pool in case there is a balancing charge when you sell it. If it is used partly privately, put it in its own pool, otherwise put it in your main pool.

NO ↓

2 Is the item a car, something you bought to lease out, or something that you have brought into your business after using it privately? **YES** → No first-year allowance (you claim a 25% writing-down allowance instead). Put each car worth over £12,000 in its own pool – the maximum writing-down allowance is 25% or £3,000 if less. All other cars go in your main pool (but see 5 below if used privately).

NO ↓

3 Deduct first-year allowance (40% or 50%, see overleaf).

↓**NEXT**

4 Do you want to claim that this is a 'short-life' asset (one you expect to dispose of within five years)? **YES** → Put it in its own pool and claim it as a short-life asset on your tax return. If you dispose of it within five years, you can claim an immediate allowance for anything left in the pool. If you don't scrap it within five years, its remaining value is added to your main pool.

NO ↓

5 Used partly privately? **YES** → Put it in its own pool. Your allowances are restricted in line with the business use (see Example 7.4 on page 148).

NO ↓

6 Any remaining costs are added to your main pool of expenditure.

First-year allowances

Small businesses can claim 50 per cent of the cost of most plant and machinery purchased in 2006–07 and 2007–08 except cars (up from 40 per cent for 2005–06 purchases). Businesses of any size can claim 100 per cent on some environmentally friendly equipment. This includes new cars with CO_2 emissions of 120g per kilometre or less bought before 31 March 2008. (There is a website listing other items that qualify – see the Fact file.) From 11 April 2007 you can also claim a 100 per cent Business Premises Renovation Allowance for renovating vacant business premises in disadvantaged areas.

Working out allowances

The cost of each new item, after deducting first-year allowance, is added to a 'pool' of expenditure. Some things have to be kept in separate pools, but everything else goes in one main pool – see Figure 7.1 on page 145. At the end of each accounting period you work out your writing-down allowance on each pool as follows:

1 Take the value of the pool at the end of the previous accounting period and add the cost of any new purchases, excluding those which qualify for a first-year allowance.
2 Deduct the proceeds of any sale from the value of the pool, or the original cost of the item if less. (The market value is deducted if you gave the item away or started to use it for non-business purposes.) If the sale proceeds are more than the value of the pool, the difference is a *balancing charge*.
3 Multiply the result by 25 per cent. This is your *writing-down allowance* on the pool. Deduct the writing-down allowance from the value of the pool so far.
4 Add the cost of any new purchases which qualified for a first-year allowance (after deducting the first-year allowance). The result is the value of your pool at the start of the next accounting period.

The total of your first-year allowances and writing-down allowances is *deducted* from your taxable profits. If you sell something in the pool for more than the value of the pool so far, the difference is a balancing charge and it is *added* to your profits.

Your allowance or balancing charge must be adjusted if:

- You use an item partly for business, partly privately. The capital allowance (or balancing charge) is restricted in line with the proportion of any business use (see Example 7.4 overleaf) and you must keep it in a separate 'pool'.
- Your accounting period is not 12 months (e.g. when starting up in business). If your accounting period is eight months long, say, you get eight-twelfths of the full writing-down allowance. But first-year allowances are not adjusted in this way.

Example 7.3: Working out capital allowances

In May 2006, Noah paid £1,500 for energy-saving equipment on which he gets a 100% first-year allowance, and £6,500 on office equipment to which a 50% allowance applied. He sold his old equipment for £2,450. Note that had Noah bought before 6 April 2006, the office equipment would have received only a 40% allowance.

		Allowances £	Pool £
Pool at start of period			4,250
Sales			−2,450
			1,800
Writing-down allowance	£1,800 × 25%	450	−450
			1,350
Purchases			
Energy-saving £1,500	× 100% first year allowance	1,500	0
Other purchases £6,500	× 50% first year allowance	3,250	3,250
Pool to carry forward			4,600
Total allowances		5,200	

Example 7.4: Capital allowances on a car

Leah's car has a written-down value of £13,000. As it cost over £12,000, the maximum allowance she can claim in any one year is 25% or £3,000 if less – £3,000 in Leah's case. However, as her business mileage in the car is only 20% of the total mileage, she can only claim 20 per cent of the full allowance: £3,000 × 20% = £600.

Changes to capital allowances

From April 2008, first-year allowances for plant and machinery will be replaced by a £50,000 annual investment allowance, and the writing-down allowance will fall from 25 per cent to 20 per cent. Allowances on industrial and agricultural buildings will be phased out, but tax credits for research and development costs will be increased. Capital allowances for business cars are also under review.

Buying on credit

You can claim capital allowances for things bought with a loan or on hire purchase, or using an alternative finance arrangement (see page 79). You cannot claim capital allowances on items bought with a finance lease unless the lease lasts at least five years, sometimes more (the lessor gets the allowance, not you).

When a pool ends

If you sell an item that is kept in a separate pool, or scrap an asset that you have nominated as a 'short-life' asset (see page 145), or you close down your business, you can claim the whole of any value remaining in your pool as a 'balancing allowance'.

Basis periods explained

Your profits are calculated for an accounting period, but you are taxed on your profits for a 'basis period'. After you have been in business for two or three years, the two periods will coincide. Until then, you may need to make an adjustment to your profits for your first, and possibly your second, accounting period. You may also have to make adjustments if you change your accounting date.

If your basis period is shorter than the period covered by one set of accounts, you pay tax on only part of the profits in your accounts. If it is longer, you add in part of the profits of the next set of accounts. Splitting up your profits is done according the number of days, weeks or months in each period.

A partner in a partnership? You have your own basis period, which may differ from that of the other partners in the first year or so after you join the partnership. Otherwise, the rules are the same as for sole traders.

First tax year you are in business
Your 'basis period' is the period between the date you start up and the next 5 April. (See page 159 for what you need to do on starting up.)

Example 7.5: **Your first tax year in business**

Archie starts up on 5 January 2007 and ends his first accounting period on 5 January 2008. His basis period for the 2006–07 tax year is 5 January 2007 to 5 April 2007 – three months. However, as his first accounts cover a 12-month period, he pays tax for 2006–07 on ³⁄₁₂ of the profits of his first accounting period.

On his tax return for 2006–07 he reports his profits for the whole of his first accounting period, but then (in box 3.77) he deducts an adjustment of ⁹⁄₁₂ of his profits.

Second tax year you are in business
Your basis period depends on the length of your first accounting period. If it is less than 12 months, you are taxed on 12 months' profits, beginning on the date you started. If it is 12 months or more, you are taxed on the profits of the 12 months up to your accounting date (see Example 7.6 overleaf).

If you had no accounting period ending in the tax year, you are taxed on the profits of the 12 months from 6 April in one year to 5 April in the next, as shown in Example 7.7.

Example 7.6: **First accounting period 12 months or longer**

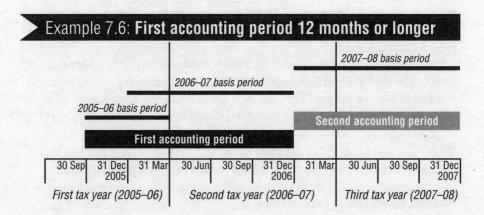

Andrew starts in business on 1 October 2005 and ends his first accounting period on 31 December 2006 – 15 months later – with a profit of £25,000. For the 2006–07 tax year (his second in business) his basis period is the 12 months up to 31 December 2006. The profits for this basis period are $^{12}/_{15}$ of the profits in his first accounting period – i.e. £25,000 $\times$ $^{12}/_{15}$ = £20,000. He must enter a negative adjustment of £25,000 – £20,000 = £5,000 in box 3.77 of his 2006–07 tax return.

Three months of the profits in Andrew's 2006–07 basis period have also been included in his 2005–06 basis period, i.e. £25,000 $\times$ $^{3}/_{15}$ = £5,000. These are called 'overlap profits'.

Give yourself time to work out your profits

If your first accounting period ends just before 31 January (the last date for sending in your return), you might have to work out your tax on the basis of provisional figures. HMRC allow this if – like Archie above – your accounting period ends within three months of 31 January, but you will have to pay interest if you underestimate your tax.

> Example 7.7: **First accounting period less than 12 months**

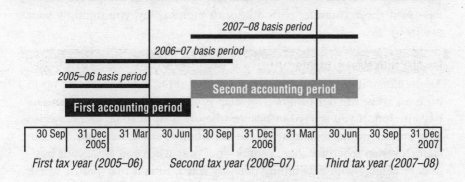

Belinda also starts in business on 1 October 2005, but she ends her first accounting period after 9 months, on 30 June 2006. Her basis period for her second tax year in business (2006–07) is the 12 months from the day she started up, i.e. 1 October 2005 to 30 September 2006. Her profits were:

1 October 2005–30 June 2006	£18,000
1 July 2006–30 June 2007	£40,000

To make up the profits of her 2006–07 basis period, Belinda is taxed on the 9 months' profit from her first accounting period (£18,000), and 3 months of the profits from her second accounting period – i.e. £40,000 × $\frac{3}{12}$ = £10,000. She will be taxed on £18,000 + £10,000 = £28,000.

Six months of these profits overlap with those included in the 2005–06 basis period (£18,000 × $\frac{6}{9}$ = £12,000), and three months overlap with those included in the 2007–08 basis period (£40,000 × $\frac{3}{12}$ = £10,000). Belinda's 'overlap profits' are £12,000 + £10,000 = £22,000.

Third tax year you are in business

From this tax year on, your basis period is the 12 months running up to your accounting date in that year – so if, for example, you make up your accounts to 30 September each year, your basis period for the 2006–07 tax year would be the period from 1 October 2005 to 30 September 2006.

Your accounting period ending in the third tax year may be longer than 12 months. If so, you will need to take just 12 months of this period's profits – so if the accounting period lasts 16 months, say, you multiply your profits by $^{12}/_{16}$.

Dealing with overlap profits

As the illustrations in Examples 7.6 and 7.7 show, when you start up in business some of your profits – 'overlap profits' – fall into more than one basis period. If you started in business before 6 April 1994, you may also have overlap profits that arose on the transition to self-assessment. You can claim 'overlap relief' for these profits – but only when you close your business or change your accounting date, by which time it may not be worth very much after taking inflation into account.

Overlap profits look as though they have been taxed twice. In practice, at the end of each tax year you will find that the number of months' profit on which you have been taxed, including the overlap period, is the same as the number of months in which you have been in business so far.

Note that if you make a loss in an overlap period, you cannot claim the whole loss in each overlapping basis period. Instead, part of the loss belongs to one tax year and the rest to the next tax year. (So if Belinda in Example 7.7 made a loss, six-ninths of it would belong to 2005–06 and three-ninths to 2006–07.)

Keeping things simple

You have no overlap profits if you end your accounting period with the end of the tax year – which doesn't necessarily mean 5 April. If your accounting period ends on any date from 31 March to 4 April, you can treat it as ending on 5 April.

When is your first tax bill due?

If you haven't received a tax return, you must tell your tax office that you have taxable profits by 5 October after the end of your first year in business. (You should in any case tell them within three months of the end of the month when you become self-employed – see page 159 for how to do so.) If you have any taxable profits in your first basis period (running up to 5 April), you will have to pay the tax on them by the following 31 January.

You may have to start making payments on account on 31 January following the end of your first tax year in business, but as Chapter 4 explains, you have to do this only if less than 80 per cent of your tax bill for the previous tax year was met from tax paid at source, and if more than £500 of your tax was *not* deducted at source. (See Example 7.8.)

Example 7.8: **When do you first pay tax?**

Craig and Darren each started a business in October 2006, making a profit of £6,000 in 2006–07. Craig was unemployed for the first half of 2006–07, and his tax for the year is £430. He must send in his tax return and pay the tax by 31 January 2008, but he has no payments on account to make for 2007–08 because his 2006–07 tax was under £500.

Darren, however, was in a good job, and his tax comes to £4,370. He will have to make a payment on account for 2007–08 if less than £4,370 × 80% = £3,496 of his 2006–07 tax was paid at source. His employer had deducted PAYE, but only £3,000, so on 31 January 2008, as well as paying the £4,370 − £3,000 = £1,370 tax outstanding for 2006–07, he must also start making payments on account for 2007–08. These are £1,370 ÷ 2 = £685, payable in January and July 2008.

For 2007–08 they again had the same profits and they each had a tax bill of £3,000, due on 31 January 2009. Darren had already paid £1,370 through his payments on account. But Craig had to pay the whole £3,000 in one go. At the same time, they both had to make their first payment on account of £1,500 for 2008–09:

		Craig	Darren
31 Jan 08	Outstanding tax for 2006–07	£430	£1,370
	First payment on account for 2007–08	–	£685
	Total tax to pay	£430	£2,055
31 July 08	Second payment on account for 2007–08	–	£685
31 Jan 09	Outstanding tax for 2007–08	£3,000	£1,630
	First payment on account for 2008–09	£1,500	£1,500
	Total to pay	£4,500	£3,130

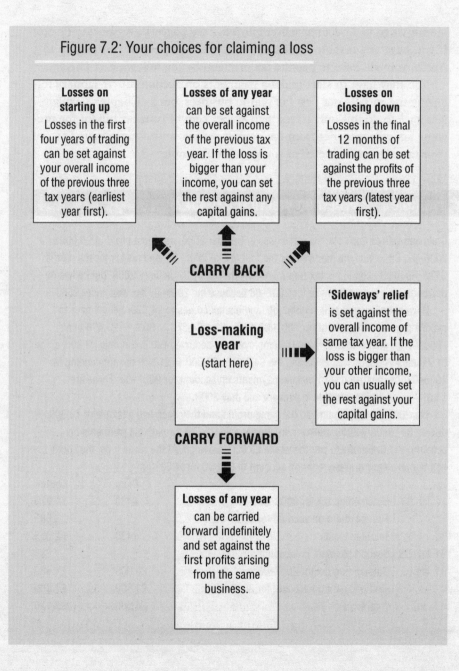

Figure 7.2: Your choices for claiming a loss

Losses on starting up
Losses in the first four years of trading can be set against your overall income of the previous three tax years (earliest year first).

Losses of any year
can be set against the overall income of the previous tax year. If the loss is bigger than your income, you can set the rest against any capital gains.

Losses on closing down
Losses in the final 12 months of trading can be set against the profits of the previous three tax years (latest year first).

CARRY BACK

Loss-making year
(start here)

'Sideways' relief
is set against the overall income of same tax year. If the loss is bigger than your other income, you can usually set the rest against your capital gains.

CARRY FORWARD

Losses of any year
can be carried forward indefinitely and set against the first profits arising from the same business.

Planning your tax

Depending on your tax outstanding after the first tax year in business, you will have to start making payments on account anything from 10 to 22 months after the end of your first tax year in business. A long delay could mean a large bill to pay in one go, so plan ahead. (See Example 7.8 on page 153.)

Choosing your accounting date

■ Depending on the date you choose, you may have a lot of overlap profits or none at all.
■ Overlaps work in your favour if your profits are rising, against you if your profits are high in the first year and then drop.
■ The simplest option is to end your first accounting period at the end of a tax year, but ending your accounting period as early as possible in the tax year means that you have longer to work out your tax bill before you have to submit your return.

When your business ends
You are taxed on your profits between the end of your basis period for the previous tax year and the date you stop trading or leave the partnership. If you have any profits when you close down, you can deduct any overlap relief brought forward. If you close with a loss, it is increased by the amount of any overlap relief.

Losses

If you make a loss, you can claim tax relief for it in a number of ways. (See Figure 7.2, and HMRC help sheet IR227 *Losses*.)

Provided you claim within the time limits (see below) you can carry the loss back to set against the income of earlier years. If so, the tax saved is worked out using the rates of tax that applied in the earlier year, and given as a credit against your statement of account. Alternatively, 'sideways relief' allows you to set your losses against your overall income of the same tax year (e.g. from investments or another job), and, if you still have losses left over, your capital gains. But you cannot claim only part of a loss.

Otherwise, once you have claimed your losses by entering them in your tax return, they are carried forward indefinitely and used in the first year in which you have profits from the same business – even if those profits are not taxable because they are less than your personal allowances, say.

A partner in a partnership? Any losses are shared out according to the partnership agreement, and each partner can use them as he or she prefers. However, partners who do not spend a significant amount of time running the business are restricted in the amount of losses that they can set against their overall income.

Time limits for using your losses

It often makes sense to set your losses against other income or carry them back, rather than carry them forward against profits that may never arise. But this depends on your tax bill in the earlier and current years, and your likely profits in future.

If you want to carry back losses, or claim sideways relief, you must claim on your tax return (or tell your tax office) within 12 months of 31 January after the end of the tax year in which you made the loss, i.e. by 31 January 2009 for losses made in 2006–07. The time limit is longer – 31 January 2013 – for losses on closing down or losses carried forward.

Example 7.9: Claiming a loss

Anji made a loss of £5,000 in her first year in business and expects her profits for the next year to be low. She can carry her loss forward, or set it against the overall income of the current tax year or any of the previous three tax years. Anji has some income from investments in the current tax year, but she will only pay basic-rate tax on this, whereas in the previous three tax years (before she left her job to set up on her own) she was a higher-rate taxpayer. She will save most tax by carrying back her loss: £5,000 × 40% = £2,000.

> ## Special rules for some trades

- Agriculture – see HMRC help sheets IR224 *Farmers and market gardeners* and IR232 *Farm stock valuation.*
- Art and literature – see help sheet IR234 *Averaging for creators of literary or artistic works.*
- Foster or adult care – see help sheet IR236 *Foster carers and adult placement carers.*
- Medicine – see help sheet IR231 *Doctors' expenses.*
- Construction – see leaflet CIS340 *Construction industry scheme* and the construction industry section on the HMRC website.

National Insurance contributions

As a self-employed person, you may have to pay both Class 2 and Class 4 National Insurance contributions.

If you have a job as well as being self-employed, you may also have to pay Class 1 employees' NICs, but there is an overall maximum. You can apply to defer paying some of your contributions (see page 30).

Class 2 NICs

These are flat-rate contributions of £2.10 in 2006–07 (£2.20 in 2007–08). When you start up in business, you must register with HMRC within three months of the end of the month in which you start trading, and then, if you are liable, payments are usually made by monthly direct debit. You will be sent a separate bill for any contributions between registering and the first direct debit. However, you do not have to pay once you are over state pension age (65 for men, 60 for women).

If your profits are less than £4,465 in 2006–07 (£4,635 in 2007–08), you can apply not to pay Class 2 contributions. But this could affect your right to state retirement pension and some other state benefits, so you may want to continue paying. (Full details are given in the application form CF10 *Self-employed people with small earnings.*)

Class 4 NICs

You do not have to pay Class 4 NICs for any tax year if, on the first day of that year, you are over state pension age. Otherwise, you pay a percentage of your profits. Table 7.3 shows the rates payable. So if your taxable profits are £37,840 in 2007–08, say, you would pay nothing on the first £5,225, 8 per cent on the next £29,615 (i.e. £2,369) and 1 per cent on anything over £34,840 (i.e. on £37,840 − £34,840 = £3,000). This comes to £2,369 + £30 = £2,399 in total.

Class 4 NICs are collected with your income tax through your payments on account. If you have more than one business, the rate payable depends on the total profit from all your businesses (see HMRC help sheet IR220 *More than one business*). If you are a partner in a partnership you pay Class 4 NICs on just your share of the partnership's profits. You do not have to pay them if you are a sleeping partner, contributing to, but not working in, the partnership.

Table 7.3: Class 4 NICs for 2006–07 (2007–08 figures in brackets)

Slice of taxable profits	Rate payable
First £5,035 (£5,225)	Nil
Next £28,505 (£29,615)	8%
Anything above £33,540 (£34,840)	1%

Use your losses

You can use losses to reduce your Class 4 NICs. However, if you choose to set your losses for income tax purposes against non-trading income (which is not liable to Class 4 contributions), you will have unused losses for National Insurance purposes. You do not have to use them the same way as for income tax, and instead you can carry them forward to set against future profits when working out Class 4 NICs. (See Example 7.10.)

Example 7.10: **How losses can reduce Class 4 NICs**

Anji (from Example 7.9) had a loss of £5,000 that she set against her non-trading income of an earlier year – but this income wasn't liable to Class 4 NICs. So she still has the whole £5,000 available to reduce her profits for the purposes of Class 4 NICs in future years.

Thinking of taking somebody on?

You will have to deduct PAYE and National Insurance if your employee's pay is above the 'earnings threshold' – £100 a week in 2007–08 (see page 16). Even if you pay less, you must register as an employer with HMRC if they have another job, or if you provide any benefits, or if you pay more than the 'lower earnings limit' of £87 a week in 2007–08, as this is the level above which they qualify for contributory benefits such as state pension. Contact HMRC's helpline for new employers (see the Fact file).

What to tell HMRC

The most important thing is to register as self-employed, or a partner, within three months of the end of the month in which you start trading. If you don't, and you have no reasonable excuse, you will have to pay a penalty of £100 unless you can show that the annual equivalent of your earnings so far is below the threshold for Class 2 NICs (£4,635 in 2007–08).

There is a helpline for the newly self-employed on which you can register (see the Fact file). Also see leaflet SE1 *Thinking of working for yourself?*, which has a registration form. This includes a box to tick if you think you will have to register for VAT. HMRC have Business Support teams that give practical advice and run free local workshops. (See the Fact file.)

Once you have registered, you should receive tax returns – though possibly only a short return if your turnover is low (see page 50). If you get the full return, start on page 2 and tick:

■ Question 3 if you were self-employed as a sole trader – you will need to complete the Self-employment supplementary pages.

■ Question 4 if you were a partner in a partnership – you will need to complete the Partnership supplementary pages.

A partner in a partnership? The partnership gets its own tax return which covers all the business profits received by the partnership. It also contains a 'partnership statement' that tells your tax office how the income and gains have been shared out between the partners. Individual partners also get Partnership supplementary pages for their own tax returns, covering their share of the profit or loss, and any adjustments claimed by them as individuals (e.g. losses).

Filling in the Self-employment or Partnership pages

The Self-employment pages and most of the Partnership tax return are very similar, so you can use the information below to help you fill in both.

Boxes 3.1 to 3.13 Business details

Enter the business or partnership's name and address, and the date the business started up or ceased (if this was between 5 April 2004 and 6 April 2007). If you (or the partnership) have more than one trade you will need to complete a separate form for each.

You will also need to complete separate forms if the figures of more than one accounting period are included in your basis period for the 2006–07 tax year – e.g. if you have just started in business. If you have included one set of figures in last year's tax return you do not have to give them again, but tick 3.10 if this applies to all your accounts.

Box 3.9 applies only if you are a foster carer or adult carer, or if you run a business completely overseas and are taxed on a remittance basis (see Chapter 10). If so, you only need to complete a few boxes in the form. (Note that most income received by foster carers is tax-free – see help sheet IR236 *Foster carers and adult placement carers*.)

The other boxes in this section give your tax office the information it needs to check your basis period.

Boxes 3.14 to 3.23 Capital allowances

See page 146 for how to work out the figures to enter in this section. Balancing charges are amounts that have to be added to your income when you make a profit on selling something for which you have previously claimed capital allowances.

Short-life assets

If you bought something in this period that you want to treat as a 'short-life asset' (so that you can claim immediate relief if you scrap it within five years), you must put in a claim within one year and ten months of the end of the tax year. You can do this by adding a note under 'Additional information' at the end of the self-employment pages.

Boxes 3.24 to 3.26 Income and expenses – annual turnover below £15,000

If your *annual* turnover is below £15,000, you don't need to fill in boxes 3.27 to 3.73 of the form – instead, just enter here your overall income, expenses and net profit and move on to box 3.74. These are called 'three-line accounts'. Don't forget to include your capital allowances with your expenses, and any balancing charges with your income.

Common mistake

You complete boxes 3.24 to 3.26 only if your turnover is below £15,000 for a full year. This means that if the accounting period you are reporting here is shorter or longer than 12 months, you must adjust the £15,000 proportionately. So if it is 8 months, say, the threshold is £15,000 × $\frac{8}{12}$ = £10,000; if it is 14 months, it is £15,000 × $\frac{14}{12}$ = £17,500.

Boxes 3.27 to 3.73 Income and expenses – annual turnover £15,000 or more

Leave this page blank if you have already completed boxes 3.24 to 3.26.

Otherwise, transfer the necessary information from your accounts or other records. You may have to make the following adjustments:

- You should enter non-trading income relating to your business in the relevant pages of your basic tax return (e.g. Question 10 if you receive interest from a business bank account). If you include such income in box 3.50 (other income/profits), also enter it in box 3.71 as a deduction, or you will be taxed on it twice.
- If your expenses include amounts that do not qualify for tax relief, enter the disallowable part in boxes 3.30 to 3.45. These are added to your profits at box 3.69. (See the table of allowable and disallowable expenses in HMRC's notes.) This is unlikely to apply, however, if you are keeping records only for tax purposes, not formal accounts, and you enter only the allowable amounts in boxes 3.30 to 3.63.
- Goods taken out of your business for private use count as a sale for tax purposes and should be added back in at box 3.67.
- Add in your capital allowances and balancing charges at box 3.70 or 3.68.

Dealing with VAT

You do not need to tick box 3.27 or 3.28 (which ask whether your figures include VAT) if you were not VAT-registered during this period, but be sure to include any VAT paid in your expenses, so that you can get tax relief on it.

If you are in the Flat Rate Scheme (see page 137), and your figures are VAT-inclusive, tick box 3.27 and enter your payments to HMRC as an expense at box 3.63. But if your figures exclude VAT, any VAT saved counts as taxable income. As well as ticking box 3.28 you will need to work out the VAT saved and enter it at box 3.50; any extra VAT incurred can be claimed as an expense in box 3.63.

Check the HMRC notes for what to enter if you are VAT-registered but you are entering figures including VAT, or supply zero-rated goods, or are partly exempt, or if you registered or deregistered for VAT during this period.

Example 7.11: **Filling in pages 2 and 3**

When Alex transferred his figures from his accounts to his Self-employment pages, he had some adjustments to make. The 'other income' in box 3.50 is interest on a bank account; as he has also entered this elsewhere in his tax return, he deducts it at box 3.71 to avoid being taxed on it twice (see Figure 7.3 on page 164).

Alex made a profit of £13,193 in this, his first accounting period (but his second basis period). As this is a 14-month period (1/11/05 to 31/12/06), he must deduct two months' profits at box 3.77, £13,193 $\times$ 2 $\div$ 14 = £1,885, leaving profits for this basis period of £13,193 − £1,885 = £11,308. As his basis period for the 2006–07 tax year overlapped with that for the 2005–06 tax year, he has overlap profits of £2,827 to carry forward in box 3.80 (see Figure 7.4 on page 165).

Boxes 3.74 to 3.93 Adjustments to arrive at taxable profit or loss

These boxes appear only in the Self-employment pages, but if you are a partner you will see the same questions at boxes 4.5 to 4.21 of the Partnership pages that go with your personal tax return.

Example 7.12: **Adjustments for service businesses**

Mark runs a research consultancy with a year end of 31 March. On 31 March 2006 his work in progress was worth £5,000. Under the new rules for service businesses, he added £5,000 to his turnover and included it in box 3.29 of his 2005–06 tax return. He also had to make an adjustment for work in progress at the end of the previous accounting period (31 March 2005). This was worth £6,000 but he must treat it as an adjustment to be entered in box 3.82 of his 2005–06 return. He is claiming to 'spread' the adjustment over three years, so he should enter £2,000 in box 3.82 in each of his 2005–06, 2006–07 and 2007–08 tax returns. However, if the spread amount comes to more than one-sixth of the profits of his business, he can spread the payments over a period of up to six years.

■   The 'Adjustments to arrive at profit or loss' (box 3.77) applies if your basis period is not the same as your accounting period. This may also

Figure 7.3: Self-employment pages (see Example 7.11)

Income and expenses - annual turnover £15,000 or more

You must fill in this Page if your annual turnover is £15,000 or more - read the Notes, pages SEN2, SEN4 to SEN7

If you were registered for VAT, will the
figures in boxes 3.29 to 3.64, include VAT? **3.27** [ ] or exclude VAT? **3.28** ✓

Sales/business income (turnover)

3.29 £ *42,302*

	Disallowable expenses included in boxes 3.46 to 3.63	Total expenses	
• Cost of sales	**3.30** £	**3.46** £ *12,002*	
• Construction industry subcontractor costs	**3.31** £	**3.47** £	
• Other direct costs	**3.32** £	**3.48** £	box 3.29 *minus* (boxes 3.46 + 3.47 + 3.48)
		Gross profit/(loss)	**3.49** £ *30,300*
		Other income/profits	**3.50** £ *434*
• Employee costs	**3.33** £	**3.51** £ *8,013*	
• Premises costs	**3.34** £	**3.52** £ *3,020*	
• Repairs	**3.35** £	**3.53** £	
• General administrative expenses	**3.36** £	**3.54** £ *540*	
• Motor expenses	**3.37** £ *320*	**3.55** £ *775*	
• Travel and subsistence	**3.38** £	**3.56** £	
• Advertising, promotion and entertainment	**3.39** £	**3.57** £ *330*	
• Legal and professional costs	**3.40** £	**3.58** £ *150*	
• Bad debts	**3.41** £	**3.59** £	
• Interest and alternative finance payments	**3.42** £	**3.60** £	
• Other finance charges	**3.43** £	**3.61** £ *85*	
• Depreciation and loss/(profit) on sale	**3.44** £ *3,150*	**3.62** £ *3,150*	
• Other expenses	**3.45** £	**3.63** £ *64*	total of boxes 3.51 to 3.63
	Put the total of boxes 3.30 to 3.45 in box 3.66 below	Total expenses	**3.64** £ *16,127*
		Net profit/(loss)	boxes 3.49 + 3.50 *minus* 3.64 **3.65** £ *14,607*

Tax adjustments to net profit or loss

• Disallowable expenses	boxes 3.30 to 3.45 **3.66** £ *3,470*	
• Adjustments (apart from disallowable expenses) that increase profits. For instance; goods taken for personal use and amounts brought forward from an earlier year because of a claim under ESC B11 about compulsory slaughter of farm animals	**3.67** £	
• Balancing charges (from box 3.23)	**3.68** £	
Total additions to net profit (deduct from net loss)		boxes 3.66 + 3.67 + 3.68 **3.69** £ *3,470*
• Capital allowances (from box 3.22)	**3.70** £ *4,450*	
• Deductions from net profit (add to net loss)	**3.71** £ *434*	boxes 3.70 + 3.71 **3.72** £ *4,884*
Net business profit for tax purposes (put figure in brackets if a loss)		boxes 3.65 + 3.69 *minus* 3.72 **3.73** £ *13,193*

Figure 7.4: Self-employment pages (see Example 7.11)

Adjustments to arrive at taxable profit or loss

Basis period begins   **3.74** *01 / 11 / 05*   and ends   **3.75** *31 / 12 / 06*

Profit or loss of this account for tax purposes (box 3.26 or 3.73)   **3.76** £ *13,193*

Adjustment to arrive at profit or loss for this basis period   **3.77** £ *(1,885)*

- Overlap profit brought forward   **3.78** £   • Deduct overlap relief used this year   **3.79** £

- Overlap profit carried forward   **3.80** £ *2,827*

- Averaging for farmers and creators of literary or artistic works *(see Notes, page SEN7, if you made a loss for 2006–07)*   **3.81** £

- Adjustment on change of basis   **3.82** £

Net profit for 2006–07 (if you made a loss, enter '0')   **3.83** £ *11,308*

Allowable loss for 2006–07 (if you made a profit, enter '0')   **3.84** £

- Loss offset against other income for 2006–07   **3.85** £

- Loss - relief to be calculated by reference to earlier years   **3.86** £

- Loss to carry forward (that is allowable loss not claimed in any other way)   **3.87** £

- Losses brought forward from earlier years   **3.88** £

- Losses brought forward from earlier years used this year   **3.89** £

Taxable profit after losses brought forward   box 3.83 *minus* box 3.89   **3.90** £ *11,308*

- Any other business income (for example, Business Start-up Allowance received in 2006–07)   **3.91** £

Total taxable profits from this business   box 3.90 + box 3.91   **3.92** £ *11,308*

- Tick box 3.93 if the figure in box 3.92 is provisional   **3.93**

Class 4 National Insurance contributions - see Notes, pages SEN9 and SEN10

- Tick box 3.94 if exception applies   **3.94**

- Tick box 3.95 if you **hold** a deferment certificate for 2006-07   **3.95**

- Adjustments to profit chargeable to Class 4 National Insurance contributions *(If you are calculating your tax enter the amount of Class 4 NICs due in box 18.28 on Page 7 of your Tax Return not in box 3.96)*   **3.96** £

Subcontractors in the construction industry

- Deductions made by contractors on account of tax (please send your CIS25s to us)   **3.97** £

Tax taken off trading income

- Any tax taken off trading income (excluding deductions made by contractors on account of tax)   **3.98** £

have created overlap profits to enter in box 3.78. (See page 152 for how to work out these figures.) Note that you can claim to deduct overlap relief this year (at box 3.79) only if your business has closed down or you have changed your accounting date.

■ Boxes 3.81 applies only if you are a farmer or market gardener, writer or artist (see page 157 for where to find more information).

■ Box 3.82 is for adjustments arising from accounting changes, e.g. if you are moving from a 'cash' basis of accounting. If yours is a service business, under the new UITF40 rules for work in progress (see page 138) you may have to enter here a one-off adjustment for any unbilled work outstanding at the end of the last accounting period before 22 June 2005. You can spread the adjustment over several years (or pay it off faster if you prefer). If you are claiming 'spreading', enter here one-third of the value of the unbilled work, or one-sixth of your profits if less, and include an explanation under 'Additional information', box 23.9. Do not include the value of unbilled work arising from any accounting period ending on or after 22 June 2005 – this goes in box 3.29, not here. See HMRC help sheet IR238 *Revenue recognition in service contracts* and Example 7.12.

■ Use boxes 3.85 to 3.89 to keep track of your losses from this business. (See Figure 7.2 on page 154 for the choices you have.) Boxes 3.85, 3.86 and 3.87 tell your tax office what you want to do with any losses from the current year. If you made a profit, and have losses from the same business made in previous years, enter the total losses in box 3.88, and the amount used in 2006–07 in box 3.89. If you want to set losses against capital gains, remember also to enter them in box 8.5 of the capital gains tax supplementary pages.

■ 'Any other business income' (3.91) is explained at step 6 on page 138. Enter the amount received in the tax year, not the accounting period.

You should tick box 3.93 if the figure in box 3.92 is estimated. Remember also to tick box 23.2 in the main tax return, and give further information in box 23.9 – see page 67.

Boxes 3.94 to 3.96 Class 4 National Insurance contributions (4.23 to 4.25 on Partnership pages)

See page 158 for how these contributions are calculated. You do not need to enter the amount in the supplementary pages. Instead, enter an overall figure for all your businesses in box 18.2B of the main tax return (see page 63), unless you are asking HMRC to calculate your tax.

However, as shown by Example 7.10 on page 159, it is important to enter any unused business losses from earlier years as an 'adjustment' at box 3.96. You may also have to enter an adjustment if you have an entry at box 3.82 (because the adjustment is not liable to Class 4 contributions) or if your trading income includes interest.

You do not need to pay contributions at all, and can tick box 3.94, if you were over state pension age on 6 April 2006, or exempt (i.e. because you are not resident in the UK, or you are a professional diver or a trustee). If you have a job as well as your business, and have a certificate from HMRC's National Insurance Contributions Office entitling you to defer your contributions (see page 30), tick box 3.95.

Boxes 3.97 to 3.98 Tax deducted (4.75 to 4.75A on Partnership pages)

Box 3.97 (4.75) applies only if you are a subcontractor in the building trade, and you have received payment with tax already deducted. The CIS25 vouchers showing the tax should be sent in with your return.

It is unlikely that you will have anything to enter in box 3.98. If you have, you may not be self-employed – contact your tax office.

Boxes 3.99 to 3.115 Summary of balance sheet

Complete these boxes only if you actually have a balance sheet in your accounts for this accounting period – you are not required to have one.

Common mistakes

- Failing to complete the Self-employment pages in full, particularly box 3.74 onwards.
- Including in expenses the amount spent on plant and machinery, instead of claiming capital allowances, or entering the full expense in box 3.14, not just the allowance.
- Not reducing your capital allowances or expenses to reflect any private use (of a car, say).
- Entering the amount of Class 4 National Insurance in box 3.96 – this should go in box 18.2B, not here.
- If you are working out your own tax, forgetting to include in boxes 18.4 and 18.5 of the main tax return any adjustment from carrying back business losses, or from averaging your income if you are a farmer, writer or artist.

Record-keeping

You do not need to send a copy of your accounts to your tax office. But you must keep records to back up your entries, and you must keep all records for at least five years and ten months from the end of the tax year (so records for the 2006–07 tax year must be kept until 31 January 2013). See page 13. As well as records of income and expenses (including receipts and invoices) remember to keep records of:

- if you are starting up, the date you registered as self-employed
- transactions between your business and your private finances (it is usually simplest to keep separate bank accounts)
- stock and work in progress at the end of the accounting period
- cash transactions, such as till rolls and a daily note of tips received
- payments to staff, including (if you are in the building trade) records of tax deducted from payments and a note of what you did to decide whether staff were employees or self-employed
- business mileage in a car used both privately and for work (and running expenses if you are not using the HMRC-approved mileage rates)
- how much of any losses you set against your profits for Class 4 National Insurance purposes (see Example 7.10).

If you keep your records on computer you must also keep your original paper records unless you microfilm them or use optical imaging.

Tax relief on pre-trading expenses

You can claim tax relief on business expenses incurred before you formally start in business. Make sure you keep records of all possible expenses. If you register for VAT, you can also claim back VAT on some pre-registration expenses, but you will need a receipt showing the supplier's VAT registration number.

Avoiding an enquiry

Unusual or unexplained items in your Self-employment pages may trigger an HMRC enquiry. Explain in the 'Additional information' box anything that might look odd and make sure that your records support your explanations, for example:

■ the basis on which you split expenses between private and business use
■ reasons for any 'blips' in turnover or expenses compared to the year before – e.g. increased premises costs
■ rounded numbers which might look like estimates
■ the basis of any valuation, and who the valuer was
■ explanations of any provisional or estimated figures.

Tax-planning hints

1 When you start up, spend some time getting your records set up to make filling in your tax return (and VAT returns if applicable) easy. Do get help to establish what expenses you can claim – and on accounting periods and whether you should set up a company or partnership rather than operating as a sole trader.
2 You can claim tax relief on some pre-trading expenses.

3   See page 155 for guidance on choosing your accounting period. The simplest option is to end it on 31 March.

4   In the January after the end of the tax year in which you first make taxable profits, you may have to pay an instalment of tax in advance, as well as tax owed so far. Put cash aside to meet the bill.

5   If you make a loss, you have a number of options that might be better than setting it against a future year's profits – but you must claim within the time limits (see page 156). Keep separate records of your losses for Class 4 National Insurance purposes (see page 158).

6   You may have paid too much National Insurance if, for example, you had losses from a previous year that you have not yet set against profits, or if you carried on paying even though you were over state pension age (see page 158). If you think you might have paid too much, contact HMRC's National Insurance Contributions Office (see the Fact file) and ask for a refund.

7   You can claim exemption from Class 2 National Insurance if your profits are low – but this may affect your right to state benefits.

8   The Flat Rate Scheme may save you VAT (see page 137).

9   If you work from home, you can claim a proportion of your household expenses, but if you use part exclusively for work, there may be capital gains tax when you sell the property (see page 268).

10 Buying a new car for business and personal use? You will need to decide whether to use the HMRC-approved mileage rates, or split the actual expenses in line with your business use (see page 143).

11 Remember to claim the VAT portion of any expense if you are not registered for VAT.

12 You can claim tax relief on the pay and National Insurance of a family member you employ – but it must be a proper job (see page 141). Consider paying them a salary below the threshold for deducting National Insurance and PAYE, but make sure that you pay a realistic rate for the job, and not less than the National Minimum Wage. And it is a good idea to pay enough to reach the lower earnings level (for 2007–08, £87 a week) to protect the employee's rights to state pension and other contributory benefits.

13 You can claim capital allowances on equipment you buy for the business – but this might not save you tax, see page 144.

14 If you buy equipment with a short useful life (such as high-tech
equipment), claim it as a 'short-life' asset on your tax return. Then if
you scrap it within five years, you can claim an immediate allowance
for its written-down value (see page 145).

15 You can get a 100 per cent capital allowance on cars with very low
CO_2 emissions, on some environmentally beneficial equipment and on
renovating vacant business premises in disadvantaged areas (see page
146).

16 Get to grips with the internet. Compulsory online filing of VAT
returns, employers' PAYE returns and company tax returns is to be
introduced between 2008 and 2012.

8

Pensions and state benefits

In most cases, money going into a pension is tax-free; money paid out, however, is usually taxable. This includes most state pensions.

Most other state benefits, but not all, are tax-free. These are listed on page 174. There are also two types of state benefits – Working Tax Credit and Child Tax Credit – that are not themselves taxable, but where the amount you get will be affected by your taxable income. Tax credits are covered in Chapter 3.

Note that if you buy your own sickness or unemployment insurance, the benefits will normally be tax-free, unless the insurance was paid for by your employer. If so, it counts as employment income, see page 101. For long-term care insurance, see page 230.

This chapter covers:

- tax relief on private pension contributions (see page 175)
- tax on a private or company pension (see page 183)
- taxable state benefits, such as state retirement pension (see page 184).

Does this affect you?

The state retirement pension, including any lump sum from deferring it, counts as taxable income, although if it is your only income it may be below your tax-free allowances.

Private pensions fall into the following categories:

■ *Occupational pension schemes.* Run by your employer, these may be either 'final salary' (you earn a pension of say, one-sixtieth of your final salary for each year of membership) or 'money purchase' (the benefits depend on the investment performance of contributions).
■ *Personal pension schemes and stakeholder pensions.* These are individual pension plans taken out with a pension company, usually an insurance company. Stakeholder pensions are a form of personal pension with low minimum contributions, low cost transfers to and from other pension schemes, and a cap on charges. Both types may be arranged through your employer, in the form of group personal pensions and employer-sponsored stakeholder pensions.
■ *Retirement annuity contracts.* These are no longer available – they were superseded by personal pensions in 1988 – but if you have one you can continue to pay in.

The government also plan to introduce a new type of pension, called a personal account, from 2012, but the same tax rules will apply.

Self-invested personal pensions (SIPPs)

A SIPP is just a personal pension, and the same tax rules apply as for other private pensions. But instead of having to invest through the pension fund of an insurance company, you can choose a wide variety of investments to sit within your SIPP, including stocks and shares, unit trusts and commercial property.

In addition to the state retirement pension, other taxable state benefits are:

■ *Bereavement allowance, widow's pension, widowed mother's allowance* or *widowed parent's allowance.*
■ *Industrial death benefit pension.* This is no longer available to new claimants, but may still be paid to widows and dependants of people

who died before 11 April 1988 as a result of an accident at work.

■ *Jobseeker's Allowance.* The taxable amount is capped: in 2007–08, the maximum taxable amount is £46.85 a week for a single person aged 18 to 24, £59.15 a week for a single person aged 25 or over, and £92.80 for a couple both aged 18 or over.

■ *Statutory sick pay* and *statutory maternity, adoption or paternity pay.*

■ *Carer's Allowance* paid to people who spend at least 35 hours a week caring for a disabled person.

■ *Incapacity Benefit.* This is taxable after the first 28 weeks of incapacity (but is not taxable if you previously claimed invalidity benefit for this disability and have claimed continuously since 12 April 1995).

Tax-free pensions and benefits

Tax-free pensions

■ Extra pension from an unregistered scheme paid if disabled at work.
■ Pension Credit.
■ Some compensation for personal pensions that were mis-sold to you.
■ Pensions and benefits paid because of death, injury or disability in the Armed Forces (but some dependants' benefits are taxable). (See HMRC help sheet IR310 *War Widow's and dependant's pensions.*)
■ 10 per cent of an overseas pension.
■ German and Austrian pensions for victims of Nazi persecution.

Tax-free state benefits for families

■ Additions to benefits paid because you have a child.
■ Bereavement payment (a one-off lump sum on bereavement).
■ Child benefit, Child Tax Credit and Guardian's Allowance.
■ Education Maintenance Allowance, for some children staying in school after age 16. See the Fact file for the EMA helpline number.
■ Maternity allowance (but not statutory maternity pay).

Tax-free state benefits if sick or disabled

■ Attendance allowance (for people over 64 who need care).
■ Disability living allowance.

■ First 28 weeks of incapacity benefit paid at the short-term rate (or if you previously claimed invalidity benefit before April 1995).
■ Industrial injury benefits (except industrial death benefit pension).

Other tax-free state benefits
■ Working Tax Credit.
■ Income support (unless on strike).
■ £10 Christmas bonus paid with some benefits and state pension.
■ Some employment grants, e.g. New Deal training allowance.
■ Cold weather and winter fuel payments for pensioners.
■ Council tax benefit and housing benefit.
■ Jobseeker's Allowance above the taxable maximum (see opposite).
■ Social fund payments.

How the tax is worked out

Tax relief for money going into a pension

Paying the right sort of National Insurance contributions will entitle you to a state retirement pension, but you do not get tax relief on them.

Contributions to occupational and other private pension schemes that have been registered by HMRC qualify for tax relief at your top rate of tax, but there is a limit on the amount of contributions on which you can get tax relief. The Financial Services Authority, the government Pension Service and the independent Pensions Advisory Service all have useful leaflets.

A major simplification of the tax rules for pensions took place on 6 April 2006. Previously, the rules differed, depending on the type of pension and when you started it, but the same rules now apply to all registered pensions. Almost all schemes are registered.

Some schemes (previously known as 'unapproved' schemes) choose not to meet the conditions for registering. You get no tax relief on your contributions to these schemes and the payouts are usually taxable. Contributions your employer pays in for you count as a tax-free benefit, but in the past they were usually taxable: if you have paid tax on employer's contributions, this will reduce the tax you pay on any payouts.

Don't lose your pension rights

If you have not paid enough National Insurance contributions to get a full state pension the HMRC National Insurance Contributions Office should write to you telling you how you can pay Class 3 voluntary contributions, and the time limits for doing so (see page 6). Make sure that they have your up-to-date address, and that you have been credited for qualifying periods of sickness, unemployment or caring for dependants. You can get a forecast of your pension from the government Pension Service, and the National Insurance Contributions Office will be able to answer questions about your contributions record (see the Fact file).

If you cannot track down a private pension company that you have saved with, the Pension Service also run a free tracing service.

Action to take now

The new tax rules that started on 6 April 2006 should make life simpler for most people. But get advice urgently if:

- You are hoping to retire at age 50 but don't reach this age until after 2010, when the normal minimum retirement age rises to 55.
- You have already built up a very large pension pot. Under the new rules your maximum tax-allowable pension savings will be capped (see below), but there are ways of protecting yourself from extra tax if you act immediately. The process of registering for this protection must be completed before 6 April 2009.

If your employer contributes

- Your employer's contributions to a pension scheme for you are a tax-free benefit.
- If your employer contributes to your personal or stakeholder pension, its contributions are included with yours for the purposes of working out whether you have exceeded the contribution limits, but you cannot claim tax relief on them.

How the tax relief is given

There are three methods of getting tax relief on pension contributions:

- *Relief at source.* You hand over the amount that is due after basic-rate tax relief. (See Example 8.1.) The pension company claims any basic-rate relief from HMRC (even if you are a non-taxpayer). If you are a higher-rate taxpayer you can then claim higher-rate relief.
- *Net pay* applies only to occupational schemes. Your employer deducts your pension contributions from your pay and then works out the tax on what's left, giving you tax relief at your highest tax rate. Since 6 April 2006, employers can use the 'relief at source' method instead.
- *Gross payment* applies mainly to retirement annuity contributions. You pay the full amount and get tax relief either through your tax return or through your tax code – if you are a taxpayer. However, the retirement annuity company can choose to move to the net pay method instead.

Note that from April 2008, when the basic rate of tax falls from 22 to 20 per cent, the basic-rate tax relief on pension contributions will also fall.

Example 8.1: **How much tax relief?**

Brandon, who is self-employed, decides to contribute £6,500 to his personal pension. But for each £1 going into his pension, Brandon pays only 78p – the remaining 22p comes in the form of tax relief that the pension company claims from HMRC. So, Brandon's £6,500 is actually worth £6,500 ÷ 0.78 = £8,333.

Brandon is a 40% taxpayer so he can also claim higher-rate tax relief. He has already had 22% relief, so he can claim the remaining 40% − 22% = 18% on his tax return or by asking his tax office to adjust his tax code. The extra relief is £8,333 × 18% = £1,500.

How much can you contribute?

In the past, how much you could pay in depended on your age. But now, as long as you are under 75, you can pay in all your earnings and get full tax relief. If you have no earnings, you can get tax relief on payments up to

£2,808 a year (made up to £3,600 by basic-rate tax relief). You can belong to any number of pension schemes, occupational or personal. There are just two limits – an annual allowance and a lifetime allowance.

The annual allowance

If the money going into all your pensions in the tax year is more than the 'annual allowance' (£225,000 in 2007–08, see Table 8.1 opposite), the excess is taxed at 40 per cent. The following count as money going in:

- your contributions (but not National Insurance rebates contributed by the government if you contract out of the state second pension)
- if you are in a money purchase scheme (where the amount going in is fixed, but not what you get out), any contributions your employer pays
- if you are in a salary-related scheme, any increase in your pension multiplied by 10, and any increase in your right to a tax-free lump sum.

The lifetime allowance

This is a limit on the overall value of all your pension savings, which is £1.6 million in 2007–08 (see Table 8.1). When you take your benefits (a pension, say), you will have to pay tax on any pension savings above this allowance. The tax is 55 per cent if you draw a lump sum, 25 per cent if you draw an income (but the income will also be taxed each year). When you draw your benefits, the pension scheme administrator should tell you how much of your allowance you have used.

The value of your pension savings includes:

- if you are in a money purchase scheme (where the amount going in is fixed, but not what you get out), the value of your pension fund
- if you are in a salary-related scheme, your annual pension multiplied by 20, plus any lump sum. So, if you get no lump sum, the maximum pension is £80,000 × 20 = £1.6 million. (See Example 8.2 opposite.)
- if you draw your benefits over a number of years, the value of benefits you have already drawn.

Any dependants' pensions paid if you die before retirement will not count towards your lifetime allowance, but any lump sum payout above the allowance will be taxed.

There is more information about the lifetime and annual allowances in the Registered Pension Schemes manual on the HMRC website (see the Fact file). Although they are not likely to restrict many people, if you are worried that you might go over them, you should seek the advice of a financial adviser with specialist pensions qualifications (see page 176).

Table 8.1 Pension allowances

Tax year	Annual allowance	Lifetime allowance
2006–07	£215,000	£1.50 million
2007–08	£225,000	£1.60 million
2008–09	£235,000	£1.65 million
2009–10	£245,000	£1.75 million
2010–11	£255,000	£1.80 million

Example 8.2: **Keeping within the lifetime allowance**

Beverley is a company director. She is entitled to a deferred pension of £22,000 from her old employer. This uses up £22,000 × 20 = £440,000 of her lifetime allowance. She also belongs to her current employer's group personal pension, in which she has built up a pension fund of £250,000. She has used up £440,000 + £250,000 = £690,000 of her lifetime allowance to date, but it is the value of her pension fund when she draws her pension benefits that matters – so whether she breaches the limit will depend on how much more she contributes, and how much her pension fund grows.

Payouts from a private pension

You get tax relief on what goes into a registered private pension and on retirement you can take a tax-free lump sum of up to 25% of your pension fund, up to a maximum of £400,000 in 2007–08. However, other money coming out is generally taxable, and there are restrictions on the benefits you can draw. The main restrictions are:

- *You cannot draw money from a pension scheme before a minimum age* (with a few exceptions, this is 60 for an occupational scheme or retirement annuity contract, 50 for a personal or stakeholder pension scheme, although this will increase to 55 by 2010). You no longer have to stop work to draw your benefits, although if you belong to an occupational scheme your employer might require you to do so.
- *Limits on the amount of benefits payable.* Benefits payable by 'money purchase' schemes are naturally limited by what your investment will buy. If you belong to a salary-related scheme you can take as much as your pension scheme allows, but any benefits above the lifetime allowance will have a one-off tax charge deducted.
- *Most of your pension money must be used to provide an income when you retire.* See opposite for how this is done.

Note that even though the tax rules may permit various options, the pension scheme you are in may not. You may have to transfer your money to a different scheme that does provide the option you want.

Very low pension savings?

If your total pension savings come to less than 1% of the lifetime allowance (i.e. £16,000 in 2007–08) you can draw the whole lot as cash. This is known as 'trivial commutation'. Up to a quarter of the cash may be tax-free, and the rest is taxed as income – so it is best to do this in a year when you have very little other income. To do this, you must draw all your pension savings within a 12-month period, and you must be aged at least 60 but under 75.

Getting your money out of a pension early

You cannot get your money out of a pension before you reach the minimum age unless you are in ill-health or you have a right to draw an earlier pension from a scheme to which you belonged on 6 April 2006. You can also claim a refund of your contributions if you leave an occupational scheme within two years of joining (but tax will be deducted).

Providing a pension income

If you belong to a salary-related occupational scheme, the scheme will provide a pension. With any other type of scheme, the tax rules give you the option of buying an annuity (a guaranteed income for a set period, usually for life, provided by an insurance company) or withdrawing income. (See Figure 8.1 overleaf.)

An annuity provides greater certainty, but the cost fluctuates with conditions in the financial markets. You may be stuck with a low income, and on your death your family may get nothing back.

Income withdrawal keeps your options open, but your income will fluctuate in line with your investments and you could run out of money. An alternative might be phasing your retirement, by splitting your pension plan into separate segments. The Financial Services Authority has useful leaflets explaining the pros and cons.

Reinvesting a lump sum

You can now take a lump sum from some types of pension scheme without having to draw your pension – but the government doesn't want you to take a lump sum simply to reinvest it in your pension, thereby getting a second lot of tax relief on the contributions. So a tax charge may apply if you draw a lump sum of £16,000 or more and reinvest more than 30 per cent of it in your pension, but only if HMRC think that the reinvestment is 'pre-planned'.

Shop around for your annuity

With a money purchase pension, you can choose to buy your annuity from a different company to that with which your pension is invested (the so-called 'open market option'). Always shop around – annuity rates vary hugely. If you have any health impairments, ask about an 'impaired life' annuity, which may pay better rates.

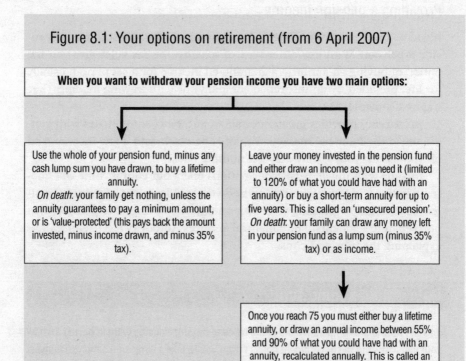

Figure 8.1: Your options on retirement (from 6 April 2007)

When you want to withdraw your pension income you have two main options:

Use the whole of your pension fund, minus any cash lump sum you have drawn, to buy a lifetime annuity.
On death: your family get nothing, unless the annuity guarantees to pay a minimum amount, or is 'value-protected' (this pays back the amount invested, minus income drawn, and minus 35% tax).

Leave your money invested in the pension fund and either draw an income as you need it (limited to 120% of what you could have had with an annuity) or buy a short-term annuity for up to five years. This is called an 'unsecured pension'.
On death: your family can draw any money left in your pension fund as a lump sum (minus 35% tax) or as income.

Once you reach 75 you must either buy a lifetime annuity, or draw an annual income between 55% and 90% of what you could have had with an annuity, recalculated annually. This is called an 'alternatively secured pension'.
On death: any money left in your pension fund may be used to provide a dependant's pension, or given to charity. Tax is payable unless the money goes to charity.

Changes to Alternatively Secured Pensions (ASPs)

ASPs were introduced as an alternative way of providing a pension income for people who had ethical objections to annuities. However, they quickly became seen as a way of passing on your unused pension fund to your family. To stop this, new rules were introduced from 6 April 2007 which mean that the fund will be heavily taxed unless you draw most of it as income, as will unused amounts passed to your family.

How money from a private pension is taxed

- Any lump sum is tax-free (within limits, see page 179). If you invest the money, the interest or dividends arising will be taxable in the same way as any other income from savings and investments.
- The pension or annuity income from an occupational pension, personal pension or stakeholder pension counts as taxable income, taxed in the same way as earnings from a job. Tax will be deducted under PAYE, and you will receive a tax code (see Chapter 2).
- The income from a retirement annuity contract is also taxable. From April 2007, the tax will be collected under PAYE, but before then income was paid with basic-rate tax deducted. If you have a retirement annuity, you should have received a PAYE coding notice. Check this carefully (see Chapter 2) and contact your tax office if it is wrong.
- Any income withdrawn from a pension fund, as an alternative to an annuity, is taxed in the same way as the income from an annuity.

Inheritance tax implications

Inheritance tax is not normally payable if a pension fund pays out to your family on your death. But it may be payable if:

- You die before age 75, and your family gets an enhanced payout because you were in very poor health but chose not to draw your pension. However, there will be no tax if the money goes to your spouse, civil partner, or somebody financially dependent on you.
- You die on or after age 75, while receiving an 'alternatively secured pension' (see Figure 8.1). Any left-over funds will be treated as part of your estate, unless paid to charity. From 6 April 2007, they can no longer be transferred tax-free to a dependant's pension fund.

A different type of annuity

Purchased life annuities bought with funds which do not come from a pension are taxed differently from pension scheme annuities and are covered in Chapter 11.

Tax on state pensions and benefits

Tax-free and taxable state pensions and benefits are listed on page 173.

When it comes to working out the taxable amount of a state retirement pension, the following additions to your pension are taxable:

■ any addition for invalidity or for an adult dependant (but not a child)
■ the age addition you get if you are over 80
■ any additional pension from the State Earnings Related Pension Scheme (SERPS) or the State Second Pension
■ any graduated pension earned before SERPS was introduced
■ any increases paid by the Pension Service to uprate your guaranteed minimum pension if you are contracted out of the State Second Pension.

A state pension is taxed as yours if it is payable to you, even if you are a married woman claiming a pension on your husband's contributions.

You can defer your state pension indefinitely. In return, you get a larger pension when you do start to draw it. This is taxable in the normal way. Alternatively, if you defer for at least a year, you can take the deferred amount as a lump sum. This will be taxable in the year you receive it, but it will not be taken into account when working out your age-related allowances (see page 72) or push you into a higher tax band. You can also put off drawing your lump sum until the year after you draw your pension. This will save tax if your top rate of tax falls.

How the tax is paid

State pensions are always paid out before tax, even when they are taxable, and so are most other state benefits. The exception is the lump sum from deferring a pension, which will be paid with tax deducted.

HMRC's preferred way of collecting any tax due on state pensions and benefits is to adjust your tax code for another source of income taxed under PAYE, such as a private pension – see Chapter 2. This will mean that more of your private pension (or other income from which the PAYE is deducted) goes in tax.

There are two state benefits that get special treatment:

■ *Incapacity Benefit.* If you receive taxable Incapacity Benefit (in most
cases, benefit paid after the first 28 weeks) and have no other income
taxed under PAYE, the DWP deduct tax before paying you.

■ *Jobseeker's Allowance.* Tax is not deducted, but you must give your P45
to the Jobcentre Plus, which keeps track of your tax liability over the
year. You will get a statement of taxable Jobseeker's Allowance from
your Jobcentre Plus at the end of the tax year. Any tax you owe is
normally collected by adjusting your tax code when you get a new job.
If you have paid too much tax you will usually get a refund, from
either the Jobcentre Plus or your new employer.

What to tell HMRC

Pension contributions
You do not need to do anything if you pay into an occupational scheme
using the net pay method (explained on page 177) – you have already had
all the tax relief you are due because your employer worked out the tax on
your pay after deducting your contributions.

If you pay into any other type of registered pension scheme, you need
to enter the contribution in Question 14 of the main tax return and in the
tax credits annual declaration form (if you get one, see Chapter 3). Even if
you have already had all the tax relief you are due by paying less to the pension company, the contribution will reduce your taxable income for other
purposes, such as claiming tax credits or age-related personal allowances
(see Chapter 5). If you do not get a tax return, write to your tax office with
details of your pension contributions – but this is only necessary if you are
a higher-rate taxpayer or over 65 (see page 72).

Exceeding the pension contribution allowances
You will need to tell HMRC if, during 2006–07, your pension rights grew
by more than the annual allowance or you drew any pension benefits that
took you over the lifetime allowance (see page 178). You must also tell them
if you are liable to tax on any unauthorised payment from a UK-registered
pension scheme or on some payments from overseas pension schemes.
Your scheme administrator can usually give you the information you need.

You will need to tick Question 25 on page 2 of the main tax return, fill in the Pensions supplementary pages, and if you are calculating your own tax enter the amount in box 18.2C of the main return (the notes to the Pensions pages will help you work it out). Note, though, that if you receive a payment from a pension scheme that is not registered, it should go in the Employment pages (see page 116).

Receiving a pension or state benefits

Make sure your tax office knows in good time if you expect to start receiving a pension in the next few months so that they can sort out your tax code, if relevant. You may be asked to complete a 'pension enquiry' form P161. With state benefits, your tax office should not need notifying.

If you get a tax return, enter the taxable amount of any UK pension, state or private, or state benefits, in Question 11 on page 4.

Filling in your tax return

Question 11 – Did you receive a taxable UK pension, retirement annuity, Social Security benefit or Statutory Payment?

Tick this if you received a pension from an ex-employer or other private pension, or if you received a state retirement pension or other taxable state benefit listed in the question. Don't tick it if you received an overseas pension or benefit – these go on the Foreign supplementary pages.

Boxes 11.1 to 11.9 State pensions and benefits

Generally, you should enter the taxable amount to which you were entitled between 6 April 2006 and 5 April 2007, whether or not you received it. And note that you should enter the total of your weekly entitlements, even if you received the income monthly or quarterly. See 'Record-keeping' on page 190 for documents that show taxable amounts, or contact the Pension Service helpline (Pensions Direct) if you are not sure what to enter.

You may have put off receiving your state pension, in return for a higher pension later on or a lump sum. The higher pension is taxed just like the normal state pension and should be entered in box 11.1. If you chose a lump sum, this will normally be paid with tax deducted. Enter the amount before tax in box 11.1B, and the tax in box 11.1A (this will be shown in the letter you receive from the Pensions Service).

Mistakes to avoid when entering state benefits

- Additions to state benefits and pensions for children are not taxable. Do not include them.
- If you received Jobseeker's Allowance for more than one period in the tax year, remember to add together the taxable amounts given on each of the P45U forms you received, plus that shown on the P60U you get if still claiming on 5 April 2007.
- Don't confuse bereavement allowance with the lump sum bereavement payment. The allowance is taxable – the payment is not.
- Don't include statutory maternity, paternity, adoption or sick pay in this section unless they have been paid to you directly by HMRC. If paid by your employer, enter them on the Employment supplementary pages.
- If you received the pension credit in addition to your state pension, only the pension itself is taxable. The pension credit is tax-free.

Boxes 11.10 to 11.14 Other pensions and retirement annuities

Enter here any pension from a UK occupational pension, personal or stakeholder pension, free-standing additional voluntary contributions (FSAVC) plan, or retirement annuity contract. If instead of buying an annuity with your pension fund you took an income withdrawal, include the amount of income withdrawn. And if you drew the whole of a small pension as a lump sum (see page 180), enter the amount of the lump sum.

Do not include:

- any tax-free cash lump sum from your pension
- a taxable lump sum from a pension scheme that is not registered – this is taxed as income from employment (see page 129)
- any tax-free amount paid because of a work-related accident or illness
- a foreign pension
- a purchased life annuity (see page 183). This goes in box 10.14.

Box 11.13 applies only if you have a UK pension, paid through an overseas government, for public service in the Commonwealth or other UK protectorate. If so, you can claim a 10 per cent deduction here. Deduct the 10 per cent from the pension received, and enter the result in box 11.12.

If you have more than one private pension, you need to give details of each. Use 'Additional information' at the end of the return if there is not enough room in box 11.14.

Question 14 – Do you want to claim relief for your pension contributions?

Don't tick the 'Yes' box if you only paid into an occupational scheme where full tax relief was given by deducting the contributions from your pay before it was taxed. But you should enter here payments made to any other UK-registered pension scheme, whether it was run by your employer or was a personal pension, stakeholder pension, free-standing voluntary contribution (FSAVC) scheme or retirement annuity contract.

Include any payments made between 6 April 2006 and 5 April 2007 (note that it is no longer possible to have contributions 'carried back' and treated as if made in a previous tax year).

Most payments these days are made with basic-rate tax relief given at source and go in box 14.1. Remember, though, that it is the gross amount that you should enter – that is, the amount you handed over, plus the basic-rate tax relief the pension company claims from HMRC. To work this out, divide the amount you paid by 0.78.

However, if you pay into a retirement annuity contract and the pension company does not allow you to make payments with tax relief deducted, enter the amount paid in box 14.2. And if, unusually, you made a payment to your employer's pension before tax (for example, you paid in more than you earned from that job), enter it in box 14.3.

Finally, use 14.4 if you paid into a pension scheme based overseas that qualifies for UK tax relief under an agreement with the country concerned.

Don't include contributions your employer paid into your plan – you don't get tax relief on these.

Mistakes to avoid when entering pension contributions

- Entering payments made with no tax relief deducted in box 14.1. If in doubt, check with the pension company.
- Entering the amount you actually paid into a personal or stakeholder pension or FSAVC plan (the net amount), rather than the gross payment.

Example 8.3: Entering your pension contributions

Oscar is a member of a group personal pension scheme to which he contributes £156 a month. The pension company reclaims basic-rate tax relief on Oscar's contributions, so the total regular payment into his plan is £156 ÷ 0.78 = £200 a month, or £2,400 each year. Oscar also paid in his annual bonus as a lump sum – £2,000 (£2,564 gross) in December 2006.

On his tax return, Oscar enters in box 14.1 his total contribution for 2006–07: £2,400 + £2,564 = £4,964.

Figure 8.2: Question 14 (see Example 8.3)

Q14 Do you want to claim relief for your pension contributions? **YES** ✓
If yes, tick this box and then fill in boxes 14.1 to 14.4 as appropriate.
If not applicable, go to Question 15.

*If your pension contributions are taken off your pay **before** it is taxed, no more tax relief is due – leave Question 14 blank. If you make **any other type of pension contribution** read page 24 of the Tax Return Guide and then complete Question 14.*

- ■ *Contributions you paid with basic rate tax deducted (called relief at source)* – contributions paid to a personal pension or stakeholder pension scheme, or group personal pension; contributions paid to a Free standing AVC Scheme; contributions paid to other pension schemes after deducting basic rate tax.

- Enter the full amount of the contribution and add back the basic rate tax deducted. *Read the notes on page 24 of your Tax Return Guide.*   **14.1** £ *4,964*

- ■ *Contributions you paid in full* – Enter the amount of contributions you paid. Read the notes on page 24 of the Tax Return Guide.

- Contributions under a retirement annuity contract paid in full without deducting basic rate tax   **14.2** £

- Contributions paid to your employer's occupational pension scheme which were not deducted from your pay before tax   **14.3** £

- Contributions paid to a non-UK registered overseas pension scheme which are eligible for tax relief, and were not deducted from your pay before tax   **14.4** £

Record-keeping

You must keep records for at least 22 months (five years and ten months if your return includes trading or letting income) from the end of the tax year to which they relate.

Pension contributions
- Keep records of all your contributions – e.g. receipts or contribution certificates.
- If you are paying in more than £2,808 to your pension, you will need proof of your earnings for the tax year.
- Keep any statements showing how much your pension is worth, and how much of your lifetime allowance you have used.

Receiving a pension, state benefits or tax credits
- Keep the letter you receive from the Pension Service each year giving the value of your basic pension, and details of other state benefits. If you are not sure how much taxable state pension you have received, ask your local Pensions Centre office for form BR735 for the relevant tax year.
- Letters from the Pension Service about any deferred state pension.
- If you have been claiming Jobseeker's Allowance, you should have received a statement of taxable amounts on either a P45U (when you stopped claiming) or P60U (at the end of the tax year). For incapacity benefit, you should receive a P45(IB) or P60(IB).
- If you have a pension from someone other than the state, you should receive a P60 or other certificate at the end of the tax year, showing the taxable amount and any tax deducted. Also keep any PAYE coding notice (P2) (see Chapter 2).

Tax-planning hints

1 Ask for a forecast of your state retirement pension, to check that your National Insurance contributions have been credited correctly (see

page 6). You can also contact HMRC's National Insurance Contributions Office for details of your contributions record.

2   You pay no tax or National Insurance on contributions your employer makes to your pension – worth remembering when negotiating pay.

3   If you are a director of your own company, you can reduce your taxable profits by making a contribution to your own pension.

4   You don't have to have an income to have a pension. You can pay in up to £2,808 and the government will add tax relief. The money can come from anywhere – investments, or a gift.

5   Always shop around for an annuity – rates vary hugely. Alternatively, consider 'income withdrawals' – but see page 181 for some risks.

6   The new pension regime that started in April 2006 means that you may be able to pay much more into your pension – but if you are nearing the £1.6 million lifetime fund limit get advice now.

7   The new rules also give you much more flexibility. You can belong to any number of pension schemes, you don't have to stop work to draw your pension benefits, and you can take a tax-free lump sum without also having to draw your pension.

8   If your total pension savings are very small – under £16,000 in 2007–08 – you can draw the whole lot as cash.

9   If your only income comes from benefits, you are unlikely to be a taxpayer. Indeed, you might be entitled to a tax refund when you start claiming benefits – ask your tax office for a repayment claim form P50.

10 You can defer drawing your state retirement pension – this may be worthwhile if drawing it would push you into a higher tax bracket or affect your age-related allowances (see Chapter 5).

9

Income from property

You take in a lodger to help with your mortgage or rent. You let out – or sublet – part of your home. You get posted abroad and let your home. You've become a buy-to-let landlord. You rent out a holiday property.

However you make money from property – whether you own it or not – if you make more than you spend on servicing the property, you'll usually be liable for income tax. And if you make a profit when you sell a property that you have let, there may also be a capital gains tax bill.

Does this affect you?

You don't need to worry about income tax if you let a room in the home you are living in to a lodger and your letting income for the tax year is less than the limit for tax-free income under the Rent-a-Room scheme (see opposite). You *will* be liable to income tax if the income you get from letting a room in your home exceeds that limit and/or you have other income from property. However, tax is not charged on the whole amount of the income because of the deductions you can make.

Capital gains tax becomes an issue only when you sell a property you have let. You don't have to worry about capital gains tax if you let a room to a lodger who shared your living space and the home qualifies for 'private residence relief' (see Chapter 12). But there may be a capital gains tax bill if the part of your home you let was self-contained (a 'separate dwelling house'), or you made major structural alterations to create the accommodation that you let. If you made no structural alterations, you may be able to claim 'lettings relief' (see page 270). If you sell property which you let but never used as your own home, the whole of the gain is subject to capital gains tax, although what you have to pay (if anything) depends on what you can claim to reduce the gain (see Chapter 12).

Stamp Duty Land Tax is payable if you buy residential property worth £125,000 or more, or non-residential property, or residential property in disadvantaged areas, worth £150,000 or more. Above these levels, the tax is 1 per cent of the purchase price if the property is worth £250,000 or less, 3 per cent if it is worth £250,001 to £500,000, and 4 per cent if worth more than £500,000. From October 2007, new zero-carbon homes are tax-free.

Tax-free income from property

Under the Rent-a-Room scheme, the first £4,250 of income each tax year from letting a room (or rooms) in your home is tax-free. This applies to owner-occupiers and those who sublet a room in a home they rent.

If you share a home, the person who lets the room gets the whole exemption of £4,250. If two (or more) share the rental income, or you rent out separate rooms in a joint home, each gets an exemption of £2,125.

If the money your lodger pays is more than the exempt amount that you're entitled to, you pay tax on the excess. So if you receive £5,000 in rent and are entitled to the full exemption of £4,250, you'll pay tax only on £5,000 − £4,250 = £750.

Rent-a-Room is usually the best option

If you claim an exemption under the Rent-a-Room scheme, you cannot claim any expenses. You do not have to claim Rent-a-Room relief, but unless you have expenses of more than £4,250 (£2,125 if you let jointly) from letting a room in your home (which is unlikely in most cases), you will be better off – and have less paperwork to deal with – if you do claim.

What counts as income from property

Although you still have to pay tax on it, some property-related income is excluded when working out the taxable profit from your rental business. Yearly interest on a business bank account – which counts as savings income – is one example. Another is income from property abroad which counts as foreign income (see Chapter 10) even though the taxable profits are calculated in broadly the same way as those on property in the UK.

If the way you make money from your land or property counts as a trade, the tax you pay on it is worked out using the rules described in Chapter 7 and you should include details of the income on the Self-employment pages of the tax return rather than on the Land and Property pages. Trading income includes income from:

■ using your home to run a guest house or to provide B&B
■ charging tenants (in a property you don't live in) for services – such as meals and laundry – which are well beyond the services normally provided by a landlord; for tax purposes, you should separate these charges from the rents you receive even if you include the cost of these services in the rent rather than charging for them separately
■ farming and market gardening
■ exploiting the natural resources on your land – this includes things like mining, quarrying and cutting timber from woodland.

Since January 2007 it has been possible to invest in property through a 'Real Estate Investment Trust'. Most income from these is taxed as property income, but the income is entered in the main tax return, not the Land and Property pages.

Rent-a-Room for traders

Although the income you get from using your home to run a B&B, guest house or small hotel counts as trading – rather than rental – income, you can still claim Rent-a-Room relief. (For more information, see help sheet IR223 *Rent a Room for traders*.)

How the tax is worked out

As far as Her Majesty's Revenue & Customs (HMRC) are concerned, the money you make from property – whether you merely take in a lodger or you are a buy-to-let tycoon – is treated as income from a rental business and you are taxed on the profits from that business. Tax is based on the profits from rental income due to you in a tax year even if you don't actually get some of the income until after the end of the tax year (see page 204) and even if you have accounts that cover a different 12-month period.

After ignoring income that is tax-free under the Rent-a-Room scheme and income that doesn't count as income from a rental business, the taxable profit on your rental business is worked out as follows:

- *Step 1:* total all income from letting holiday property which qualifies for special treatment (see overleaf).
- *Step 2:* subtract expenditure on letting holiday property in the form of allowable expenses (see page 197) and capital allowances (see page 199).
- *Step 3:* add the total of rents from letting part of your home and/or other properties which don't qualify for special treatment and all other income from property (see page 200).
- *Step 4:* subtract the total of allowable expenses on all other properties (see page 200) and/or any exempt amount you're entitled to under the Rent-a-Room scheme (if applicable).
- *Step 5:* subtract any qualifying losses (see page 202) to arrive at your taxable profit for the year.

If you have made a taxable profit, it is added to your other non-savings income and taxed at 10 per cent, 22 per cent or 40 per cent, according to what falls into the lower-, basic- and higher-rate income tax bands (see Chapter 1).

HMRC no longer have a printed booklet explaining the taxation of property. Instead, full information is given in the *Property Income Manual* on the HMRC website.

A simpler way of working out your profits

Strictly speaking, when working out your taxable profits, you should include rent (and other income from property) which is earned from the tenant's use of the property in a tax year – called the 'earnings basis' – irrespective of when you actually got the money. However, you may be able to work out your profits using the simpler 'cash basis' where you base your figures on the cash paid and received in the tax year provided that:

■ your gross rental business income is less than £15,000
■ you always use the cash basis when working out your profits
■ using the cash basis doesn't mean that your profits are substantially lower than they would be if you had used the stricter earnings basis to calculate them.

Tell HMRC under 'Additional information' in your tax return if you are doing this.

Working out profits on holiday homes

You don't *have* to calculate the profits from letting holiday property separately from your other rental business income, but if the property passes the 'furnished holiday lettings' test (see below), you can:

■ claim capital allowances on furniture and furnishings
■ use losses from the property to reduce tax on non-property income
■ use the profits to pay more into a pension (see page 177)
■ claim special reliefs from capital gains tax when you sell the property.

The furnished holiday lettings test

You can take advantage of the special rules for holiday property provided it is furnished and all of the following conditions are met in the 12 months covered by the tax year. However, in the first year of letting, the 12 months run from the date the property is first let; in the final year of letting the 12 months run to the date of the last letting. Whichever time period applies, the property must:

■ be in the UK – the special rules don't apply to foreign property

- be available for letting at a commercial rent for a minimum of 140 days
- be let for at least 70 days – or, if you have more than one property, at least 70 days on average for the properties involved (see Example 9.1). If you want to claim to average several lettings, you must tell your tax office by 31 January after the end of the tax year.
- not be rented out on longer-term lets (i.e. more than 31 days) for more than 155 days in total during the year.

If the property you let doesn't pass the test, you work out your profits according to the rules for other property given on page 200.

Example 9.1: Dealing with multiple properties

Ryan lets out three holiday cottages. One of them fails the 70-day test, but otherwise they all meet the tests to qualify as furnished holiday lettings. Cottage 1 is let for 90 days, cottage 2 for 78 days and cottage 3 for 66 days.

Ryan divides the total (234 days) by the number of properties (3) to arrive at an average of 78 days, so all three properties still pass the furnished holiday lettings test.

Allowable expenses for holiday property

You don't pay tax on all the income you receive from letting holiday property (which qualifies for special treatment) because, when calculating your taxable profits, you can deduct the expenses involved in letting it. You cannot deduct 'capital expenditure' which includes the purchase price of the property and the cost of any improvements to the property – although you may be able to claim capital allowances for some things.

To be able to deduct the full amount of other costs, they must be incurred 'wholly and exclusively' in letting the property. HMRC divide deductible expenses into six main categories.

Rent, rates, insurance, ground rents etc.
- rent if you lease a property which you then sublet
- buildings, contents and rental guarantee insurance

- business rates, council tax, water rates, ground rents, feu duties (in Scotland), service charges (for flats)
- gas and electricity bills, less any amount your tenants contribute towards them

Repairs, maintenance and renewals
- repairs and maintenance, but not most improvements (see opposite)
- painting and decorating – inside and out
- other work necessary to prevent the property from deteriorating – e.g. stone-cleaning and damp treatment
- renewing and replacing moveable objects such as furniture, domestic appliances, cutlery and crockery – unless you claim capital allowances instead (see opposite)

Finance charges, including interest
- interest on a mortgage or another type of loan to buy the property and any charges involved in taking out the loan, such as arrangement fees or booking fees for fixed-rate loans
- payments on an alternative finance arrangement (see page 79)
- bank charges and overdraft interest on a separate business account

Legal and professional costs
- legal fees for renewing a lease (provided it is for less than 50 years) or evicting a tenant
- fees charged by an accountant for drawing up your accounts
- management fees for the cost of letting – e.g. you employ an agent to deal with the business of letting the property

Costs of services provided, including wages
- costs of services you provide such as cleaning and gardening, but only if you pay someone else to provide them; you cannot claim the cost of your own time

Other expenses
- advertising costs
- stationery, phone calls and other incidental expenses

■ travel costs provided travel was solely for business purposes –
   travelling to inspect your holiday cottage and then coming straight
   back will count but travelling to inspect your holiday home while
   taking a holiday in it will not
■ expenses incurred before you started letting, provided they would
   have been allowable if incurred once the letting had begun.

If you incur an expense partly for private use (e.g. you use a holiday property for your own holidays or let friends and family use it rent-free), you
can deduct only the proportion of the expense which relates to the commercial letting of it. So if you use the property for your own holidays for a
month each year, you will be able to claim only $^{11}/_{12}$ of any expenses that do
not arise wholly from the letting.

Combining repairs with improvements

If you combine repair work with improvements to the property none of the cost of the work
can be claimed as an allowable expense. Similarly, if you replace fixtures and fittings, such
as kitchen units, and upgrade them at the same time – you replace cheap units with de-
signer versions, for example – the cost counts as capital expenditure and so is not allowable (but in holiday property, you may be able to claim a capital allowance). However, if an
'improvement' occurs in order to meet modern building standards, the cost is allowable. A
good example is replacing single-glazed windows with double-glazed or installing insulation (see page 201). So keep good records of your maintenance work and try to keep any
'improvements' separate.

Capital allowances for holiday property
The main advantage of having a holiday property treated for tax purposes
as a furnished holiday letting is that you can claim capital allowances (explained in detail in Chapter 7) for the cost of furnishing and equipping the
property. This makes good financial sense, but remember that when you
replace items, you must claim capital allowances for the replacements *instead of* claiming the cost as an allowable expense.

You can also claim capital allowances for equipment you need to run the letting business. This includes things like ladders, lawnmowers, tools, fax machines, computers, filing cabinets and other business furniture.

As with expenses, if you claim a capital allowance for something used partly for business and partly for your own personal use, you can claim only a proportion of the allowance.

Working out the profits on other property

Other income from property is lumped together, so if you have more than one property, you don't need to work out the profit (or loss) separately for each one. As well as rents, income from other property includes:

- rent charges, ground rents and feu duties (Scotland)
- income from sporting rights such as fishing and shooting permits
- income from allowing waste to be buried or stored on your land
- payments for allowing other people to use your property – e.g. to store things in your shed or as a location for a film
- grants from local authorities or others for repairs (but not improvements) to a property
- income from caravans or houseboats which never go anywhere
- service charges
- refunds of running costs you claimed previously as allowable expenses
- payments from rental guarantee insurance (which provides cover against non-payment of rent)
- lump sums you receive when you grant a lease of less than 50 years.

How you arrive at the profit (or loss) figure for other property is the same as how you calculate profits on holiday property, but there are important differences in the tax reliefs you can claim.

Allowable expenses on other property

All the expenses which are allowable as deductions for holiday property (see page 197) are allowable as deductions for other property. But, in addition:

- If you let furnished property, instead of claiming the actual cost of renewal and replacement of furniture and so on, you can claim a 'wear and tear' allowance. This is 10 per cent of the rent you receive, minus council tax and other bills which you, rather than your tenant, pay.

■ If you let out residential property, you can claim the cost of draught-proofing, or insulating walls, lofts or hot water systems as an allowable expense (up to £1,500 per property). From 6 April 2007, you can also claim for floor insulation. This is called Landlord's Energy Saving Allowance, but you cannot claim for property on which you are also claiming Rent-a-Room relief, or for furnished holiday lettings.

Wear and tear advantage

The advantage of choosing to claim a wear and tear allowance rather than deducting the cost of replacement items is that you can make the deduction every year even if you haven't actually replaced anything. It also makes record-keeping simpler. But once you have chosen the way in which you are going to get tax relief on renewals, you can't change your mind.

Capital allowances on other property

You cannot claim capital allowances for furnishing and equipping the property. But you can claim them for equipment needed to run your rental business as you can for holiday property. From 11 April 2007, you can also claim a 100 per cent allowance for renovating vacant business premises in disadvantaged areas (see page 146).

Flats over shops

If you buy a flat above a shop to rent out, you can claim the cost of renovations as a 100% capital allowance even though such expenditure is not normally allowable. The same allowance is available for the cost of converting vacant or underused space above business premises into a flat to let. There are guidance notes on the HMRC website.

Using losses

A loss you make on letting out any type of property can be used to reduce the size of your taxable profit. And all losses can be carried forward if you can't make use of them in the current tax year. However, losses carried forward can be set only against future profits from your rental business. A loss on qualifying holiday property is treated as a business loss, so you have the options shown in Figure 7.2 on page 154, including setting it against other income in the same tax year, or even the income of earlier years. Any loss left over is carried forward to set against rental income in future years.

What to tell HMRC

If you don't get a tax return and your only income from property is rent below the tax-free Rent-a-Room scheme limit, you don't need to tell HMRC anything. But you must tell your tax office if either of the following apply:

- you have been receiving Rent-a-Room relief but no longer qualify e.g. you have moved but are still receiving the lodger's rent, or the rent has risen above the tax-free amount
- you receive any other income from property.

You must notify your tax office by 5 October after the end of the year in which you received the income – i.e. by 5 October 2007 for income received in the 2006–07 tax year. You will usually be sent a tax return, but if you are taxed under PAYE the tax may be collected by adjusting your tax code. If you prefer, you can ask your tax office to take your property income out of your tax code. This will increase your regular income, but you will have to fill in a tax return and pay the tax in one or two lump sums each year. You will have to do this in any case if you have no income taxed under PAYE.

If you have not been sent a tax return, 5 October is also the deadline for telling your tax office if you have sold a property you let and have made a taxable capital gain (see Chapter 12).

If your income from property counts as trading income (see page 194), you must register as self-employed (see Chapter 7).

If you get a tax return and receive any income from property, you should tick Question 5 in the main tax return and fill in the Land and Property supplementary pages *unless*:

■ the way you make money from your home counts as a trade (see page 194), in which case you should tick Question 3 or 4 in the main tax return and fill in the relevant supplementary pages

■ the property is abroad – if so you should tick Question 6 in the main tax return and fill in the Foreign supplementary pages

■ the income comes from a Real Estate Investment Trust (see page 245). This income should be entered in Question 13 of the main tax return.

Filling in the Land and Property supplementary pages

The Land and Property supplementary pages ask for details of all your income from property in the UK. If the only income you receive is money from a lodger who shares your home and this amounts to less than £4,250 (£2,125 if you let jointly), all you have to do is tick 'Yes' in answer to the first question.

Furnished holiday lettings

Complete the rest of this page only if you let out holiday property that passes the 'furnished holiday lettings' test (see page 196).

Boxes 5.1 to 5.9 Income from furnished holiday lettings

Enter in box 5.1 the total amount of income you received from letting holiday property that passes the 'furnished holiday lettings' test. If your total property income is £15,000 or less over a whole year, you can:

■ *either* break down your expenses according to HMRC's headings in boxes 5.2 to 5.7 (see page 197 for what comes under each heading)

■ *or* you can simply enter the total figure for all your expenses in box 5.7 and again in box 5.8 without giving any details.

If your total income from letting furnished holiday property is more than £15,000, you must fill in boxes 5.2 to 5.7 and give the total in box 5.8.

Relating income and expenses to a tax year

Unless you are using the 'cash basis' (see page 196) for working out your profits, you must give details of income due to you in a tax year and expenses which relate to a particular tax year even if you paid the bill at an earlier or later date. For example, if you had your holiday property repainted in March 2007 but didn't pay the bill until the end of April, the expense still belongs to the 2006–07 tax year. In addition, if you have an expense that straddles two years, you need to divide the payment between the two tax years, in line with the number of days between the date you incurred the expense and the end of the tax year (see Example 9.2).

Example 9.2: Splitting expenses between tax years

Lucy's buildings insurance on her rental property runs from 5 October 2006 to 5 October 2007 and she pays a lump-sum premium of £300: half of the premium belongs to the 2006–07 tax year (which ends on 5 April 2007), and half to the 2007–08 tax year.

Boxes 5.10 to 5.14 Tax adjustments

Before you arrive at the figure for your taxable profit from letting holiday property, you may need to:

■ add back the proportion of your expenses which relate to private use in box 5.10, unless you have already taken this into account in the expenses figures entered in boxes 5.2 to 5.7
■ add any 'balancing charges' in box 5.11, if you have made a profit from selling something on which you previously claimed capital allowances
■ subtract capital allowances you can claim in box 5.13 (see page 146 for how to calculate them). If you are claiming enhanced allowances for environmentally friendly or water-saving equipment tick box 5.13A.

Boxes 5.15 to 5.18 Losses

If you have made a loss at box 5.15, you need to tell your tax office what you want to do with the loss. If you want to use it to reduce your tax bill on:

- *non-property income and/or capital gains*, enter the loss in box 5.16 (remember to include it in box 8.5 of the capital gains tax supplementary pages if you're using it to reduce that tax)
- *income from earlier tax years*, enter the loss in box 5.17 and give the amount and the tax year you want the loss to be used for in box 23.9 in the main tax return
- *other income from property*, enter the amount in box 5.18 and copy it to box 5.38.

Other property income

The second page of the Land and Property supplementary pages deals with property that doesn't pass the 'furnished holiday lettings' test. You must give details of not only rents you receive but also all other property income (see page 200).

Boxes 5.19 to 5.23 Income

- Ignore box 5.19 unless you filled in the first page of the form. If so, copy the figure you entered in box 5.14.
- In box 5.20 give a total figure for all your income from property in the UK which hasn't already been accounted for.
- Box 5.21 applies only to landlords who are resident abroad – their tenants may be required to deduct basic-rate tax from the rent and pay the tax to HMRC.
- The 'chargeable premiums' referred to in box 5.22 apply only if you received a lump-sum payment from your tenant when granting a lease of less than 50 years. If this applies, fill in the working sheet on page LN5 of the Land and Property notes to get the correct figure to enter.
- Ignore box 5.22A unless you sublet a leased property and received a lump-sum payment (a 'reverse premium') to encourage you to take on the lease. Check with your tax office if you think that this may apply.
- Total all the figures in this section and enter them in box 5.23.

Boxes 5.24 to 5.30 Expenses

You don't need to fill in this part of the form if your income from property is made up solely of one or more of the following:

■ income from a lodger who lives with you and you are claiming relief under the Rent-a-Room scheme (see page 193)
■ rent from property which passes the 'furnished holiday lettings' test – you have already given details of expenses in boxes 5.2 to 5.8
■ joint income from property and you know only your share of the income after expenses has been deducted.

Unless any of the above apply:

■ if your property income is less than £15,000 over a full year, enter a total figure for all your expenses in boxes 5.29 and 5.30
■ if your property income is more than £15,000, enter separate figures split according to the headings given in boxes 5.24 to 5.29 with a total of these figures in box 5.30.

Example 9.3: Filling in the Land and Property pages

Edgar has rent of £5,250 from a buy-to-let property and £3,000 from a lodger (see Figure 9.1). He enters the total – £8,250 – in box 5.20. As he is claiming Rent-a-Room relief on his lodger's rent, he can claim expenses only on his buy-to-let property, which come to £3,500. His rent is less than £15,000 over a full year, so he doesn't need to break down his expenses and he enters the total in box 5.29. He claims the tax-free amount of rent from his lodger in box 5.35, and 10% wear and tear for his buy-to-let property in box 5.37. This gives him a total profit at box 5.40 of only £1,225. However, his buy-to-let property was empty for part of 2005–06 and he made a £1,845 loss, which he enters in box 5.42. This wipes out his profit and leaves £1,845 – £1,225 = £620 of unused loss to carry forward to 2007–08.

Figure 9.1: Land and property, Questions 5.19 to 5.47 (see Example 9.3)

Other property income (not including dividends from a UK Real Estate Investment Trust - go to box 13.1 - 13.3 on page 5 of the Tax Return)

■ **Income**

		copy from box 5.14	
● Furnished holiday lettings profits	**5.19** £		
● Rents and other income from land and property	**5.20** £ *8,250*	Tax taken off **5.21** £	
● Chargeable premiums	**5.22** £		
			boxes 5.19 + 5.20 + 5.22 + 5.22A
● Reverse premiums	**5.22A** £		**5.23** £ *8,250*

■ **Expenses** (do not include figures you have already put in boxes 5.2 to 5.7 on Page L1)

● Rent, rates, insurance, ground rents etc.	**5.24** £		
● Repairs, maintenance and renewals	**5.25** £		
● Finance charges, including interest	**5.26** £		
● Legal and professional costs	**5.27** £		
● Costs of services provided, including wages	**5.28** £		
			total of boxes 5.24 to 5.29
● Other expenses	**5.29** £ *3,500*		**5.30** £ *3,500*

		box 5.23 minus box 5.30
Net profit (put figures in brackets if a loss)		**5.31** £ *4,750*

■ **Tax adjustments**

● Private use	**5.32** £		
● Balancing charges - including those arising under Business Premises Renovation Allowance which should also be included in box 23.8	**5.33** £	box 5.32 + box 5.33 **5.34** £	
● Rent a Room exempt amount	**5.35** £ *3,000*		
● Capital allowances - including those arising under Business Premises Renovation Allowance which should also be included in box 23.7	**5.36** £		
● Tick box 5.36A if box 5.36 includes a claim for 100% capital allowances for flats over shops	**5.36A**		
● Tick box 5.36B if box 5.36 includes enhanced capital allowances for designated environmentally beneficial plant and machinery	**5.36B**		
● Landlord's Energy Saving Allowance	**5.36C** £		
● 10% wear and tear	**5.37** £ *525*		
	copy from box 5.18		total of boxes 5.35 to 5.38
● Furnished holiday lettings losses	**5.38** £		**5.39** £ *3,525*

		boxes 5.31 + 5.34 minus box 5.39
Adjusted profit (if a loss, enter '0' in box 5.40 and put the loss in box 5.41)		**5.40** £ *1,225*

	boxes 5.31 + 5.34 minus box 5.39
Adjusted loss (if you have entered '0' in box 5.40)	**5.41** £

	box 5.42
● Loss brought forward from previous year	**5.42** £ *1,845*

	box 5.40 minus box 5.42
Profit for the year	**5.43** £ *0*

■ **Losses etc.**

● Loss offset against total income - read the note on page LN8	**5.44** £
● Loss to carry forward to following year	**5.45** £ *620*
● Tick box 5.46 if these Pages include details of property let jointly	**5.46**
● Tick box 5.47 if **all** property income ceased in the year to 5 April 2007 **and** you do not expect to receive such income again, in the year to 5 April 2008	**5.47**

Now fill in any other supplementary Pages that apply to you.
Otherwise, go back to page 2 of your Tax Return and finish filling it in. ➡

Boxes 5.32 to 5.35 Tax adjustments

Before you arrive at the figure for your taxable profit from UK property, you may need to:

- add back the proportion of your expenses which relates to private use in box 5.32, unless you have already taken this into account in the expenses figures entered in boxes 5.24 to 5.29 (see page 200)
- add any 'balancing charges' referred to in box 5.33 if you have made a profit from selling something on which you previously claimed capital allowances (see page 199)
- if you get rent which is tax-free under the Rent-a-Room scheme, enter in box 5.35 the amount of relief you are claiming – i.e. £4,250 (£2,125 if you let the property jointly) or the amount of rent to which the relief applies if less
- subtract any capital allowances you can claim in box 5.36 (see page 146 for how to calculate them) and tick box 5.36A if you are claiming a 100 per cent allowance for a flat over a shop (see page 201), box 5.36B if claiming for environmentally friendly expenditure and box 5.36C if claiming landlord's energy saving allowance
- subtract your 'wear and tear' allowance (see page 201) if you let furnished property and you have chosen not to claim the actual cost of repairing and replacing furniture and so on
- subtract any loss on holiday property which you have chosen to set against other income from property (from box 5.18).

Jointly owned property

If you receive income from jointly owned property, enter only your share of the income, expenses and any allowances or reliefs claimed.

Follow the instructions on the form to find your adjusted profit in box 5.40, or loss in box 5.41. Finally, subtract any losses made in an earlier tax year and so far unused and enter the result in box 5.43. However, if the brought-forward loss is bigger than your adjusted profit, don't forget to enter the difference in box 5.45 to carry it forward to future years.

Boxes 5.44 to 5.47 Losses etc.

■ Box 5.44 applies only if you have made a loss – either partly or wholly – as a result of claiming capital allowances and you want to set this loss against other income rather than carrying it forward to set against future income from property. You cannot claim to do this for any other loss, unless it is a loss made on furnished holiday lettings.

■ You will have losses to carry forward to a future year either if you made a loss in this year or if you made a profit but it was less than your loss brought forward from previous years. Enter in box 5.45 any losses brought forward and not used this year, plus any loss made this year, minus any loss which you are claiming to use against other income in box 5.44.

■ Tick box 5.46 only if you have given details of income from jointly owned property of any type. If you have not given details of expenses because your co-owner deals with that side of things and so you only know your profit after expenses have been deducted, give the name and address of your co-owner in box 23.9 in the main tax return.

■ Tick box 5.47 if this is the last tax year in which you expect to receive taxable income from property (this may affect your tax code).

Record-keeping

The records you have to keep if you have income from property are similar to those you have to keep if you run any kind of business (see page 168). You must keep them for at least five years and ten months after the end of the tax year. However, in addition to keeping documentary evidence of all your income and relevant expenditure, you should keep a record of the number of days:

■ a property was not offered for letting at a commercial rent (so that you can work out the proportion of an expense that counts as personal use – see page 199)

■ a holiday property was let so that you can check whether it passes the 'furnished holiday lettings' test (see page 196).

Tax-planning hints

1 If you take in a lodger, you pay no tax on the income you receive if you charge less than the Rent-a-Room limit, £354 a month or less, or £177 if letting jointly.

2 If you are claiming Rent-a-Room relief you cannot deduct expenses. If you are just over the threshold of £354 a month, get your lodger to pay some bills separately. If you include them in the rent, the money for bills counts as income and you'll have to pay tax on it.

3 A holiday property in the UK may qualify for favourable tax rules if it is available for letting for at least 140 days in the year, and is actually let for at least 70 days (see page 196).

4 If you make a loss on letting holiday property which passes the test above, try to set it against other income and/or capital gains in the same tax year as you made the loss. If you carry the loss forward, it can only be used to reduce future income from property.

5 There are tax advantages for purchasing non-residential property in disadvantaged areas. You may qualify for higher capital allowances, and exemption from business rates.

6 There are also favourable tax rules if you buy a flat above a shop (or other commercial premises) to rent out (see page 201).

7 You can claim tax relief on a mortgage to buy a property you let out, but not on a mortgage on your own home (unless you let part out).

8 If you employ your partner or children to do the cleaning or gardening at the properties you let you can claim what you pay them as an allowable expense – you can't do this if you do the work yourself. But they must actually do the work and be paid at a realistic rate.

9 You can claim a deduction of up to £1,500 if you install loft, wall or floor insulation, draught-proofing or insulation for hot water systems in a property you let out.

10 If you have a tax code your tax office will normally adjust it, so that tax on your property income is deducted from your pay or pension – but can you ask them not to, if this would help your cashflow.

11 Living for a period in a home you buy to let can reduce the capital gains tax when you sell – see page 268.

10

Income from abroad

You still have to think about UK tax if you go overseas to work, or have an income from overseas property, investments or pensions. If you are resident in the UK, overseas income and capital gains are taxed in much the same way as other income or gains.

For tax purposes, the Channel Islands and Isle of Man count as 'overseas'; the UK covers England, Wales, Scotland and Northern Ireland.

Does this affect you?

This chapter affects you if you are resident or 'ordinarily resident' (see page 213 for definitions) in the UK, but you have income from outside the UK, or you own property or other assets abroad. If so, you will have to declare your foreign income and capital gains, and may have to pay tax on them.

Non-residents do not have to pay UK tax on foreign income. But they may still have to pay it on UK income, and (if only temporarily non-resident), UK capital gains. This is covered on page 220.

Whether resident or non-resident, you may still have to pay overseas tax on any foreign income. The UK has 'double taxation agreements' with many countries which may reduce the overall tax bill.

There are flow-charts to help you work out your residence status in the notes to the Non-residence pages of the tax return. HMRC's Residency office also has a useful website and helpline (see the Fact file).

Tax-free foreign income and gains

Table 10.1 on page 216 shows which types of income and gains are tax-free if you are not resident in the UK.

If you are a UK resident, the same types of income and capital gains that are tax-free in the UK are tax-free if they come from overseas. So, for example, foreign social security benefits that correspond to tax-free UK social security benefits are also tax-free. But some special tax reliefs, such as the Rent-a-Room scheme (see Chapter 9) do not apply overseas.

Note that you have to be living in the UK to claim tax credits (see Chapter 3), although temporary absences of up to eight weeks (occasionally 12 weeks) are ignored.

Foreign pensions are favourably taxed

Ten per cent of the income from a foreign pension is tax-free for UK residents. See Chapter 8 for other tax-free pensions, and note that a UK pension lump sum might also be partly or fully tax-free if it came from a job that involved working overseas. (See HMRC help sheet IR204 *Lump sums and compensation payments*.)

How the tax is worked out on foreign income and gains

- *Step 1: check your residence status* (see opposite).
- *Step 2: check how much of your foreign income and gains is taxable in the UK.* You may not have to pay tax on all of it (see Table 10.1).
- *Step 3: check whether any special rules apply,* if you are working abroad, or have investments or a property overseas (see page 217 onwards).
- *Step 4: convert to sterling.* Use the rate of exchange at the time the income arose, unless it is taxable only when you bring it in to the UK (if so, use the rate at the time it is brought in). You can use the average exchange rates on the HMRC website (see the Fact file).
- *Step 5: claim relief for any foreign tax already paid* (see page 221).

Any taxable foreign income or gains are then taxed at the same rate as any UK income or gains of the same type.

Checking your residence status

There are three types of 'residence' that might affect your tax: residence, 'ordinary' residence, and 'domicile'. The effect that they have is summarised in Table 10.1 on page 216, and see Example 10.1.

Are you non-resident?

If you are non-resident, your foreign income is not taxable in the UK. You can claim to be non-resident if:

- *either* you go abroad to work full-time as an employee (or accompany a husband, wife or civil partner who is working abroad)
- *or* you show that you have gone abroad to live permanently, or for at least three years – e.g. by buying a permanent home abroad and selling your UK home. If you have no such evidence, you may still be able to claim if you have gone for a particular purpose that is likely to cover an extended period of time.

And you meet both of the following conditions:

- you are away from the UK for at least one whole tax year
- your visits to the UK since leaving have totalled less than 183 days in any tax year and averaged less than 91 days in a tax year. (The average is worked out over four tax years, or the period of your absence if less, and excludes days in the UK for exceptional reasons, such as illness.)

If you become non-resident during the tax year

You may be able to claim 'split-year' treatment. If so, only the amount of your foreign income arising before you left the UK is taxable here.

Are you ordinarily resident?

If you are not resident, you are usually not ordinarily resident as well. But you might be classed as non-resident but ordinarily resident if, say, you usually live in the UK but have gone abroad for an extended holiday and do not set foot in the UK during a whole tax year. If so, your foreign income is not taxable in the UK but any foreign capital gains will be.

If you come to the UK, you may become resident but remain not ordinarily resident, for example if it is clear that you intend to stay less than three years (four years for students). If so, your foreign income and capital gains may become taxable in the UK, but this depends on whether you are 'domiciled' in the UK – see Table 10.1.

Example 10.1: **Claiming non-residence**

Nigel and Ben both go abroad to work full-time for 15 months and both spend only 42 days in the UK during their absence. However, only Nigel is treated as non-resident. That's because he left in February 2006 and returned in May 2007, and so was away for the whole of the 2006–07 tax year. Ben, however, left, in May 2006 and returned in August 2007 – so he did not meet the condition of being away for a whole tax year.

Are you non-domiciled in the UK?

Broadly speaking, your domicile is the country regarded as your permanent home. It will normally be the country in which your father was domiciled at the time of your birth (not necessarily the country where you were born), or, for women married before 1974, their husband's domicile. You can change your domicile but it is difficult.

If you are not UK-domiciled, foreign income and capital gains are taxable here only if you bring them into the UK. Your overseas assets may also be free of UK inheritance tax – see opposite.

Note that the residence and domicile rules are currently under review, and in particular how they affect non-domiciled individuals living in the UK.

Long-term planning for inheritance tax

You cannot escape UK inheritance tax on your overseas property by a last-minute move abroad, because you are still treated as UK-domiciled for inheritance tax if you were domiciled in the UK in the previous three years, or if you were a UK resident in 17 of the previous 20 years. (See the inheritance tax customer guide on the HMRC website.)

How much of your foreign income is taxable in the UK?

If you are a UK resident, all your income and gains from abroad are normally liable to UK tax from the date they become yours, even if they stay overseas. This is called the 'arising' basis. However, there are two cases in which you might not have to pay tax on the income immediately.

If you are not domiciled or not ordinarily resident in the UK, you can claim to pay UK tax only when you actually bring the money into the UK. This is called the 'remittance' basis (see Table 10.1). Make your claim in the 'Additional information' section of the foreign supplementary pages each year. Note that you cannot claim the remittance basis when you are working out your income for Working Tax Credit or Child Tax Credit purposes.

Whatever your residence status, if you cannot bring the money into the UK, because of exchange controls, say, you can claim that it is 'unremittable'. You pay tax on it when it does become possible to transfer it to the UK (even if you choose to leave it where it is).

UK tax on foreign capital gains

If you part with assets overseas – a property, say – you are liable to UK capital gains tax on any gains, unless you are non-resident and not ordinarily resident. However, you can put off paying tax on 'unremittable' gains (see above), and if you are not UK-domiciled, you pay tax only on gains brought into the UK. See Chapter 12 for more on capital gains tax.

You cannot escape UK capital gains tax by going abroad for a year or two. You are still liable to UK tax if you are away for less than five years and part with UK or overseas assets that you owned before you left. (See HMRC help sheet IR278 *Temporary non-residents and capital gains tax*.)

Table 10.1: Summary of how foreign income and gains are taxed in the UK

If you are	Taxable	Taxable only if remitted to UK	Not taxable in UK
Resident and			
■ ordinarily resident, domiciled	all foreign income (minus 10% of foreign pensions); foreign capital gains		
■ ordinarily resident, non-domiciled	earnings from working abroad for a UK-resident employer	all other foreign income and capital gains	
■ not ordinarily resident, domiciled	foreign capital gains	foreign income (in most cases)	
■ not ordinarily resident, not domiciled		all foreign income and capital gains	
Not resident and			
■ ordinarily resident, domiciled	foreign capital gains		all foreign income
■ ordinarily resident, non-domiciled		foreign capital gains	all foreign income
■ not ordinarily resident, (domiciled or non-domiciled)			all foreign income; foreign capital gains unless only temporarily non-resident

Working abroad

Provided that you go to live and work abroad for at least a whole tax year, and your visits back do not average more than 91 days in a tax year, you will be non-resident. All your earnings abroad will be free of UK tax from the day after your departure until the day of your return.

If you are a non-resident employee, but your job involves working partly abroad and partly in the UK, your UK earnings (allocated on daily rate) are taxable unless they are 'incidental' to your work abroad. However, you may be able to claim full relief under a double taxation agreement with the other country involved.

If you are self-employed and non-resident, your business has to be controlled overseas for the profits to be tax-free, and the profits of any UK branch or agency are taxable here.

If you are UK-resident, your foreign earnings as an employee are taxable in the UK. However, you may be able to claim extra deductions:

■ At the start or end of the job, travel costs between the UK and your workplace abroad, provided that your employer is UK-resident.
■ During the course of the job, travel to and from the UK, provided that your employer pays the costs or reimburses you.
■ The cost of board and lodging overseas, provided that this is paid or reimbursed by your employer, who must be UK-resident.
■ If your job keeps you abroad for 60 days or more, travel costs for your spouse and children, provided that your employer bears the cost.
■ Seafarers who are out of the UK for a 'qualifying absence' of 365 days or more can claim to have their foreign earnings tax-free (see HMRC help sheet IR205 *Seafarers' earnings deduction*).
■ If you are not domiciled in the UK, a deduction for earnings you do not bring into the UK (see HMRC help sheet IR 211 *Employment – residence and domicile issues*).

You may get special treatment if you are working at sea, or in the gas and oil industries, or in entertainment or sport, or if you are an employee of the Crown or European Union, or a citizen of the Commonwealth, Republic of Ireland, Isle of Man or Channel Islands. Contact HMRC's Residency office (see the Fact file).

National Insurance contributions while abroad

Whether you pay social security contributions in the country in which you are working or the UK depends on the country you are visiting and how long you expect to be away. Contact HMRC's Residency office.

Not paying UK contributions means that your right to some UK state benefits, such as a state pension, may be affected. If you plan to return to the UK, it may be worth paying Class 2 or Class 3 National Insurance contributions in the UK to protect your pension. (See HMRC leaflet NI38 *Social Security Abroad* and DWP leaflet SA29 *Your social security insurance, benefits and healthcare rights in the European Economic Area.*)

Frequent flyers

Even if you spend more than 183 days abroad, and are home for less than 91 days a year, HMRC are unlikely to treat you as non-resident if you have no settled home abroad, no intention of staying abroad indefinitely, and return to a UK base and UK home at the end of each assignment.

Investing abroad

If you are a UK resident, income from an 'offshore' investment is still liable to UK tax. You may be able to claim relief for any tax already deducted by the overseas government (see page 221), but this does not apply to dividends from some countries. Foreign dividends do not currently qualify for the 10 per cent tax credit that applies to UK dividends, but from April 2008 the government plan to introduce a tax credit for small shareholders who have less than £5,000 of dividends a year from non-UK companies.

Most foreign investment income you get is added to any UK income of the same type and taxed at the same rate – so interest is taxed at 20 per cent if you are a basic-rate taxpayer, and dividends at 10 per cent. Investment income to which the remittance basis applies (see Table 10.1) is taxed in the same way as earnings, except that the top rate of tax on foreign dividends is 32.5 per cent, not 40 per cent. For the 2005–06 tax year HMRC's computers wrongly charged 40 per cent, so if you have foreign

dividends taxed on the remittance basis, and are a higher-rat
check with your tax office that the mistake was corrected.

When you sell your overseas investments, you are liable to capital gains
tax in the same way as if you sell UK investments, except for some offshore
funds. With these, your gains when you sell are taxed as income, unless the
fund has had 'distributing status' throughout your period of ownership (in
which case part or all of the gain is subject to capital gains tax). There is a
list of 'distributing' funds on the HMRC website.

Don't count on avoiding tax by investing overseas. HMRC have the
right to information from a bank about their customers' offshore accounts,
and most European countries share information about savings interest
paid to non-residents. Some deduct a special 'withholding' tax instead, as
well as any normal tax, unless you agree to have the interest disclosed to
HMRC. If tax is deducted, make sure you enter it in your tax return (see
page 224).

A property abroad

Your profits from renting out property overseas are worked out in the same
way as your profits on UK property (see Chapter 9), except that Rent-a-
Room relief and the special rules for holiday properties do not apply. As in
the UK, if you have more than one overseas property, the income and expenses for all the properties are added together. You can claim tax relief for
interest on a loan to buy the property, adjusted to allow for any private use.

Although the same *method* for working out your profits is used as for
UK property, your overseas property is treated as a separate rental business. This means that overseas expenses cannot be deducted from UK
rental income (or vice versa) and, if you make a loss on overseas property,
you cannot use it to reduce your UK profits unless it arises from some capital allowances (see the HMRC notes). All other losses must be carried forward to set against any future profits from overseas property.

If you own a property through a company (a common set-up in many
countries), your personal use of the home could be taxed as an employment benefit. But the government have now said that they will not apply
this rule to companies owned by individuals and set up purely to hold the
property.

Your UK tax if you are non-resident

If you are not resident in the UK for tax purposes, you still have to pay UK tax on income arising in the UK. But:

- *You cannot claim UK personal allowances* (see Chapter 5), unless you are a citizen of the UK, the Commonwealth or the European Economic Area, or are resident in the Isle of Man or Channel Islands. You can also claim if you are a missionary, a servant of the Crown, abroad for health reasons, or entitled to allowances under a double taxation agreement. However, you still get the first £8,800 (in 2006–07) or £9,200 (in 2007–08) of capital gains tax-free.
- *Your tax bill is capped.* The maximum is the amount deducted at source from your investment income *plus* the tax due on any other income. But this is worked out without deducting any personal allowances. If you can claim allowances, you may pay less tax by working out your tax as if you were a UK resident. (See HMRC help sheets IR300 *Non-residents and investment income* and IR304 *Non-residents – relief under Double Taxation Agreements*.)
- *You may still have to pay UK capital gains tax.* See page 215.
- *If you let out your UK property,* your tenant or letting agent may have to deduct basic-rate tax from the rent before paying you. You can apply to receive rent before tax. Information for non-resident landlords is on HMRC's website (see the Fact file).

Tax-free interest

If you are not ordinarily resident in the UK, you can receive interest from a bank, building society, unit trust or OEIC in the UK without having tax deducted by completing form R105 (from the financial organisation, the HMRC website or your tax office). Also, interest from British Government Stock is completely tax-free if you are not ordinarily resident.

Claiming relief for foreign tax

You may find yourself having to pay tax on foreign income and gains both in the UK and in the country from which they arise. You can claim tax relief for foreign tax in one of two ways:

- *Tax credit relief* – a special credit against your UK tax bill. Usually, the credit is equal to the amount of UK tax on the foreign income or gain, or the amount of the foreign tax if less (so overall your foreign income is taxed at the higher of the two national rates – see Example 10.2 overleaf).
- *Deducting the foreign tax from the foreign income* before you work out UK tax. If, say, you paid £50 overseas tax on £500 income, you pay UK tax on £450.

Usually, tax credit relief saves you most money because it credits you with the whole amount of the tax. Deducting the tax just saves you the UK tax payable on the foreign tax. But:

- If the UK has a double taxation agreement with the other country, the foreign tax on which you can claim tax credit relief may be restricted. Agreements in force are summarised in the notes to the Foreign pages of the tax return.
- If there is no double taxation agreement, you can claim relief only if the foreign tax corresponds to UK income tax or capital gains tax.
- You can claim tax credit relief only if you are a UK resident.

Note that these rules do not apply to special withholding tax (see page 219). This is deducted from your tax bill in the same way as UK tax paid.

Example 10.2: **Claiming relief for foreign tax**

Hannah has interest of £860 from a foreign bank account, from which tax at 15% (£129) was deducted before she received it. However, as she is a basic-rate taxpayer, the interest is liable to 20% tax in the UK: £860 × 20% = £172. She can claim tax credit relief of either the UK tax (£172), or the foreign tax (£129), whichever is lower. So her tax credit relief is £129 and in the UK she pays tax of £172 − £129 = £43.

Claiming tax back from the overseas tax authority

If more tax has been deducted from your foreign income than allowed for under any double taxation agreement, reclaim the excess from the foreign tax authorities. If you get a rebate but have already claimed relief for the excess tax in the UK, you will have to tell your tax office and repay the relief. Ask the payer if the income can be paid gross in future.

What to tell HMRC

If you have any foreign income or gains that are taxable in the UK, and are not sent a tax return, you need to declare them to HMRC by 5 October after the end of the tax year. You will usually be sent a tax return (see Chapter 4). But if your only foreign income is less than £300 (gross) of overseas dividends, and you would not otherwise have to fill in a full return, you may be able to use a short return or other method – ask your tax office.

If you are claiming to be non-resident or non-domiciled in the UK, it is up to you to 'self-certify' yourself as not resident or not domiciled by ticking the boxes on the Non-residence pages of the tax return, and Question 9 on page 2 of the main tax return. HMRC may then decide to start an 'enquiry' into your return – they will not issue rulings on your residence status in advance. But you may be able to pre-empt problems by sending a form P85 to your tax office when you leave the country. You may also have to complete form P86 (on your arrival in the

UK) or DOM1 (if you are claiming non-domicile). Remember to notify HMRC's Tax Credit office if you go abroad (see page 46).

You do not need to declare foreign income or gains that are not taxable in the UK. Otherwise enter:

- *Income from working abroad* on the Employment or Self-employment pages (see Chapters 6 and 7). If you want to claim tax credit relief on this income, enter the relief in box 6.9 of the Foreign pages.
- *Taxable overseas capital gains* on the Capital Gains pages (see Chapter 12). Again, if you want to claim tax credit relief on your gains, you must enter the relief in box 6.10 or 6.10A of the Foreign pages.
- *Any other foreign income* on the Foreign pages. Remember to tick Question 6 on page 2 of the main tax return.

Filling in the Foreign supplementary pages

First, enter separately the income from each overseas source – e.g. each foreign savings account – in the relevant category on pages F1 or F2. However, if you have foreign property income, fill in pages F4 and F5 first (see page 225) and just enter the total on page F2. Finally, work out the tax credit relief you are claiming and enter it on page F3.

Pages F1 and F2 – Foreign savings and income etc.

Broadly the same information is needed for each type of income.

Column A Country

Enter the name of the country from which the income comes. In the section for 'Interest and other income from overseas savings' at the top of page F1 you should also write in [I] if the income is interest, and [O] if it is any other type of overseas savings income.

Tick box if income is unremittable

No tax is payable on income that you are prevented from transferring to the UK, but you still need to declare it and tick this box. Enter the amount of income and any tax in the currency in which you received it (cross out the £ sign) but leave column E ('Amount chargeable') blank.

Column B Amount before tax

Enter the amount before deducting any UK or foreign tax. Generally, you should enter the income earned, even if you left it in the overseas country, reinvested it, or received it late. But if part of the income was unremittable, or taxed on the remittance basis, enter only the amount you brought into the UK. Enter the amount in sterling, unless it is unremittable.

Column C Foreign tax

Enter the amount of any foreign tax paid on the income, but if a double taxation agreement applies, do not enter more than the maximum allowed (see HMRC's notes to the Foreign pages). Enter the amount in sterling (or in the overseas currency if the income is unremittable).

Column D Special withholding tax and UK tax

If the income comes from a European country that charges the special withholding tax (see page 219), enter the amount deducted. You can also enter any UK tax deducted, but this is unusual, so enter details on page F5.

Column E Amount chargeable

This is the amount that is included in your taxable income.

- *If the income is unremittable* – leave this column blank.
- *If part of the income is tax-free* (e.g. 10 per cent of a foreign pension) – only include the taxable amount.
- *If you are claiming tax credit relief* – copy the figure from column B, minus any tax-free amount, and tick the 'foreign tax credit relief' box. Do not deduct any amount in columns C or D.
- *If you are not claiming tax credit relief* – enter the amount in column B, minus the foreign tax in column C, and minus any tax-free amount.

See example 10.3 and Figure 10.1 on pages 226 and 227.

Boxes 6.3–6.4A, 6.5A Overseas trusts, companies and other entities

These boxes (and the reference to overseas trusts and companies in box 6.5) appear so that HMRC can apply various anti-avoidance rules. Read HMRC's notes carefully before you enter anything.

Box 6.5 Disposals of holdings in offshore funds

If you have sold part or all of an offshore fund, your gain may be liable to income tax, rather than capital gains tax – check with the fund manager.

Boxes 6.6 to 6.8 Gains on foreign life insurance policies

A foreign policy is one issued by an insurer from outside the UK, or by an overseas branch of a UK insurer. A policy issued by the UK branch of an overseas insurer is treated as a foreign policy. If in doubt, check with the insurer. You will need to read HMRC help sheet IR321 *Gains on foreign life insurance policies* to find what to enter in these boxes.

Page F3 – Foreign tax credit relief

You need to complete the two tables on this page if you are claiming tax credit relief on income or capital gains that you have entered elsewhere in the tax return, e.g. the Employment or Capital Gains pages.

If you are working out your own tax, you must enter the amount of tax credit relief to which you are entitled in boxes 6.9, 6.10 and 6.10A – otherwise leave these boxes empty. The relief is worked out separately for each item of foreign income, starting with the item on which you have paid the highest rate of foreign tax. The notes to the Foreign pages include a working sheet, and there is one for capital gains in HMRC help sheet IR261 *Foreign tax credit relief: capital gains*. Non-residents should see IR304 *Non-residents: relief under Double Taxation Agreements*.

Pages F4 and F5 – Income from land and property abroad

The general principle is that you fill in a separate page F4 for each foreign property you let, because tax credit relief has to be worked out separately for each. However, if all your properties are in the same country, or if no foreign tax has been deducted, and you are not claiming that any income is unremittable, you can enter all the information on one page F4.

Figure 10.1: Foreign supplementary pages (see Example 10.3)

Foreign savings

Fill in columns A to E, and tick the box in column E to claim foreign tax credit relief.

Country A		Amount before tax B	Foreign tax C	Special Withholding Tax D	Amount chargeable E	
(tick box if income is unremittable ▼)					*(tick box to claim foreign tax credit relief ▼)*	
RURITANIA (1)		£ 860	£ 129	£	£ 860	✓
		£	£	£	£	
		£	£	£	£	
		£	£	£	£	
		£	£	£	£	
		£	£	£	£	
		£	£	£	£	
		£	£	£	£	
		£	£	£	£	
		£	£	£	£	
		£	£	£	£	

Interest, and other income from overseas savings - see Notes, pages FN3 to FN4

total of column above 6.1A £   total of column above 6.1 £ **860**

Dividends - see Notes, pages FN...

		£	£		£	
		£	£		£	

Foreign tax credit relief for foreign tax paid on employment, self-employment and other income

See Notes, pages FN14 to FN15

Enter in this column the Page number in your Tax Return from which information is taken. Do this for each item for which you are claiming foreign tax credit relief ▼	Country A	Foreign tax D	Amount chargeable E (tick box to claim foreign tax credit relief ▼)
			£
		£	£
		£	£
		£	£
		£	£
		£	£
		£	£

- If you are calculating your tax, enter the total foreign tax credit relief on your income in box 6.9 - see Notes, pages FN15 to FN16.

6.9 £ **129**

Your taxable profit is worked out in the same way as for rental income in the UK, so see Chapter 9 for how to complete page F4.

Page F5 pulls together your taxable profits from all your overseas let properties, to enter on page F2.

Example 10.3: Filling in the Foreign pages

Hannah (from Example 10.2) is a UK resident with £860 income from an offshore savings account, on which she paid £129 foreign tax. As shown in Figure 10.1, she enters the income on page 1, writing [I] after the country to show that it is interest. She is claiming tax credit relief, so the chargeable amount in column E is also £860. As she is working out her own tax, she claims tax credit relief of £129 in box 6.9 on page F3 (she does not need to complete the table above box 6.9 because she has already entered the details on page F1).

Record-keeping

Keep the same records as for UK income of the same type, plus:

■ Dividend counterfoils from overseas companies.
■ Records of any overseas tax deducted.
■ Notes of exchange rates used in converting between currencies, and, if taxed on the remittance basis, the dates on which income was received in the UK.
■ Records of any calculations you carried out to arrive at the figures entered in the Foreign pages (e.g. tax credit relief working sheets).
■ Records to support any claim to be non-resident or non-domiciled in the UK, such as records of living overseas and the dates of travelling to and from the UK, and employment contracts.

Tax-planning hints

1 If you can organise your overseas visits so that you are classed as non-resident in the UK, your foreign earnings will be free of UK tax. Note that this may not save UK inheritance tax or capital gains tax and may affect your tax credits (see pages 46 and 215).

2 If you are not ordinarily resident, you can register to have your UK interest paid without tax deducted. Interest from British Government Stock is tax-free altogether.

3 Foreign pensions qualify for a 10 per cent deduction, but part or all of a UK pension may also be tax-free if it arose from work overseas.

4 Some extra expenses are tax-free if you work abroad (see page 217).

5 Even if you do not have to pay UK National Insurance contributions, it may still be worth doing so to protect your rights to UK benefits.

6 If you have income from working abroad, you may qualify for tax relief on contributions to an overseas pension fund. Ask your tax office or see help sheet IR211 *Employment – residence and domicile issues*.

7 If you want to claim non-residence, sending in HMRC form P85 when you leave and asking for confirmation that you will be regarded as non-resident may reduce the chance of problems later.

8 A special tax relief can save you UK tax if you have already paid foreign tax (see page 221).

9 Don't invest offshore in the hope of saving tax. Any foreign investment income is still liable to UK tax if you are resident or domiciled in the UK and HMRC are tightening up on people who fail to declare it.

10 If you let out UK property while abroad, apply to have the rent paid out gross. Otherwise, it will be paid with tax deducted (see page 220).

11

Income from your savings

Everybody with savings and investments needs to take tax into account: a 5 per cent interest rate is worth only 4 per cent to you if you are a basic-rate taxpayer, 3 per cent if you pay higher-rate tax. Even non-taxpayers may find themselves paying tax.

Fortunately, there are several tax-free schemes, which are covered in this chapter, to encourage you to save. See also Chapter 8 for the generous tax rules on pension contributions. If the income came from overseas, or you are not resident in the UK, see Chapter 10. And capital gains tax may be an issue if you disposed of investments – see Chapter 12.

Does this affect you?

You will need to read this chapter if you have:

- interest – e.g. from a bank or building society account
- dividends from companies, unit trusts, investment trusts and open-ended investment companies (OEICs – a modern form of unit trust)
- taxable gains from a life insurance policy
- income from a purchased life annuity
- income from a trust that is taxed as yours (a trust is a legal arrangement for holding investments or other assets)
- income from the estate of someone who has died.

Tax-free income from savings and investments

You can save tax on money when you put it *into* a savings or investment scheme only if you invest in a pension plan (see Chapter 8), Community Investment schemes (see page 81) or Venture Capital Trusts and Enterprise Investment Schemes (see page 246). However, there is no tax to pay on the interest or dividends coming *out* of the following investments:

■ ISAs (Individual Savings Accounts) and PEPs (Personal Equity Plans).
■ Venture Capital Trusts.
■ Savings Certificates from National Savings & Investments (both fixed-interest and index-linked versions) and Children's Bonus Bonds.
■ Ulster Savings Certificates, if you normally live in Northern Ireland, and were living there when they were bought or repaid.
■ Child Trust Fund accounts.
■ Premium Bond prizes, lottery prizes and other gambling winnings.
■ Save As You Earn schemes (now available only in conjunction with employer's share option schemes – see Chapter 6).
■ Tax-exempt friendly society life insurance polices. In practice, you do not usually have to pay tax on other life insurance policies (see page 240).
■ Income from a family income benefit life insurance policy.
■ Special annuities to cover the immediate costs of long-term care, if paid direct to the care provider. Payouts from long-term care policies taken out before the need for care became apparent are also tax-free.
■ *Part* of the income from purchased life annuities (ones you buy independently, not in connection with a pension – see page 239).
■ If you are not ordinarily resident in the UK (see Chapter 10), British Government Stock.

Individual Savings Accounts (ISAs)

ISAs offer tax-free saving in the following categories (or 'components'):

■ cash, e.g. a savings account
■ stocks and shares, including unit trusts, OEICs, investment trusts,

corporate bonds, British Government Stock, some life insurance
policies and Real Estate Investment Trusts (REITs, see page 245).

Any money coming out of your ISA is free of income tax and capital
gains tax. Your ISA is run by an 'ISA manager', such as a bank, building
society, credit union or National Savings & Investments, and many investment firms. You can withdraw all or part of your money at any time, although the ISA manager may impose a minimum investment period.

Are stocks and shares ISAs worthwhile?

Share dividends are paid with 10 per cent tax deducted, which cannot be reclaimed even if
the shares are held in an ISA. This means that buying share-based investments through
ISAs saves you tax only if you are a higher-rate taxpayer, or likely to pay capital gains tax.
Investing in corporate bonds or cash-based unit trusts through ISAs has tax advantages,
though, as these pay interest which is tax-free.

Your ISA choices for 2007–08

You can invest up to £7,000 in ISAs in the tax year. You can choose either
one 'Maxi-ISA' or up to two 'Mini-ISAs', but you cannot take out both a
Maxi and a Mini in the same year. (See Figure 11.1 overleaf.) Investments
must be in cash, so if you have investments that you want to move into an
ISA, you will have to sell them and reinvest – except for shares from an employer's SAYE share option scheme, approved share incentive plan or approved profit-sharing scheme (see page 98). You can transfer these shares
without having to sell them.

If you buy more than one Maxi-ISA in a tax year, or more than one
Mini-ISA of the same component, or both a Mini-ISA and a Maxi-ISA,
you will be liable for tax on the most recent ISA investment.

Your choices start afresh the next tax year, so you can end up with a col-
lection of Mini- and Maxi-ISAs. You can also transfer your ISA to a different ISA manager, or switch your money from one investment to another
offered by the same ISA manager, provided that you keep your money in

the same category (i.e. cash, stocks and shares). However, these are only the tax rules; your ISA manager may impose other restrictions.

As Figure 11.1 below shows, the only way you can put more than £4,000 in stocks and shares in 2007–08 is to choose a Maxi-ISA.

Changes on the way

The government originally introduced ISAs for a limited period, until April 2010. It has now announced that they will continue after that, and be simplified. From 6 April 2008, there will be no 'Mini' or 'Maxi' ISAs, just one overall limit of £7,200. You will be able to put the whole amount in stocks and shares, or up to £3,600 in cash and the rest in stocks and shares. You will also be able to transfer cash savings into stocks and shares (but not vice versa).

Withdrawing money from an ISA

Think twice before withdrawing money from an ISA in the same tax year in which you invest it. If, say, you put the maximum £3,000 in a cash ISA in May 2007, and then withdraw £1,000 in July 2007, you will not be able to put in another £1,000 in the 2007–08 tax year.

Figure 11.1: Your ISA choices in 2007–08

You can invest up to £7,000 overall.
You can choose to invest through either of the two routes below:

Either   *Or*

THE MAXI ROUTE	THE MINI ROUTE
Put all your money in one Maxi-ISA, from one ISA manager, with: ■ Up to £3,000 in cash ■ The rest in stocks, shares and life insurance, i.e. up to £7,000	Split your money between two Mini-ISAs, one for each component, from separate ISA managers, and with: ■ Up to £3,000 in cash ■ Up to £4,000 in stocks, shares and life insurance

Example 11.1: **Your ISA choices**

James puts £5,000 a year into an ISA. In 2006–07 he put the maximum in a Mini cash ISA (£3,000) and the remaining £2,000 in a Mini stocks and shares ISA.

In 2007–08, James puts £5,000 in unit trusts, but to do this he has to follow the Maxi-ISA route, with one ISA manager only. He also switches his 2006–07 Mini cash ISA to a new manager with better rates. The rules allow this, but until 2008–09 he must keep the money in cash, he cannot switch it into stocks and shares.

From 2008–09, James can put the whole of his £5,000 in one ISA, with up to £3,000 of this in cash, if he wants, or the whole lot in stocks and shares. And he will be able to transfer his cash ISAs from previous years into stocks and shares – but not the other way round.

PEPs and TESSAs

These tax-free investments have not been available since 1999, but you may still have one.

A TESSA was a tax-free way of saving in a bank or building society, similar to a cash ISA. Once your TESSA matured, any further interest or bonuses became taxable. However, provided that you did so within six months, you could transfer the money you put into your TESSA (but not any interest on it) into a cash ISA or a special 'TESSA-only' ISA.

PEPs were the predecessor of the stocks and shares component of an ISA, and have the same tax advantages. If you have one, you can keep it, or transfer it to a new PEP manager, but you cannot put more money in. From April 2008, all PEP accounts will become stocks and shares ISAs.

Pitfalls when transferring an ISA

If you want to transfer your ISA, you have to open your new ISA first, and then ask your existing ISA provider to transfer the money across for you. (Often, the new provider will organise this for you.) Do not just take the money out and then open your new account – your money may lose its tax-free status.

Investing for children

- Children are taxed the same way as adults. The first slice of their income is tax-free (£5,035 in 2006–07 and £5,225 in 2007–08) but they pay tax on any income above that.
- Children are normally non-taxpayers so if yours have savings accounts make sure you register for the interest to be paid gross – i.e. without tax deducted. (See page 236.)
- To stop parents investing in their children's name purely to use their allowances, any income arising from gifts to your own child is taxed as yours, *unless* it comes to less than £100 a year (per parent per child). If this is likely to affect you, choose a tax-free investment for your child. The rule doesn't apply to gifts from grandparents.

Child Trust Fund

All children born after 31 August 2002 are entitled to a £250 voucher from the government, or £500 if they are in a low-income household (children in care get extra). They will receive another £250 or £500 voucher when they reach age 7. The money must be invested for them in a range of special accounts, until they reach 18. The accounts are tax-free (in the same way as ISAs, see page 230). Other people can contribute a total of £1,200 a year to a child's account.

It's up to you to choose and open the account for your child. If you fail to do so by the expiry date on the voucher, HMRC (who administer the scheme) will open one for you, although you can transfer the money later to an account of your choice.

How tax is worked out on investment income

- *Step 1: identify any tax-free income* (see page 230). You can ignore this when working out your tax.
- *Step 2: sort income into categories.* Different types of investment income are taxed at different rates, so first your income is sorted into interest, dividends and life insurance gains.
- *Step 3: add any investment income from trusts or estates.* If you have received income from a trust, or the estate of someone who has died, the money may count as yours for tax purposes (see page 245).

■ *Step 4: work out which tax band each type of investment income falls within.* Your income is taxed in this order: first your non-investment income, then your interest, then dividends, then any taxable life insurance gains. So first you need to work out how much of your allowances, starting-rate tax band and basic-rate tax band are used up by your non-investment income (see Figure 1.1 on page 5).

■ *Step 5: decide how much tax you have to pay, taking into account any tax already paid.* Multiply each category of investment income by the appropriate rate of tax (shown in Table 11.1 overleaf) and then deduct any tax already paid on the income before you received it. You may be able to claim tax back – or you may have more to pay.

Alternative finance

Under Islamic Shari'a law, the payment and receipt of interest is forbidden. As a result, alternative finance contracts have been developed to avoid interest, by providing the return either in the form of a profit share, or through the purchase and re-sale of assets. The return from these investments is now taxed in the same way as interest. This means that tax is deducted unless you complete form R85 to have it paid before tax.

Interest

As well as interest from a bank or building society, interest includes:

■ income from taxable National Savings & Investments products
■ income from lending money to people, organisations, or governments (for example, British Government Stock and corporate bonds)
■ interest distributions from a unit trust or OEIC
■ the return from an alternative finance arrangement (see above).

Unless you have invested through an ISA, the interest is taxable. It is paid out to you either without any tax deducted (gross) or with 20 per cent tax taken off (i.e. 'net', 'with tax deducted at source').

If the income is paid out after tax, you have no further tax to pay

Table 11.1: Total tax payable on different types of investment income

Type of income	Non-taxpayer	Starting-rate taxpayer	Basic-rate taxpayer	Higher-rate taxpayer
Non-savings income	0%	10%	22%	40%
Interest	0%	10%	20%	40%
Dividends	10%	10%	10%	32.5%
Life insurance	None – because the insurance fund is taxed			20% if the policy is 'non-qualifying'

provided that all your taxable income – including the interest, but after deducting your allowances – is less than £33,300 in 2006–07 (£34,600 in 2007–08). Indeed, if your taxable income is less than £2,150 in 2006–07 (£2,230 in 2007–08), you will be able to claim part or all of the tax back, using form R40 if you do not get a tax return (see Chapter 2). On income above £33,300 in 2006–07 (£34,600 in 2007–08), you will have a further 20 per cent tax to pay to bring the overall tax up to 40 per cent. This is done by adjusting your tax code or through your tax return.

Bank and building society interest
This is usually paid with 20 per cent tax taken off, unless you are a non-taxpayer and have registered to receive the interest gross by completing form R85 (from the bank or building society or the HMRC website, or in leaflet IR111 *Bank and building society interest. Are you paying tax when you don't need to?*). With a joint account, the other person must be a non-taxpayer too, unless the bank or building society agrees to pay half of the interest gross. See page 244 for more on investing as a couple.

British Government Stock, corporate bonds and other loan stocks
These are effectively interest-paying loans to various organisations. The interest you receive is taxable, but paid as follows:

■ *British Government Stock* (or 'gilts'): the interest is normally paid gross, but you can opt to have it paid net – contact the Gilts Registrar, Computershare (see the Fact file).

- *Corporate bonds* (loans to a company): the interest is paid gross.
- *Local authority stocks*: the interest is paid with tax taken off but if you are a non-taxpayer you can apply to have it paid gross.
- *Permanent Interest Bearing shares* (PIBs – loans to a building society): the interest is paid gross.

Once issued, all these loan stocks can be bought and sold, which means that the price goes up and down to reflect demand. In particular, if you buy stocks after they are first issued, or sell them before they mature, part of the price may reflect the right to receive the next interest payment – i.e. the 'accrued' interest. The contract note for the sale should show the amount.

If the face value of all your stocks and bonds is below £5,000, the accrued interest will not affect your tax. Otherwise, you are within the 'accrued income scheme', which is a way of deciding whether the purchaser or the seller is taxed on the accrued interest. The government is reviewing the accrued income scheme, but this is how it currently works:

1 Find the tax year in which the first payment of interest after the transaction falls. You must apply the rules if, at any point within that tax year or the preceding tax year, you owned stocks with a total face value (not 'price') of more than £5,000.
2 Check whether the accrued interest was added to the price, or deducted from it (this should be on the contract note).
3 If the accrued interest is added to the price (the normal practice), the interest counts as the taxable income of the seller and is called a 'charge'. It is deducted from the income of the purchaser as a relief.
4 If the accrued interest is deducted from the price, the purchaser pays tax on the accrued interest and the seller gets relief on it.

Any tax is payable, or any relief is given, in the tax year of the first interest payment, not the tax year in which the sale took place. (See Example 11.2, overleaf, and HMRC factsheet *Accrued income scheme*, available on the HMRC website.)

Example 11.2: **Dealing with accrued income**

In January 2007, Frances sold some British Government Stock with a face (or 'nominal') value of £4,000. The next interest payment is due in May 2007. She also has corporate bonds with a face value of £3,000, so she is within the accrued income scheme. Five months of accrued interest is added to the price she gets for her stock. This is a 'charge' on which she must pay tax but, as the next interest payment is not due until May 2007, she pays tax on it in 2007–08, not the tax year in which she sold her stock.

'Strips' and 'discounted securities'

The right to receive interest can sometimes be bought and sold separately from the right to the capital repayment when a stock or security matures. The process of separating the interest from the capital is called 'stripping'. Alternatively, a security may be issued where little or no interest is paid and the return comes from the difference between the issue price and the amount payable on redemption. With such 'discounted securities' or 'strips', both the interest and any profit on the 'capital' element of the security or gilt are taxable as interest, but the exact rules depend on the type of security.

Credit union share interest

The 'dividend' from credit unions is paid gross but is taxable.

National Savings & Investments products

All of these are taxable, *except* for Savings Certificates, Children's Bonus Bonds and Premium Bonds. The taxable products fall into two groups:

- The Investment Account, Easy Access Savings Account, Income Bonds, Capital Bonds, Pensioners' Guaranteed Income Bonds and Guaranteed Equity Bonds: income from all these products is paid out before tax. The income is still taxable, but any tax due is collected either by adjusting your tax code or through your tax return.
- Fixed Rate Savings Bonds: 20 per cent tax is *always* deducted from the income paid out by these bonds. You can reclaim overpaid tax, but non-taxpayers should pick more suitable products.

A downside of Capital Bonds

You are taxed each year on the income earned on National Savings & Investments Capital Bonds – even though it is not paid until the end of the five-year term.

Interest from a unit trust or OEIC

Unit trust or OEIC funds that are invested in gilts, loan stocks and other interest-producing investments pay out interest distributions instead of dividend distributions. The tax voucher will show the type of distribution.

Unless you have invested through an ISA, 20 per cent tax will be deducted. From April 2007, non-taxpayers can register to have the interest paid gross (ask your tax office for the appropriate form R85). You can reclaim any tax overpaid in previous tax years.

Purchased life annuities

A purchased life annuity is a lifetime income payable by a life insurance company, in return for a lump sum. Do not confuse it with an annuity that is bought with your pension savings – it is taxed very differently.

Part of the income from a purchased life annuity – the 'capital element' which will depend on your age at purchase – is tax-free. The rest is taxable as interest, with 20 per cent taken off. Non-taxpayers can get the interest paid gross by completing form R89 (or R86 for joint annuities).

Dividends

The main types of dividend income are cash payouts, such as:

■ share dividends from UK companies and investment trusts (note that zero dividend investment trusts pay no income and therefore are not liable to income tax). See page 245 for income from REITs
■ dividend distributions from UK unit trusts and OEICs (but 'cash' type unit trust funds pay out 'interest' distributions, see above).

With both types, you are treated as if 10 per cent tax has been paid before you receive the dividend. This is called a 'tax credit'. The taxable amount is the dividend you received, *plus* the tax credit, but you can then set the tax credit against your tax bill. So if, for example, you receive a dividend of £90, the tax credit is £90 × ⅑ = £10: you are taxed on £90 + £10 = £100 but you can deduct the £10 tax credit from your tax bill.

If you are a starting-rate or basic-rate taxpayer, you have no further tax to pay on your dividend. But if you are a higher-rate taxpayer, you will have a further 22.5 per cent to pay, to bring the overall tax up to 32.5 per cent. So on a dividend of £90, with its £10 tax credit (a taxable amount of £100), you pay further tax of £22.50: £32.50 tax in total.

Note that you cannot reclaim the tax credit on share dividends, even if you are a non-taxpayer, and even if the shares are held in an ISA.

Non-cash payouts
The following non-cash payouts to shareholders also count as dividends:

- Dividends payable as extra shares instead of cash ('stock' or 'scrip' dividends).
- Bonus redeemable shares or bonus securities. These are potentially taxable both when they are issued (as 'non-qualifying distributions') and when they are redeemed (as a 'qualifying distribution').

You are treated as having paid 'notional tax' at 10 per cent on these payouts. This is effectively the same as a dividend tax credit: non-taxpayers cannot reclaim the tax and higher-rate taxpayers will have more to pay.

The tax voucher should make it clear what sort of payment it is, and whether you get a tax credit. With 'scrip' dividends, the tax voucher will also show the taxable value of your extra shares (look for 'the appropriate amount in cash' or 'the cash equivalent of the share capital').

Life insurance

The life insurance fund in which your money is invested is taxed. When the money is paid out to you, you are treated as if you have already paid 'notional tax' of 20 per cent of the amount received. If you are a non-taxpayer, starting-rate taxpayer or basic-rate taxpayer, you have no further tax to pay. But you will have more to pay if:

- You have a 'non-qualifying' policy *and*
- You make a taxable gain on the policy (such a 'gain' is liable to income tax, not capital gains tax) *and*
- You are a higher-rate taxpayer, or a basic-rate taxpayer but the taxable gain on your policy pushes you into the higher-rate tax band. Even so, a special 'top-slicing relief' may be due.

See HMRC help sheet IR320 *Gains on UK life insurance policies.*

What is a non-qualifying policy?

This is one into which you are not expected to pay regular premiums over a period of at least ten years. So, for example, a life insurance bond into which you pay a single premium is non-qualifying. Your insurance company will be able to tell you if the policy does or doesn't qualify.

A savings-type insurance policy, e.g. an endowment policy or a 'whole life' policy, is usually qualifying and therefore no tax is payable on the proceeds. But it will become non-qualifying if you stop paying into the policy, sell it or receive benefits from it within the first ten years (or, if the policy is intended to last less than 13.4 years, within the first three-quarters of the intended term, for example 7.5 years for a ten-year policy).

Have you made a taxable gain?

You may make a gain during your lifetime when your non-qualifying policy matures, or if you surrender or sell it or withdraw money from it. There may also be a gain when the policy pays out on your death – though the gain is worked out using the surrender value immediately before your death, which may differ from the amount actually paid out.

If you have made a taxable gain, the insurance company should issue a 'chargeable event' certificate which tells you the taxable amount.

At its simplest, a gain occurs when you get more out of a policy than you put in. So if you invest £10,000 in a policy that eventually produces £15,000, your gain is £5,000. But it is common to surrender only part of a non-qualifying policy – to top up income, say. If so, you can put off paying tax on these partial withdrawals until the policy finally ends.

You can put off paying tax if, in any one year, you withdraw less than 5 per cent of the amount you paid in to the policy *plus* any unused '5 per cents' from previous years. Note that 'year' in this context means years you have had the policy, not tax year.

If you make no withdrawals in the first year you have the policy, you can withdraw 10 per cent in the second year. The maximum you can withdraw without triggering a taxable gain is 100 per cent (i.e. the amount you put in) after 20 years (see Example 11.3). If you withdraw *more* than your accumulated 5 per cents, your taxable gain is the total amount withdrawn to date (on which you have not so far paid tax), minus the accumulated 5 per cent allowances.

When the policy comes to an end, you are taxed on your total benefits from it, minus the amount you paid in, and minus any taxable gains so far (i.e. withdrawals above your accumulated 5 per cents).

How much tax on your taxable gain on a non-qualifying policy?

Even if you make a taxable gain, you do not have to pay tax on it unless it falls within the higher-rate band. And you do not have to pay the full top rate of 40 per cent on any gain in the higher-rate band, because almost all policies are treated as if 20 per cent tax has already been deducted. So only a further $40 - 20 = 20$ per cent tax is payable by you.

A problem with insurance policies is that the one-off lump sum paid out can push your income into the higher-rate tax bracket. Top-slicing relief compensates for this. It works by first dividing the total gain by the number of complete years you have had the policy to find the average annual gain. If the average annual gain, when added to the rest of your income:

- *falls within the basic-rate tax band* – the whole of your gain is tax-free
- *falls within the higher-rate band* – top-slicing relief does not save you any tax
- *falls partly in the basic-rate band, partly in the higher-rate band* – you do not pay the full top rate of tax on your insurance gain. This is achieved by charging you higher-rate tax on the amount of the average annual gain that falls within the higher-rate band, and multiplying the tax by the number of complete years you have had the policy.

Example 11.3: **Tax on a non-qualifying insurance policy**

Ten years ago Patrick invested £10,000 in a single-premium insurance bond (a non-qualifying policy). From year 2 he withdrew £600 a year to top up his income, which he increased to £700 from year 7. In year 7 his total withdrawals so far came to more than his total 5% allowances so far, and he made a taxable gain of £200 in that year and the following year. He did not have to pay tax on these gains because they did not push him into the higher-rate tax bracket.

In year 9, Patrick cashed in his policy for £8,545. This, plus his regular withdrawals, made a total gain of £12,945. From this he can deduct the money he put in (£10,000) plus his taxable gains in years 7 and 8 (£400). His overall taxable gain is £12,945 − £10,000 − £400 = £2,545.

Patrick's other income in year 9 is just £400 below the top of the basic-rate band and the insurance gain would push him into the higher-rate band. But top-slicing relief comes to his rescue. His average annual gain is £2,545 divided by the 8 complete years he has had the policy − £318. As none of this falls within the higher-rate tax band, he has no tax to pay.

Year	1	2	3	4	5	6	7	8	9	Totals
Paid in	10,000									**10,000**
Annual 5% allowance		500	500	500	500	500	500	500	500	
Previous years' unused allowance			500	400	300	200	100	0	0	
Withdrawals			600	600	600	600	600	700	700	8,545	**12,945**
Taxable gains during policy								200	200		**400**

Warning: over 64 or eligible for tax credits?

Even if you do not have to pay higher-rate tax on your insurance gain, it is taken into account in deciding how much tax credit you can claim (see Chapter 3) and whether you are over the limit (£20,900 in 2007–08) above which age allowance is reduced (see page 72). And top-slicing relief will not apply – so in Example 11.3, Patrick's full £2,545 gain would be included in his income for these purposes.

Tax relief for a loss on a non-qualifying policy

If you make a loss on a life insurance policy (because stock markets have fallen, say), you may qualify for a special relief called 'deficiency relief' which saves higher-rate tax. You can claim relief only if you have previously paid tax on the policy, and you are a higher-rate tax-payer. (See HMRC help sheet IR320, *Gains on UK Life insurance policies*.) The relief is restricted if you bought the policy second-hand.

Taxable insurance policies: points to remember

- The 5% allowance is just a way of putting off tax on an insurance gain – it is not a tax-free allowance.
- It might be better to draw more than 5% during the life of the policy if you are not a higher-rate taxpayer, rather than build up a big gain at the end of the policy.
- The 5% withdrawals are 5% of the premium – not the policy value.

Investing as a couple

- If you are married or a registered civil partner, and own an investment jointly, you are normally each taxed on half of the income from it. If you contributed unequal proportions to the investment you can, instead, opt to have the income taxed in line with the proportion you each invested, by asking your tax office for Form 17. However, you cannot use this for bank accounts or life insurance nor for jointly owned shares in your own company (these are now always taxed in line with your entitlement to dividends).
- You can save tax by giving investments to the partner who pays the lower rate of tax.
- Married couples and civil partners can give each other investments without incurring inheritance tax or capital gains tax. See Chapters 12 and 13.

Real Estate Investment Trusts (REITs)

REITS – a type of investment trust that invests in property – were introduced from January 2007. Unlike other property funds, the trust itself is
not taxed if it pays out 90 per cent of its profits as dividends. Any dividends
you receive from these untaxed profits are treated as property income, not
share dividends: they are paid out with basic-rate tax deducted, but non-
taxpayers can reclaim this and higher-rate taxpayers have a further 18 per
cent tax to pay. However, REITs may also pay out other dividends, taxed
like share dividends.

Note that REITs are tax-free altogether if bought through an ISA.

Income from trusts

A trust is a legal arrangement designed to hold investments or other assets
in the care of trustees for the benefit of one or more 'beneficiaries'. The
person who provides the assets is called the 'settlor'. If you are a beneficiary or a settlor of a trust, some or all of the income received by the trust
may be taxed as yours – and, since trusts are often set up to hold investments, the income paid is often investment income. Life insurance policies
are often held in trusts for inheritance tax purposes (see Chapter 13).

There are various types of trust, to which different tax rules apply. See
HMRC factsheet, *Trusts. An introduction*, available on the HMRC website.

Part or all of a trust's income may be taxed as yours if:

■ You are a beneficiary of a 'bare' trust (one where you have an
  unconditional right to the trust's property and income). All the trust's
  income is treated as if it were yours. If the beneficiary is a child and
  the trust funds were provided by a parent, the income is taxed as if it
  were the parent's.
■ You are the settlor of any type of trust (apart from a bare trust) and
  you, your child, spouse, or civil partner have any right to the trust's
  property and income (or 'retain an interest' in tax-speak).
■ You are a beneficiary of any type of trust apart from a bare trust. The
  trust itself (or rather, the trustees) may pay tax and receive its own tax
  returns. Any income to which you are entitled is taxed as yours, but
  you get a credit for tax paid by the trust (see overleaf).

The trustees should give you form R185 showing how much income is taxable as yours, and how much the tax credit is. Note that income from a discretionary trust (one where the income is not automatically paid out and the trustees have a right to decide who will benefit) is paid out with a tax credit. The value of the tax credit varies, depending on the type of income and the amount of income received by the trust, but you can reclaim some or all of the tax deducted, if this is more than you are liable to pay.

Some trusts set up for 'vulnerable' people such as disabled people or orphan children qualify for special, more favourable tax treatment.

Income from estates

When someone dies, there is a gap between the paperwork being completed and the distribution of the estate to the people named in the will. During this period, the estate may still be receiving income, such as interest on a bank account or dividends from investments. If you are a beneficiary of the estate, some or all of this income may be taxed as yours.

If so, it is taxed in the same way as any other income within the same category – e.g. dividends or interest. Whoever is administering the estate should give you a form R185 stating how much income you have received in each category, and how much tax has been paid on your behalf.

Tax relief on investments

Only a few investments give you tax relief on the money you pay in. The most important is a private pension (see Chapter 8). The Enterprise Investment Scheme (EIS) and Venture Capital Trusts (VCTs) are ways of investing in unquoted companies that give you income tax relief on the amount invested. If you sell your shares for a profit, there is no capital gains tax, but don't invest purely for the tax breaks.

With both schemes, you can claim your tax relief either through your tax return, or by sending the certificate provided by the company or trust to your tax office.

Reinvesting to avoid capital gains tax

If you make a taxable capital gain on any asset, you can put off paying the tax by reinvesting the proceeds in the Enterprise Investment Scheme. (See HMRC help sheet IR297 *Enterprise Investment Scheme and capital gains tax.*)

Enterprise Investment Scheme (EIS)

You get tax relief either if you buy shares in an unquoted trading company that has been approved under the scheme, or if you invest via a special investment fund. You cannot use the scheme to invest in a company with which you are 'connected', for example as a paid director or as a major shareholder, unless, possibly, you come into the company after the shares are issued. You may also lose relief if you receive some benefit, apart from normal dividends, from the company.

You get tax relief of 20 per cent of the amount you subscribe for shares, up to a maximum of £400,000. If the shares are issued in the first six months of the tax year, you can claim to have half of your investment (up to a maximum of £50,000) treated as though made in the previous tax year. But you lose tax relief if you part with your shares within three years. (See HMRC help sheet IR341 *Enterprise Investment Scheme – income tax relief.*)

Any gain you make on the shares is free of capital gains tax provided you have held them for at least three years. But if your shares become worthless, you can claim tax relief on the amount of your loss, *minus* the amount of tax relief received when you bought the shares. You can set the loss either against your taxable income for the year of the loss (or the preceding year), or against any taxable capital gains.

Venture Capital Trusts (VCTs)

With Venture Capital Trusts you invest through a company that is itself listed on the Stock Exchange. You get income tax relief at 30 per cent on the amount you invest in new ordinary shares, but not shares bought 'second-hand'. The maximum investment is £200,000 per tax year. You lose tax relief if you part with your shares within three years (five years for shares issued after 5 April 2006).

You do not have to pay any tax on the dividends, but the 10 per cent tax credit on the dividend cannot be reclaimed and does not count as tax paid.

Any profit on shares is free of capital gains tax, but unlike the Enterprise Investment Scheme you cannot claim relief on any losses.

What to tell HMRC

If you do not get sent a tax return, you should contact your tax office if:

- You are a taxpayer receiving taxable investment income paid out before tax (for example, from British Government Stock), or a higher-rate taxpayer, and any tax due is not already collected through PAYE. If so, you must tell your tax office by 5 October after the end of the tax year (that is, 5 October 2007 for income received in 2006–07).
- Tax on your investment income is collected through your tax code but your circumstances change – e.g. you expect to receive more or less investment income in future.
- You want to claim tax relief for an investment in an EIS or VCT.
- You have a tax-free investment and somehow breach the conditions – e.g. you have taken out a Mini-ISA and a Maxi-ISA in the same tax year.
- You are a starting-rate taxpayer or a non-taxpayer, and think you might be able to claim tax back. In this case, there is also a special helpline (see the Fact file). You might be asked to fill in a form R40 to claim a tax repayment. (There is more about this in Chapter 2.)

If you do get a tax return, it will guide you through what you need to disclose about your investment income. There are special supplementary pages if you receive foreign investment income (see Chapter 10) or taxed income from trusts or the estate of someone who has died. However, if you get income from trusts that is paid gross, or scrip dividends from a trust, they should be included with any other income of the same type.

Updating your bank or building society

If you are currently receiving interest gross, and you become a taxpayer, let your bank or building society know so that they can start to deduct tax.

Filling in your tax return

Information about UK investments is collected on pages 3 and 4 of the main return. Remember, you do not have to enter tax-free investment income, listed at the beginning of this chapter; most income from a REIT goes in Question 13 (see page 62) and foreign investments go on the Foreign pages (see Chapter 10). You should be able to get the details you need either from your regular statements, or from the certificates of interest paid that are supplied at the end of each tax year by some payers of interest, e.g. banks and building societies.

Question 10 – Did you receive any income from UK savings and investments?

Note that you need to enter the total income you have in each category (there is a working sheet in HMRC's tax return guide to help you tot up your bank and building society interest).

If you receive interest with tax taken off (net), you need to show the before-tax (gross) figure as well. See overleaf for how to work this out.

Boxes 10.1 to 10.4 Interest and alternative finance receipts from banks and building societies

Remember that you need to enter amounts paid with no tax deducted in box 10.1, separately from those paid with tax deducted, which go in boxes 10.2 to 10.4. If the income comes from a foreign-currency account with a UK bank (e.g. euros), convert it to sterling before you enter it.

Boxes 10.5 to 10.7 Interest distributions from unit trusts and OEICs

The figures you need should be shown on the tax voucher accompanying the payment.

Boxes 10.8 to 10.11 National Savings & Investments

You should get a statement of interest received towards the end of April each year.

Boxes 10.12 to 10.14 Other income from UK savings and investments

Enter here income from British Government Stock, corporate bonds, other loan stocks and purchased life annuities (see page 236 onwards).

If you bought or sold stocks and the first interest payment after the transaction falls in the 2006–07 tax year, see page 237 to work out whether your tax is affected by accrued interest. If it is affected:

- *add* together any accrued interest *charges* (amounts of accrued interest on which you are taxed)
- *deduct* any amounts of accrued interest on which you get *reliefs*.

If the result is a positive number (i.e. you have more charges than reliefs), add it to the figure you enter in box 10.14. Do not change the figure in boxes 10.12 or 10.13. If the result is negative, your charges are reduced to nil and you add nothing to the figure in box 10.14. You can carry forward the unused reliefs (i.e. reliefs minus charges) to set against any charges in future years.

Finding the gross or net amount of interest

If you receive interest after tax (net), you will need to show in your tax return the before-tax (gross) figures as well as the tax itself. To find the gross figure if you know the net amount, divide the net figure by 0.8. To find the net figure if you know the gross amount, multiply the gross amount by 0.8. The tax is, of course, the difference between the gross and net figures.

Common mistakes

Double-check your entries if you find that you have figures in both box 10.1 (gross interest) and boxes 10.2 to 10.4 (taxed interest). It suggests either that you could claim to get interest paid gross, or that you have incorrectly been claiming gross interest on one account.

Boxes 10.15 to 10.26 Dividends

Income that is classed as dividends is listed on page 239. A cash payment from a company or unit trust goes in the top two rows, as appropriate. But if you get a non-cash distribution, you need to check which row to enter it in – if in doubt, contact the company's registrar. Remember, income from the untaxed profits of a REIT goes in Question 13, not here.

Boxes 10.15 to 10.23 Dividends, dividend distributions and scrip dividends

The information needed should be shown on the tax voucher that accompanies each payment. Add up the total dividends (or distributions) in each category, and the tax credits, and transfer the totals to the tax return. Then add the total tax credits (or notional tax, as appropriate) to the total dividends or distributions and enter the result in the right-hand column.

You can work out the tax credit (or notional tax, for scrip dividends paid out as shares rather than cash) simply by dividing the dividend or distribution by 9.

There are a few traps you should be aware of:

■ If you are affected by the IR35 rules as an employee of your own service company (see Chapter 6), you *may* be able to claim that dividends received from your company are tax-free. (See page 12 of HMRC's tax return guide.)

■ When entering unit trust or OEIC distributions, include any distributions from 'accumulation' units – these are retained in the trust, rather than paid out to you, but they count as taxable income and you should get a tax voucher. You do not have to enter any figures shown as 'equalisation' – these are relevant only for capital gains tax.

■ If you have higher-rate tax to pay on the redemption of bonus shares or securities, you may be able to claim tax relief (in box 15.12 of the tax return) for any higher-rate tax that you paid when the shares were first issued (see HMRC's notes to the tax return and page 87).

■ A 'qualifying distribution' catches things like receiving goods at cheap rates. This is most likely to apply to employee shareholders, in which case it would be taxable as earnings and should not be entered here. The same applies to a loan written off (see overleaf).

Hang on to tax vouchers and certificates of tax deducted

You should not send these in with your tax return, but you must keep them in case your tax office asks to see them in future. See page 255 for records you should keep.

Boxes 10.24 to 10.26 Non-qualifying distributions and loans written off

The tax you are treated as having paid is calculated differently for each type:

- For non-qualifying distributions (see page 240), leave box 10.24 blank. Instead, enter the taxable amount of the distribution in the *last* box (10.26). Multiply box 10.26 by 10 per cent – this gives you the amount of notional tax to enter in box 10.25.
- For loans written off, enter the amount of the loan written off in box 10.24. Enter ⅑ of the figure in box 10.24 in box 10.25. Add the two boxes together and enter the result in box 10.26.

Question 12 – Gains on UK life insurance policies etc.

Boxes 12.1 to 12.5 Gains on UK life insurance policies

Complete this section only if you have made a taxable gain on a non-qualifying life insurance policy. If so, the insurance company should send you a 'chargeable event' certificate showing the taxable amount. See HMRC help sheet IR320 *Gains on UK life insurance policies* if it does not.

First check on the certificate whether the policy is treated as having had tax paid on it. This will almost certainly be the case.

Assuming your policy is treated as having paid tax, enter the taxable amount in box 12.5. If it is a joint policy, only enter your share (see Help sheet IR320). Divide the figure in box 12.5 by five and enter the result in box 12.4 – this is the tax you are treated as having paid. Finally, enter in box 12.3 the number of years you had had the policy at the date of the 'chargeable event'.

Note that if you have made a taxable gain on the partial surrender of a policy, you should report it in the tax return for the tax year in which the *next* anniversary of taking out your policy falls. A surrender in January 2007, say, should go in your 2007–08 return if you bought the policy in May. This applies only to partial surrenders – other gains are taxable in the tax year they occur.

More than one policy?

You should enter the total gains from all your policies, and the total tax treated as paid. However, if you have more than one policy, do not complete the 'Number of years' box (12.1 or 12.3). Instead, give details of the gain, tax paid and number of years for *each* policy in the 'Additional information' box at the end of the return.

Sometimes, insurance policies are sold in 'clusters' – your money is invested in several identical policies to give flexibility when cashing them in. If you have identical gains from any such policies you can add all the gains together and enter them as one policy.

Boxes 12.6 to 12.8 Gains on life insurance policies in void ISAs

This will apply only if you have invested in the insurance component of an ISA which is invalid because of a breach of the ISA rules (see page 231). Your ISA manager should tell you what to enter.

Box 12.9 Deficiency relief

This will apply only if you paid tax on a partial withdrawal from a policy in the past, the policy has now come to an end and the tax you paid earlier proves to have been too high. You can claim tax relief only if you are a higher-rate taxpayer. (See help sheet IR320.)

Boxes 12.10 to 12.12 Refunds of surplus funds from AVCs

If you left a job, or retired, your employer may have notified you that you paid in too much to your pension scheme and refunded the excess, minus tax. If so, you need to check whether this is an authorised payment under the tax rules. Unauthorised payments should be entered in the Pensions supplementary pages (see page 185): only enter here any authorised payments. The pension company will give you the information you need.

This does not apply if you receive a refund of your contributions to an employer's pension scheme that you left in the first two years.

Figure 11.2: Question 10 (see Example 11.4)

INCOME *for the year ended 5 April 2007*

Q10 Did you receive any income from UK savings and investments?　YES ✓

If yes, tick this box and then fill in boxes 10.1 to 10.26 as appropriate. Include only your share of any joint savings and investments. If not applicable, go to Question 11.

■ *Interest and alternative finance receipts*

● Interest and alternative finance receipts from UK banks or building societies including UK Internet accounts. *If you have more than one bank or building society account enter totals in the boxes.*

- enter any bank or building society interest and alternative finance receipts that **have not had tax taken off**. (Interest and alternative finance receipts are usually taxed before you receive them so make sure you should be filling in box 10.1, rather than boxes 10.2 to 10.4.) Enter other types of interest and alternative finance receipts in boxes 10.5 to 10.14, as appropriate.

Taxable amount
10.1 £

- enter details of **taxed** bank or building society interest and **taxed** alternative finance receipts. *The Working Sheet on page 11 of your Tax Return Guide will help you fill in boxes 10.2 to 10.4.*

Amount **after tax taken off**	Tax taken off	Gross amount **before tax**
10.2 £ *248*	**10.3** £ *62*	**10.4** £ *310*

● Interest distributions from UK authorised unit trusts and open-ended investment companies (dividend distributions go below)

Amount **after tax taken off**	Tax taken off	Gross amount **before tax**
10.5 £	**10.6** £	**10.7** £

● National Savings & Investments (other than First Option Bonds and Fixed Rate Savings Bonds and the first £70 of interest from an Ordinary Account)

Taxable amount
10.8 £

● National Savings & Investments First Option Bonds and Fixed Rate Savings Bonds

Amount **after tax taken off**	Tax taken off	Gross amount **before tax**
10.9 £	**10.10** £	**10.11** £

● Other income from UK savings and investments (except dividends)

Amount **after tax taken off**	Tax taken off	Gross amount **before tax**
10.12 £ *772*	**10.13** £	**10.14** £ *772*

■ *Dividends*

● Dividends and other qualifying distributions from UK companies (Enter distributions from the tax exempt profits of a Real Estate Investment Trust at Q13)

Dividend/distribution	Tax credit	Dividend/distribution **plus** credit
10.15 £ *153*	**10.16** £ *17*	**10.17** £ *170*

● Dividend distributions from UK authorised unit trusts and open-ended investment companies

Dividend/distribution	Tax credit	Dividend/distribution **plus** credit
10.18 £	**10.19** £	**10.20** £

● Stock dividends from UK companies

Dividend	Notional tax	Dividend **plus** notional tax
10.21 £	**10.22** £	**10.23** £

● Non-qualifying distributions and loans written off

Distribution/loan	Notional tax	Taxable amount
10.24 £	**10.25** £	**10.26** £

Example 11.4: **Entering your taxable investment income**

Page 4 of Andy's tax return is shown in Figure 11.2. He received £248 after tax from his two building society accounts: he enters this in box 10.2 and then divides it by 0.80 to find the before tax amount (£310) to enter in box 10.4. The tax (which goes in box 10.3) is £310 − £248 = £62. Andy also received dividends of £153 in total, which go in box 10.15. He divides this by 9 to find the tax credit to enter in box 10.16 (£17), and then adds the dividend and tax credit together. The result (£153 + £17 = £170) goes in box 10.17.

Andy's other investment income (£712 from British Government Stock) is paid out before tax, so he just enters the amount received in boxes 10.12 and 10.14.

Record-keeping

You must keep your savings income records for at least 22 months from the end of the tax year to which they relate (five years and ten months if you also have business or letting income). Remember to keep copies of any relevant emails or online statements. This is the sort of thing to keep:

- *Shares and unit trusts:* tax vouchers sent with any dividend or distribution (you should get one even if the dividend is paid direct to your bank account).
- *British Government Stock:* you will get an annual statement of interest if the interest is paid direct to a bank, otherwise a tax voucher is attached to the cheque. Keep any contract notes when you buy or sell.
- *Enterprise Investment Scheme or Venture Capital Trusts:* certificates provided by the company.
- *Interest and annuities:* you may get a 'certificate of tax deducted' at the end of each year. If you are not sent one automatically you can ask for one. Otherwise the after-tax amount of interest paid will be shown on your statements or passbook.
- *Life insurance:* policy documents; notes of date and amount of any withdrawal; any 'chargeable event' certificates from the insurer.
- *Trusts and estates:* details of any income received and any vouchers or form R185 from the trustees or executors.

Tax-planning hints

1 Always compare the after-tax return from different investments. Higher-rate taxpayers may benefit from tax-free investments even if the headline interest rate is not the best.

2 Non-taxpayers should consider investments that pay out before tax (e.g. most National Savings or British Government Stock) and remember that the tax credit on shares and unit trusts cannot be reclaimed. With a bank or building society, you can register to receive interest gross.

3 If you give your child investments that produce an income of more than £100 a year, it is treated as your income and you may have to pay tax on it. You can avoid this by choosing a tax-free investment.

4 You can choose to have interest from British Government Stock paid gross or net.

5 If you are 65 or over, and expect to receive income of more than £20,900 in 2007–08, plan your investments to avoid the income affecting your age-related allowances (see page 72).

6 You do not have to pay tax directly on a taxable life insurance policy unless you are a higher-rate taxpayer. But a taxable insurance gain may affect your age-related allowance or tax credit even if you are not taxed directly on it (see page 243).

7 Gains on withdrawals from an insurance bond are taxable, but you can put off paying tax until the policy ends if you withdraw no more than 5 per cent per year of the premium value.

8 Couples may be able to save tax by transferring investments to the lower-income partner.

9 If you are a beneficiary of a discretionary trust you may be able to reclaim tax on income paid out to you.

10 Use your annual ISA allowance. ISAs are free of capital gains tax, and there is no income tax to pay on the interest from cash ISAs, or from corporate bonds and cash-based unit trusts held in ISAs.

11 Do not choose an investment just because it has tax advantages – an unsuitable investment could cost you more than it saves in tax.

12

Capital gains tax

You sell some shares at a profit. You retire and your children take over your business. You sell a property that you've been renting out.

All these transactions, and some others, may have capital gains tax implications. Capital gains tax is simply a tax on the capital sum produced when you 'dispose' of an 'asset'. The most common disposal arises when you sell something, but you also make a taxable disposal if, for example, you give something away (or sell it at an artificially low price).

If you do have to pay capital gains tax, your gains are taxed as if they were extra investment income you received.

Does this affect you?

You don't need to worry about paying capital gains tax if your total capital gains in a tax year are less than the annual tax-free amount (£8,800 in the 2006–07 tax year, rising to £9,200 in 2007–08). However, you should notify your tax office if you have made a loss on selling a capital asset, as this can usually be set against any future taxable gains.

Even if your total gains in 2006–07 came to more than £8,800, there are deductions and reliefs which will reduce the tax, or bring the gain below the £8,800 limit. And some gains are completely tax-free – they don't count towards the £8,800 limit, and don't have to be declared.

Tax-free gains

Gains on the following items
- Private cars.
- Foreign currency for your and your family's use.
- Decorations for valour (unless you bought them).
- Personal effects and goods disposed of for £6,000 or less, such as household furniture, paintings and antiques (HMRC call these 'chattels'). If the disposal proceeds are more than £6,000, you pay tax on either your gain, or five-thirds of the amount over £6,000 if less.
- 'Wasting assets', with a predicted life of 50 years or less, providing they were not eligible for capital allowances for use in a business. Machinery is treated as a wasting asset – including antique clocks and vintage cars – if owned personally and not used in a business.

Gains on the following investments
- Investments held in a Personal Equity Plan (PEP), Individual Savings Account (ISA) or Child Trust Fund.
- National Savings Certificates.
- SAYE schemes.
- Shares in a Venture Capital Trust or (with some conditions) an Enterprise Investment Scheme.
- Life insurance policies (unless you bought the policy second-hand) – but gains might be liable to income tax, see page 240.
- Pension plans (assuming the scheme is registered with HMRC).
- British Government Stock and most types of corporate bond.

Other tax-free gains
- Premium Bond prizes, and betting, lottery or pools winnings.
- Gifts to charity or for 'public benefit' (e.g. art given to the nation).
- Gifts to amateur sports clubs open to the whole community.
- Gains when an estate is disposed of at death (but watch out for inheritance tax instead, see Chapter 13).
- Cashbacks received as an inducement to buy something (e.g. a new car) or take out a loan.
- Compensation for personal injury or pension mis-selling (on policies sold between 28 April 1988 and 30 June 1994).

■ Compensation for loss or damage (such as insurance payouts), unless you use all of it to replace or repair the damaged property.

On gains made when selling your main home, and transfers of property between spouses and civil partners, special reliefs mean there is usually no tax to pay (see page 268). There are also many business reliefs.

One downside of tax-free assets such as investments in an ISA is that if you make a loss on them, the loss cannot be set against your gains. The exception is shares in the Enterprise Investment Scheme.

Note that gains you make on assets overseas are not tax-free, and the tax is worked out in the same way as for UK assets (see page 215).

How capital gains tax is worked out

Capital gains tax is notorious for being complicated, but the basic principles are quite simple.

1 Work out your gain on each asset you have disposed of in the tax year.
2 Add together the taxable gains on all the assets you have disposed of in the tax year, deduct any losses, and deduct the annual tax-free amount.
3 Work out the tax on what's left.

These principles apply to all your gains that don't fall within one of the tax-free categories above. However, there are many different tax reliefs and exemptions you can claim.

Working out the gain or loss on each asset

Start with the disposal proceeds. This is the sale price, if you sold the asset. If you didn't sell it (or you sold it for less than its full price) the disposal proceeds are the market value of the asset at the time.

From the disposal proceeds you can deduct the allowable costs of the asset. The main allowable cost is usually the purchase price if you bought the asset, its probate value if you inherited it, or its market value if you acquired it in some other way. You can also deduct other allowable expenses, such as the costs of buying and selling the asset, stamp duty and anything spent improving the asset (but not ordinary maintenance costs).

Selling something you acquired before April 1982

Only gains made since 31 March 1982 are taken into account. This works by using the market value of the asset on that date as the allowable cost. This can exaggerate your gain or loss and you should use the original cost instead if that produces a smaller gain or loss. If one method produces a gain and the other a loss, you are treated as having made neither a gain nor a loss. You may be able to use the March 1982 value for all your assets instead. (See HMRC help sheet IR280 *Rebasing – assets held at 31 March 1982*.)

Indexation allowance

After deducting allowable costs, you end up with either a gain or an allowable loss. If you made a gain and you owned the asset before 1 April 1998, you can also deduct indexation allowance, to compensate for inflation running from April 1982 up until April 1998. You cannot claim it for periods starting after 31 March 1998 – instead, you may be able to claim taper relief, but this is worked out at a later stage.

To work out indexation allowance, multiply your allowable costs by the 'indexation factor' for the month in which each cost occurred (see Example 12.1 opposite). Indexation factors are given in the Fact file or you can get them from your tax office. However, you can use indexation only if you made a gain – you cannot use indexation to create or increase a loss. So if the indexed allowable cost is more than the proceeds of the disposal, your gain is zero.

Summing up

Disposal proceeds
Minus
Allowable costs
(multiplied by indexation factor if cost incurred before April 1998)
Gives
Your gain (after indexation) *or* your allowable loss

Example 12.1: **Indexation factors**

Philip bought some shares for £10,000 in July 1990 and sold them in 2007. The indexation factor for assets bought in July 1990 and sold after April 1998 is 1.282. So the indexed cost of Philip's shares is £10,000 × 1.282 = £12,820. If Philip sells his shares for £15,000, he has made a gain of £15,000 − £12,820 = £2,180. But if his shares sell for only £11,000, he cannot use the indexation to claim a loss − he has made no gain and no loss. He can claim a loss only if he sells for less than the unindexed cost, i.e. £10,000.

Working out your overall gains for the year

Once you have worked out your gains or losses on all the disposals you have made in the year, add up all your gains and deduct all your losses:

■ If the overall gain for the year is below the level of the annual tax-free amount (£8,800 in 2006–07 and £9,200 in 2007–08), you can stop here – there is no tax to pay.

■ If your losses are more than your gains, you can carry any unused losses forward to future years, but you must notify your tax office (by letter or through your tax return) within five years and ten months after the end of the tax year (that is, by 31 January 2013 for losses made in 2006–07).

■ If the overall gain for the year is above £8,800, look back to see if you have any unused losses from earlier years. If so, you deduct just as much of those losses as you need to reduce your gains (before taper relief) to £8,800.

Note that the government is clamping down on tax avoidance schemes that create artificial losses to set against gains. But this will not affect you if you make a genuine loss on a genuine disposal.

Taper relief

If your gains are still above £8,800, you can apply taper relief. This was introduced in 1998 as a replacement for indexation allowance. It works by charging tax on only a percentage of your gain. The percentage of the gain

geable (the 'taper rate', shown in Table 12.1) is reduced in line
umber of complete years you owned the asset after 5 April 1998.

Table 12.1: Taper relief for disposals after 5 April 2002

No. of whole years after 5 April 1998	Taper rate (% of gain chargeable)	No. of whole years after 5 April 1998	Taper rate (% of gain chargeable)
Non-business assets*		Business assets	
Under 3	100	Less than 1	100
3	95	1	50
4	90	2 or more	25
5	85		
6	80		
7	75		
8	70		
9	65		
10 or more	60		

*Add extra year's ownership for non-business asset owned on 17 March 1998

You don't get taper relief for periods before April 1998, but any non-business assets that you owned on 17 March 1998 (budget day in that year) qualify for an extra year. Otherwise, taper relief is much more generous for business assets – defined on the next page.

Example 12.2: **Taper relief**

In May 2007 Susie sold some shares she inherited in January 1998, with a gain of £4,000. She has owned the shares for nine complete years since 5 April 1998, and can add an extra year because they are non-business assets owned on 17 March 1998. Her ten years mean that only 60% of her £4,000 gain is taxable, i.e. £2,400. As Susie has already used up all her tax-free amount on other gains, and she is a basic-rate taxpayer, she will pay tax of £2,400 $\times$ 20% = £480.

Business assets

Business assets are widely defined, and you don't have to own your own business to have them. Business assets are currently:

- shares or securities in an unlisted trading company
- shares or securities in a listed trading company in which you can exercise at least 5 per cent of the voting rights
- shares or securities in a company which employs you (listed or unlisted), unless it is a non-trading company and you have an interest of more than 10 per cent in it
- assets which you use in your own trading business, either as a sole trader or partner, or through a trading company which is unlisted or where you have at least 5 per cent of the voting rights. From 6 April 2004, this includes assets used by other sole traders (e.g. let assets)
- assets that you use for your work if you are an employee or director of a trading company.

'Trading' excludes businesses set up purely for investment or property development. It also excludes letting out most property – though letting furnished holiday accommodation counts as a trade (see Chapter 9).

The definition of business assets was more restrictive before 6 April 2000 – see HMRC help sheet IR279 *Taper relief*. Also see this help sheet if you own something which you use partly privately; the gain is split between the private and business use before working out the taper relief. So if a gain on your home is taxable because you use part of it exclusively for business (see page 268), you can claim some business taper relief.

Making the most of your losses

You make the most of your losses by setting them first against the gain that qualifies for the least taper relief. This is because taper relief is worked out after you have deducted your losses: you don't get full benefit from the loss if the taper relief itself would bring your gains down below the annual tax-free amount (£8,800 in 2006–07). You can't get round this by only deducting enough of the loss to bring your tapered gains down to £8,800.

Summing up

Total gains for the year (after any indexation)

Minus

Total losses for the year

Minus

Any unused losses from previous years
(but only enough to reduce your overall gains to £8,800)

Minus

Taper relief on each gain

Minus

Annual tax-free amount (£8,800 in 2006–07)

Gives

Your taxable capital gains

Working out the tax

Finally, after you have multiplied each remaining gain by the appropriate taper rate, deduct the annual tax-free amount of £8,800 in 2006–07 (£9,200 in 2007–08). What's left is your taxable capital gains for the year.

You pay tax on your taxable capital gains at 10, 20 (the basic rate applied to capital gains) or 40 per cent, depending on how much taxable income you have. Your tax bands are used first by your income, and then by any capital gains. Your capital gains will be taxed at your top rate of income tax – so you will have to pay a higher rate of tax on gains that when added to your income fall within a higher tax band (see Example 12.3).

Example 12.3: **Which rate of tax?**

Hannah's total taxable income in 2006–07 is £29,300. This all falls within the lower- and basic-rate bands. Her unused basic-rate band is £33,300 minus £29,300, that is £4,000. If she has taxable capital gains of £5,000, Hannah will pay tax at 20% on the first £4,000 of her gains (£800) and at 40% on the remaining £1,000 (£400). This gives a capital gains tax bill of £800 + £400 = £1,200.

Which shares or unit trusts are you selling?

Imagine you bought some shares in British Utility plc when the company
was privatised, and you bought more later on. Now you are selling half the
holding. To work out which shares you are selling you need to sort them
into the following groups. Group 1 shares are sold first, then any Group 2
shares and so on. The full rules are in HMRC help sheet IR284 *Shares and
Capital Gains Tax*, but Example 12.5 on page 267 shows how it works.

- *Group 1:* shares acquired on the same day as the disposal in question.
- *Group 2:* shares acquired in the 30 days *following* the sale. This is a way
  of discouraging 'bed-and-breakfasting' (see page 266).
- *Group 3:* shares acquired after 5 April 1998, taking the most recent
  acquisitions first.
- *Group 4:* shares acquired before 6 April 1998 but after 5 April 1982, on
  a 'pooled' basis (see below and Example 12.4).
- *Group 5:* shares acquired before 6 April 1982 but after 5 April 1965.
  These are also pooled, but separately from Group 4 shares, usually
  using the market value of the shares on 31 March 1982.
- *Group 6:* shares acquired before 6 April 1965. You will probably need
  to speak to your tax office about what to use as the allowable cost.
- *Group 7:* shares acquired more than 30 days after the sale.

The same rules, with added touches, apply to unit trusts and shares in investment trust companies and Open Ended Investment Companies
(OEICs), but you can avoid any worries about capital gains tax if you invest through an Individual Savings Account (see Chapter 11).

Pooling
The cost of all the shares in a pool is added together. The allowable cost of
each share is the average value of all the shares. Indexation allowance is accounted for by adjusting the value of all the shares in the pool each time
you change the number of shares in the pool (to do this, you need various
indexation factors, see the Fact file.)

Example 12.4: How pooling works

Ernie bought 2,000 shares in British Bottles plc in July 1985 for £2,000 and another 2,000 shares in July 1990 for £3,000. These form a Group 4 pool. To work out the indexed cost, he takes the allowable cost of the first group of shares (£2,000) and multiplies it by the indexation factor for the period between July 1985 and his next purchase in July 1990 (1.332). This gives him the indexed value of the first 2,000 shares in his pool at July 1990 (£2,000 × 1.332 = £2,664). He adds the cost of the next 2,000 shares (£2,664 + £3,000 = £5,664).

Finally, he multiplies the cost at July 1990 by the indexation factor for the period between July 1990 and April 1998, when indexation was frozen (£5,664 × 1.282 = £7,261). £7,261 is the allowable cost of all Ernie's Group 4 shares. But as he is selling only one-quarter of them, the allowable cost of the shares sold is £7,261 × ¼ = £1,815.

Employee share schemes

Special treatment applies when you sell shares you acquired free or cheap in your employer's company. Any gain you make may still count for capital gains tax purposes, but the way the tax is worked out will depend on how the scheme is set up. You may also be eligible for business assets taper relief. Guidance is available in the share schemes area of the HMRC website.

Bed-and-breakfasting

'Bed-and-breakfasting' means selling shares and buying them back the next day. The advantage of doing this used to be that it allowed you to realise a gain to set against your annual tax-free amount, but now, if you buy the shares back within 30 days, the price of the new purchase is used as the cost of the shares you have sold. This means that you won't realise a gain unless the share price falls within the 30 days. Selling and buying back may still be worthwhile if your spouse or civil partner buys back the shares, or if you wait 30 days, but check with a financial adviser first.

Example 12.5: **Which shares have you sold?**

Ernie acquired shares in British Bottles plc on four occasions:

July 1985   2,000 shares bought for £2,000 { ('pooled' in Group 4,
July 1990   2,000 shares bought for £3,000   see Example 12.4)
January 2000   2,500 shares bought for £6,000 (Group 3)
July 2002   500 shares bought for £1,000 (Group 3)

When Ernie sells 4,000 shares in May 2007, he takes the shares from Group 3 first (he has no Group 1 or 2 shares). This gives him 2,500 + 500 = 3,000 shares. He takes the remaining 1,000 shares he is selling from Group 4.

Mergers, takeovers and other reorganisations

If a company in which you have shares has issued extra shares, or has been taken over, merged or otherwise reorganised, the company will usually tell you how the reorganisation is treated for tax purposes in the circular or prospectus sent to shareholders. Also see HMRC help sheet IR285 *Share reorganisations, company take-overs and Capital Gains Tax*.

Scrip or stock dividends

These are extra shares issued instead of a cash dividend. The dividend voucher will tell you the amount of the dividend on which income tax is payable (see page 239). For capital gains tax purposes, you are treated as if you paid that amount in cash for the new shares.

Unit trusts and Open Ended Investment Companies (OEICs)

These are treated like shares, but there is some special treatment:

■ You might see a figure for 'equalisation' on the tax voucher that accompanies distributions. This is a repayment of the capital you used to buy the units and should be deducted from the allowable cost.
■ With 'accumulation' units, any income is reinvested automatically by increasing the value of your existing units. The increase in value is

treated as extra expenditure on your original holding, and taper relief runs from the date of original purchase.

■ If you make regular investments, each counts as a new purchase. To simplify the calculations for indexation allowance, you can treat all your investments in one year as one payment made in the seventh month of the fund's accounting year. This is not necessary for taper relief, as that is worked out on an annual basis anyway.

Tax reliefs you can claim to reduce your capital gains

There is a checklist of reliefs starting on page CGN18 of HMRC's notes to the Capital Gains pages, but here are the main ones.

Your only or main home

If you sell your only or main home, 'private residence relief' makes any gain tax-free. However, you may lose part or all of your relief if:

■ you have tenants (you may be able to claim lettings relief instead, see page 270). You do not lose relief if you have a single lodger
■ part of your home is used exclusively for business (see page 142)
■ you sell off part of your property
■ the garden is larger than necessary 'for your reasonable enjoyment' (HMRC use half a hectare as a guide to what is reasonable)
■ HMRC think you are in the business of property development.

If only part of your home qualifies, the gain will be split between parts of the home which qualify and parts which do not. There are no set rules for how the gain is split, but it is usual to take into account the number of rooms and the relative value of each part.

You may also lose part of your relief if the home was classed as your only or main home for just part of the time. The gain is split depending on how long it was your only or main home – so if you owned the house for 120 months, say, and lost relief for 40 of those months, $4/120$ of the gain is potentially taxable. You can ignore the period before April 1982 provided you use the value at the end of March 1982 to work out the allowable cost; and you do not lose the relief for:

■ the first year of ownership (exceptionally two years) if you have not been able to live in the home because you are doing it up or have still to sell your old home
■ absences if you are living in job-related accommodation
■ the final three years of your ownership.

Other absences that count as periods of residence, providing you lived in the property before and after the absence and had no other main home are:

■ absences because you are employed outside the UK
■ absences of up to four years, if you have to be away for work
■ other absences which add up to less than three years altogether.

Example 12.6: **Is your home tax-free?**

Martin and Fiona bought a Cotswolds cottage in January 1997 and sold it in January 2007 for a gain of £200,000 (£100,000 each, see page 271). It was their main home for the first two years, but then they moved, letting out the cottage until they sold it. The first two years qualify for private residence relief and the final three years always do – five years in total. They each qualify for private residence relief on $\frac{5}{10}$ of their gain, i.e. £100,000 × $\frac{5}{10}$ = £50,000.

More than one home

You can choose which home is your main one, but you must do so within two years of the date you had a particular combination of homes. A new two-year period begins on any further change in your combination of homes. If you do not choose, HMRC will. See HMRC help sheet IR283 *Private residence relief*. Note that property rented on a tenancy agreement can still be your 'residence' – so if you move from a home you own to one rented on this basis, nominate the home you own as your main residence.

Property you let

When you sell a property that you let, the whole of any gain is potentially liable to tax and it will not normally qualify for business assets taper relief (see page 263 for the exceptions). But you can reduce the tax if you occupy the property as your main residence at some point. That way you qualify for private residence relief for at least the final three years of ownership (see Example 12.7 below). You may also qualify for lettings relief.

Lettings relief

This relief is available only if you let out residential accommodation in what is or has been your only or main home, or part of it. It is part of your home if you have made no structural alterations, even if the let part has its own kitchen and bathroom, but you cannot claim it for a self-contained flat.

Lettings relief is worth the same as private residence relief, up to a ceiling of £40,000. So if your private residence relief is:

- £40,000 or less, just double the private residence relief
- over £40,000, you add £40,000 to your private residence relief.

Example 12.7: **Tax on a home that you let**

Martin and Fiona made a gain of £100,000 each on their cottage, £50,000 of which qualifies for private residence relief (see Example 12.6). The remaining gain is £50,000 each, on which they can claim lettings relief. This is the same amount as their private residence relief, or £40,000 each if less. So their taxable gain is reduced to £50,000 – £40,000 = £10,000. Taper relief means that only 65 per cent of the gain is taxable – £6,500. As they made no other gains in 2006–07, this is within their £8,800 annual exemption, so they have no tax to pay.

Property abroad?

Gains on a property abroad may be liable to UK capital gains tax (see page 215). However, you can still claim private residence relief and lettings relief, provided that it has been your only or main home at some time.

Tax on your home if you have a partner

If you are married or a civil partner, your main home (for private residence relief) must be the same for both of you, unless you are separated and living apart. But whether or not you are married, if you make a taxable capital gain on a property you own with someone else, the gain will be split between you. And both partners and spouses can claim lettings relief on their share of a gain – so lettings relief of up to £80,000 on one property may be available. (See Example 12.7 opposite.)

Reliefs for spouses and civil partners

Husbands and wives each get their own annual tax-free amount. If you give (or even sell) something to your husband or wife, there is no tax to pay at the time, provided that you are living together, or in the year of separation. Any tax is payable only when your spouse disposes of the asset – but at that stage, the gain is worked out as if your spouse had owned the asset from the moment you acquired it. The same rules apply to civil partners, but other couples do not qualify for this special treatment.

Reliefs for your business

As well as the generous taper relief for business assets, there are the following reliefs from capital gains tax:

■ *Roll-over relief* allows you to put off paying tax on disposing of business assets if you reinvest the gains in new business assets. (See HMRC help sheet IR290 *Business asset roll-over relief*.)
■ *Incorporation relief* allows you to put off paying tax if you transfer your business to a company in exchange for shares.

Note that if you have unused losses from self-employment, a partnership or furnished holiday lettings, you can choose to set them against your capital gains rather than carry them forward to future years (see page 155). The capital gains pages of the tax return call these 'income losses'.

What to tell HMRC

If you aren't sent a tax return, you should tell your tax office by 5 October after the end of the tax year in which you make the gain if you have a taxable capital gain above the annual tax-free amount. If you get a return (including the short version), ask for the capital gains tax pages.

If you have losses that you want to set against gains made in past or future years, notify your tax office by 31 January in the sixth year after the tax year in which they were incurred. That means by 31 January 2013 for losses made in 2006–07. There is no time limit for losses made before 6 April 1996. Once losses have been notified, you can carry them forward indefinitely – they do not have to be used within the six-year time limit.

Filling in the Capital Gains supplementary pages

To see whether you need to fill in the Capital Gains pages, go to Question 8 on page 2 of your main tax return. Tick the relevant box if:

■ you sold your home and, for any of the reasons on page 268, any gain you have made on it is not completely tax-free
■ you disposed of taxable assets worth more than £35,200 in total
■ your taxable gains come to more than £8,800 after taper relief
■ your gains are above £8,800 before taper relief but you have losses
■ you have any other claim or election – e.g. you made a loss overall.

Figure 12.1: Question 8 – capital gains

Q8 Capital gains - read the guidance on page 7 of the Tax Return Guide.

• If you have disposed of your only or main residence do you need the Capital Gains Pages? [YES]
• Did you dispose of other chargeable assets worth more than £35,200 in total? [YES]
• Answer 'Yes' if:
– allowable losses are deducted from your chargeable gains, which total more than £8,800 before deduction and before taper relief, **or**
– no allowable losses are deducted from your chargeable gains and after taper relief your taxable gains total more than £8,800, **or**
– you want to make a claim or election for the year. [YES ✓] CAPITAL GAINS ✓

If you ticked any box in Question 8, now go to the Capital Gains supplementary pages. Everyone has to complete page 8 of these – it records your overall gains for the tax year and provides a record of your losses (past and present). You also have to complete either pages 2 and 3 or, if your disposals were straightforward disposals of quoted shares, just page 1.

Pages 4, 5 and 6 apply only if you have disposed of unquoted shares, property or other assets and page 7 is for additional information. It's important to explain on these pages how assets were valued, and who by, how you have calculated any reliefs, and how any joint gains were split.

Page 1

This simplified version of pages 2 and 3 is for people with straightforward capital gains that don't qualify for taper relief (i.e. you have owned them for less than three years, or one year if they are classed as a business asset) on UK unit trusts, or quoted stocks and shares. In addition, it cannot be used if you are claiming any reliefs.

Pages 2 and 3

These pages are for details of each disposal, if you cannot use the simplified version on page 1.

Enter each transaction on a different row, giving brief details of the asset in column A. If necessary, photocopy the page. In column AA, you need to code each disposal as Q, U, L, T or O, depending on the type of asset. Write Q if the asset is quoted shares. If it consists of unquoted shares (U), you must give further details on page 4; for land or property (L), further details go on page 5; and for other assets (O) use page 6. Code T applies only if a gain of a trust you set up is treated as yours (this is covered in HMRC help sheet IR277 *Trusts with settlor interest and trusts for the vulnerable: taper and losses*). Tick column B if you had to estimate any figures or are relying on a valuation.

Tick column C if you owned the asset concerned on 31 March 1982, because only gains arising after that date are taxed (see page 260). Similarly, in column D you enter either 16 March 1998 or the date of acquisition if later, because taper relief applies only after this date. However, you must enter the date of disposal at E in all cases, and the disposal proceeds (which may be the sale price or the market value, see page 259) in column F.

Column G is for details of any tax reliefs you want to claim, such as private residence relief when you dispose of your home. Check the HMRC notes in case you also have to complete a claim form.

Gains on assets which are partly business assets and partly non-business assets (e.g. a home you let out) go in rows 9 and 10. Once you have completed columns A to G with the overall information for the asset, split the gain into two parts (business and non-business) when completing the other columns, because different taper rates apply.

Enter the taxable gain after deducting allowable costs and any indexation allowance in column H, showing any loss in brackets. Write 'Bus' in column I if the asset is a business asset (see page 263 for a definition) and write the relevant taper rate (from Table 12.1 on page 262) in column J.

Deduct any losses in columns K1, K2 and K3. Taper relief is worked out after losses have been deducted, so losses have to be set off against each gain in turn. Losses for the year come from box 8.2 at the bottom of the page; you can only work out what income losses (i.e. trading losses) you have once you have completed your Self-employment, Partnership or Land and Property supplementary pages. Unused losses on disposing of capital gains from earlier years will come from your records (such as page 8 of previous years' Capital Gains pages).

Remember: if you have both gains and losses, enter first the gains with the highest taper rate (i.e. those with a taper rate of 100 per cent at the top, then those at 95 per cent and so on). Then work down the rows, taking just as much as you need from each category of loss to reduce each gain to the optimum amount. That way, you'll make the most of your losses.

Attributed gains

There are various tax avoidance rules to stop people using trusts to avoid capital gains tax. If you fall foul of these rules, gains made by the trust may be 'attributed' to you and taxed as yours. See the HMRC notes to the Capital Gains supplementary pages.

Using losses

When entering income losses in column K2 (trading losses which you are claiming to set against gains) and unused losses from earlier years (in column K3), remember there is no point deducting more than you need to reduce your overall gains to the level of the annual tax-free amount (£8,800 in 2006–07). You have to deduct the whole of any losses for the current year, but any other losses can be carried forward.

Example 12.8: **Filling in pages 2 and 3**

Andrea made overall gains of £12,000 in 2006–07. Because these take her above her annual tax-free amount, she also decides to get rid of some shares that have fallen in value, giving her a £2,000 loss at box 8.2 (see Figure 12.2). She gives details of her gains in all the columns up to column K, listing the gain with the highest taper rate first, and enters the total in box 8.1.

Next Andrea carries her £2,000 loss for the year to column K1. This leaves gains after losses for the year at £12,000 − £2,000 = £10,000. She also has £3,000 unused losses from earlier years, but she needs only £1,200 of these losses to reduce her gains to the tax-free amount of £8,800. She takes £1,000 of the losses from earlier years to reduce her gains in row 1 to zero, and sets another £200 against the losses in row 2. She has £3,000 − £1,200 = £1,800 in losses left to carry forward.

Moving to column L, Andrea's gains are now zero, £4,800 and £4,000. She multiplies the gains by the relevant taper rate in column J and enters the results in row M. Adding up column M, her gains after taper relief (in box 8.3) are now £5,320 – below her annual tax-free amount. She has no tax to pay but some of her losses brought forward are wasted.

The way the tax rules are written means that Andrea cannot choose to deduct fewer losses to compensate for the taper relief. But she could have chosen to hang on to her under-performing shares, instead of selling them for a £2,000 loss. She would have used up all her £3,000 loss from earlier years against her first gain, but her taper relief would still have reduced her other gains below the level of the tax-free slice.

Figure 12.2: Capital gains (see Example 12.8)

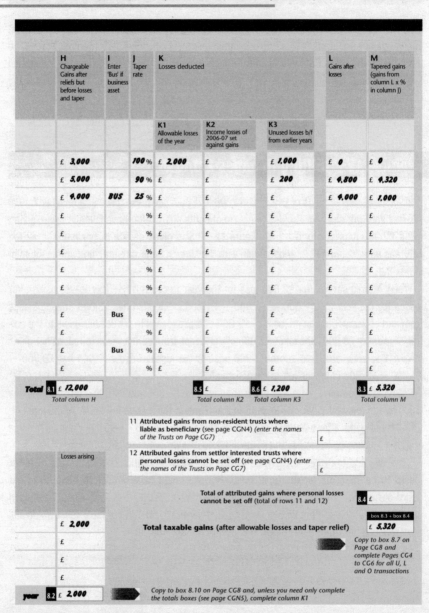

H Chargeable Gains after reliefs but before losses and taper	I Enter 'Bus' if business asset	J Taper rate	K Losses deducted			L Gains after losses	M Tapered gains (gains from column L x % in column J)
			K1 Allowable losses of the year	K2 Income losses of 2006-07 set against gains	K3 Unused losses b/f from earlier years		
£ 3,000		100 %	£ 2,000	£	£ 1,000	£ 0	£ 0
£ 5,000		90 %	£	£	£ 200	£ 4,800	£ 4,320
£ 4,000	BUS	25 %	£	£	£	£ 4,000	£ 1,000
£		%	£	£	£	£	£
£		%	£	£	£	£	£
£		%	£	£	£	£	£
£		%	£	£	£	£	£
£		%	£	£	£	£	£
£	Bus	%	£	£	£	£	£
£		%	£	£	£	£	£
£	Bus	%	£	£	£	£	£
£		%	£	£	£	£	£

Total 8.1 £ *12,000*
Total column H

8.5 £   8.6 £ *1,200*
Total column K2   *Total column K3*

8.3 £ *5,320*
Total column M

11 Attributed gains from non-resident trusts where liable as beneficiary (see page CGN4) *(enter the names of the Trusts on Page CG7)* £

12 Attributed gains from settlor interested trusts where personal losses cannot be set off (see page CGN4) *(enter the names of the Trusts on Page CG7)* £

Total of attributed gains where personal losses cannot be set off (total of rows 11 and 12) 8.4 £

Losses arising

£ *2,000*

£

£

£

box 8.3 + box 8.4
Total taxable gains (after allowable losses and taper relief) £ *5,320*

Copy to box 8.7 on Page CG8 and complete Pages CG4 to CG6 for all U, L and O transactions

year 8.2 £ *2,000*

Copy to box 8.10 on Page CG8 and, unless you need only complete the totals boxes (see page CGN5), complete column K1

If you don't know the market value

You can estimate an asset's market value if necessary. You should tell HMRC (on your tax return) how you reached the estimate and their specialist valuers may check it. You can appeal if you do not agree with their valuation. You can also ask your tax office to check a valuation before sending in your return (ask for form CG34).

Connected persons and clogged losses

A 'connected person' is your husband or wife, close family member, civil partner, business partner or a company or trust you control. There are rules designed to stop you using your connections to avoid tax. In particular, if you give or sell something to a connected person (except your spouse or civil partner, see page 271), the price used when working out the tax is replaced by the market value. Any loss on a transaction with a connected person is a 'clogged loss' that can only be set against a future gain made on a disposal to that same person.

Page 8

This is a summary of your capital gains for the year. There are just a few things to note:

■ *Additional liability in respect of non-resident or dual resident trusts* (box 8.9) applies if you received a benefit from an offshore trust which is caught by anti-avoidance rules. See HMRC help sheet IR301 *Capital gains from non-resident, dual resident and immigrating trusts.*
■ In a very few circumstances, you do not have to set this year's losses against this year's gains (boxes 8.12, 8.13A and 8.13B). If you have made a loss on shares in an unlisted trading company, or an Enterprise Investment Scheme, you can claim to set these against your income. See HMRC help sheets IR286 *Negligible value claims* and IR297 *Enterprise Investment Scheme and capital gains tax.*
■ If you have carried forward unused losses made before 6 April 1996, at

boxes 8.15 to 8.21, you have to record these separately from losses made on or after that date, because the losses made after 6 April 1996 have to be used up first.

Record-keeping

The tax return doesn't ask you to give details of how you arrive at the taxable value of any gain. But in case of enquiries keep the following for at least 22 months or, if you have a business or rental income, for five years and ten months from the end of the tax year to which they relate. If you can, it's best to keep the records for as long as you own the asset, or until you use any loss arising from it.

- Contract notes, correspondence or other documentation when you buy, sell, lease or exchange assets such as investments.
- Scrip dividend vouchers.
- Invoices or other evidence of payment records (e.g. bank statements) for costs you claim for the purchase, improvement or sale of assets.
- Documentation describing assets you acquired but did not buy yourself, such as gifts or an inheritance.
- Details of assets you have given away or put into a trust.
- Copies of valuations taken into account in your calculation of gains and losses (e.g. probate values for inherited assets).
- If you acquired or disposed of quoted shares in any other way than on the open market (e.g. if you gave shares away), a copy of a newspaper showing the share price for that day.
- If you use an asset partly for business, partly privately, records to show what proportion of the use is for each purpose.
- If you start using an asset for a purpose that might change its tax treatment (e.g. you start letting out part of your home, or you start using an asset for work), notes of dates on which the use changes.
- If you have more than one property, records of dates when you lived in them and copies of any elections to choose one as your 'main' home (see page 268).

Tax-planning hints

1 Keep careful records – not least because any losses can usually be used to reduce your capital gains in future years.

2 If you made a loss in 2006–07, remember to notify HMRC by 31 January 2013 – otherwise you will not be able to use it.

3 If you don't use all your tax-free amount in one tax year, you can't carry it forward. So if you expect to make capital gains, it can be worth spreading your disposals over more than one year.

4 You get a greater rate of taper relief for each full year of ownership. You can maximise this by selling just after the anniversary of purchase, but this won't make any difference if you owned the asset on 6 April 1998.

5 Married? You each have an annual tax-free amount, so consider splitting assets between you so that you can both make full use of it.

6 You don't have to worry about capital gains tax if you invest in British Government Stock or via an ISA (see Chapter 11).

7 If you have more than one home, nominate which one you want as your 'main' home within two years of acquiring the second home. Choose either the home you think you will make the biggest gain on, or the one you are more likely to sell.

8 Property you let? Living in it yourself for a period (provided it is genuinely your main residence) can reduce the tax bill (see page 268).

9 Taper relief is much more generous for business assets, and the definition of a 'business asset' is quite broad and may apply even if you are an employee (see page 263).

10 If you have assets that become worthless, you can claim relief for your loss immediately, and if the assets are shares in an unlisted trading company you can set the loss against either capital gains or income. See Help Sheet IR286 *Negligible value claims*.

11 Beware of giving taxable assets to 'connected persons' such as family. You will still be liable to pay capital gains tax on the full market value.

12 The rate of capital gains tax depends on your taxable income. So if you have an unavoidable capital gain in a year when you are on the verge of paying higher-rate tax, consider reducing your taxable income through, say, a one-off pension contribution.

13

Inheritance tax

Inheritance tax is a tax on gifts. A gift includes whatever you leave when you die (your 'estate'), and lifetime gifts of cash, property or anything else you own, to individuals, trusts or companies.

The tax is payable when the taxable value of your estate, including any home you own, is above a threshold. The threshold is £285,000 in 2006–07, and is scheduled to rise to £300,000 in 2007–08, £312,000 in 2008–09, £325,000 in 2009–10 and £350,000 in 2010–11. The tax is 40 per cent of everything above this, with reductions for lifetime gifts.

Do you need to worry about inheritance tax?

Inheritance tax may affect you if you are:

- making a gift during your lifetime (a 'lifetime transfer' in tax-speak)
- planning how to pass on your money after your death
- the recipient – or likely recipient – of a lifetime gift or an inheritance
- sorting out someone's estate on their death.

Lifetime gifts

Some lifetime gifts are tax-free (see page 283) and almost all other lifetime gifts are 'Potentially Exempt Transfers' (PETs). A PET is completely tax-free if you survive for at least seven years after making the gift, and taxable on a reducing scale if you die after three years but within seven years.

However, a few lifetime gifts, called 'chargeable transfers', are taxable immediately if, within a seven-year period, they come to more than the inheritance tax threshold. For individuals, chargeable transfers include a gift to most trusts (see page 288). The tax rate is 20 per cent, but on death the tax is recalculated and more may be payable.

Example 13.1: **Using the tax-free threshold**

George and Ethel have a £500,000 estate between them – £400,000 in George's name and £100,000 in Ethel's. When George dies in May 2007, leaving his £400,000 to Ethel, there is no tax to pay because they were married. But when she dies in August 2007, leaving an estate of £500,000, there is tax on £500,000 − £300,000 = £200,000 × 40% = £80,000. They have lost nearly a sixth of their joint estate in tax.

Had George left £200,000 to someone else, it would have been within his tax-free threshold, leaving Ethel's tax-free threshold to cover the remaining £300,000: no tax to pay. It can be difficult to do this if your money is tied up in property. But even if George had left just £50,000 to someone else, there would be £20,000 less tax to pay overall.

Gifts on death

Tax is payable after a death if the value of the estate, plus any PETs made in the previous seven years, but minus tax-free legacies and debts, comes to more than the inheritance tax threshold. Even so, if you received a gift or legacy you only need to worry about having to pay the tax if:

■ The will says your legacy is before tax ('subject to the payment of taxes' or must 'bear its own tax'). If not, the estate pays the tax.
■ The estate pays the tax, but there is not enough left after all legacies have been paid. If so, specific bequests may have to be reduced.
■ You received a PET in the seven years before the donor's death. If so, you are liable to pay any inheritance tax on it – though the money may be provided by a further gift from the estate.

> ## If you received a Potentially Exempt Transfer (PET)

After the donor's death, all PETs must be declared to HMRC's Inheritance Tax office by the executors. HMRC will contact you if you have tax to pay on a PET, so make sure you keep records of PETs received, and that your records are consistent with the donor's.

An executor or personal representative

You are responsible for sorting out the paperwork and paying at least part of any tax due before the money in the estate can be distributed. (See page 292 and the Inheritance Tax Customer Guide on the HMRC website.)

Planning to pass on your money

Inheritance tax is a concern to many people with only modest estates, but the rules are increasingly complicated. If a lot of money is at stake, get professional advice. This chapter concentrates on the basics:

1 Use your exemptions. See the list of tax-free gifts on page 283.
2 Make sure both you and your partner use your tax-free threshold. If you are leaving everything to your husband or wife, or civil partner, there is no immediate tax to pay, because gifts between you are tax-free. But you may merely be postponing, or even increasing, the overall bill, because you are wasting one person's tax-free threshold (see Example 13.1).
3 Make gifts early – they will be tax-free if you survive for seven years – but don't jeopardise your own financial security. Remember that capital gains tax may be payable (this does not apply on death, see Chapter 12).

Benefiting from something you no longer own

A gift in name only – such as giving away a house you continue to live in – is a 'gift with reservation' and will still count as part of your estate unless you pay a market rent for it.

'Pre-owned' assets

From 6 April 2005 you may have to pay income tax each year if you continue to benefit from something you used to own (a 'pre-owned asset') that is not already caught by the 'gift with reservation' rules. This may affect gifts, and possibly sales, going back to 18 March 1986. You are also affected if you gave cash or a loan to someone to buy something from which you now benefit (such as a house you now live in). Other cash gifts are usually exempt, except some gifts to trusts.

The rules do not apply if you pay a full market rent for the asset, or if you sell your home to an equity release company. Nor do they apply to gifts to a spouse or civil partner, or to maintain a dependent relative, or small gifts (the £250 and £3,000 exemptions, see below), or if you were left something which you gave away under a 'deed of variation' (see page 290).

If you are affected, the annual taxable amount is 5 per cent of the asset's value, or the rental value of land. Amounts below £5,000 are tax-free; larger amounts must be entered in Question 13 of your tax return and you will have pay income tax on them every year. Alternatively, you can elect to have a 'pre-owned asset' treated as part of your estate, and liable to inheritance tax rather than income tax. If you wish to make this election, you should do so by 31 January after the end of the tax year for which tax would be payable, but if you miss that date HMRC have discretion to accept late elections. See the 'pre-owned assets' area of the HMRC website.

Tax-free gifts

Tax-free lifetime gifts

■ Gifts to someone getting married – up to £5,000 if you are a parent of one of the couple, £2,500 if you are a grandparent, otherwise £1,000.
■ Payments to maintain your family or dependent relatives. This includes ex-wives, ex-husbands and ex-civil partners.
■ Gifts that are normal expenditure out of your income – e.g. regular payments into an insurance policy for the benefit of your children.
■ Small gifts – up to a maximum of £250 per recipient in any tax year.
■ An annual exemption of £3,000 in each tax year, plus any unused

balance of £3,000 from the previous tax year. If you give more than £3,000, the amount above £3,000 counts as a PET.

You can combine tax-free gifts, with the exception of the small gifts exemption – e.g. you could give a grandchild a £2,500 wedding gift plus £3,000 under your annual exemption, but not a 'small gift' of £250 as well.

Always tax-free

- Gifts to spouses or civil partners, but if they are 'domiciled' abroad (see Chapter 10), only £55,000 in total is tax-free.
- Gifts to good causes – i.e. UK charities, community amateur sports clubs or housing associations.
- Gifts to some institutions, such as universities and the National Trust.
- Gifts to qualifying political parties.
- Gifts of decorations for valour or gallant conduct, provided that these have never been sold.
- The estate of someone who dies on active service.

Saving tax as a couple

If you are married or a civil partner, you each have your own tax threshold and your own set of tax-free gifts, and transfers between you are also tax-free. This means that if one of you has most of the money, you can give some to your partner, so that he or she can make use of the exemptions. (But any gift to your partner must be outright, without strings.) And when making a will consider leaving the maximum tax-free allowance to someone other than your partner – unless he or she needs the money (see Example 13.1 on page 281).

How inheritance tax is worked out on death

- *Step 1:* set the tax-free threshold applying at the date of death (i.e. £285,000 for deaths in 2006–07, £300,000 in 2007–08) against any PETs made in the seven years before death, starting with the earliest gift (see Example 13.2 opposite).

- *Step 2:* work out the tax on any PETs above the tax-free threshold. This is 40 per cent of the taxable amount, reduced by taper relief if death occurs three or more years after the gift (see Table 13.1).
- *Step 3:* work out how much tax-free threshold is left, after deducting any PETs. So if someone dies in 2006–07 with PETs of £135,000, say, the remaining tax-free threshold is £285,000 − £135,000 = £150,000.
- *Step 4:* calculate the taxable value of the estate on death (see page 287).
- *Step 5:* if the taxable value of the estate is below the remaining tax-free threshold (from step 3), there is no tax to pay on it. If it is above, deduct the tax-free threshold. So if someone dies with an estate of £300,000, and has a tax-free threshold after PETs of £150,000, tax is payable on £300,000 − £150,000 = £150,000.
- *Step 6:* work out tax at 40 per cent on everything above the tax-free threshold, i.e. £150,000 × 40% = £60,000.
- *Step 7:* share out the tax bill between the beneficiaries of the estate (see page 289).

See the Inheritance Tax Customer Guide on the HMRC website. Note that if you made lifetime gifts that were not PETs (see page 289), this will affect the calculation and you may need professional advice.

Example 13.2: **Tax on PETs**

Mr Kumar gave £110,000 to each of his children when they reached 21. The first child reached 21 in 2000, the second in 2002 and the third in 2004. He died in September 2006. All the gifts were made in the seven years before his death, but the first £3,000 of each gift falls within the annual exemption for each year, and a further £3,000 within the annual exemption unused in the previous year, so the taxable amount of each gift is £104,000.

The first two gifts fall within the £285,000 tax-free threshold, leaving only £285,000 − £104,000 − £104,000 = £77,000 of the threshold available. So his third child must pay tax on £104,000 − £77,000 = £27,000. This amounts to £27,000 × 40% = £10,800, and no taper relief is available because the gift was made less than three years before Mr Kumar died. Because the tax-free threshold has been used up by his PETs, the whole of Mr Kumar's estate on death is taxable, apart from any tax-free gifts.

Table 13.1 Taper relief on lifetime gifts

Years between date of gift and death	Percentage of full tax payable	Equivalent to tax rate of
Less than 3 years	100%	40%
More than 3 but less than 4	80%	32%
More than 4 but less than 5	60%	24%
More than 5 but less than 6	40%	16%
More than 6 but less than 7	20%	8%
7 or more years	No tax	No tax

Example 13.3: **How taper relief works**

If you have to pay tax on a lifetime gift that was made at least three years before death, a reduced rate of tax is payable. So in Example 13.2, Mr Kumar's youngest child received a PET of £27,000 within three years of his father's death, on which £10,800 tax was payable. But if Mr Kumar had made the gift during the fourth year before his death, only 80 per cent of the full tax bill would have been payable: £10,800 × 80% = £8,640.

Lifetime gifts can increase the tax

The tax-free threshold (£285,000 for deaths in 2006–07, £300,000 in 2007–08) is set first against your lifetime gifts, with anything left over set against your estate on death. So tax is not payable on a PET, even if this was made within seven years of death, unless your total taxable lifetime gifts come to more than the tax-free threshold. But even if your gifts in the seven years before death are not themselves taxable, they can still push your estate on death above the inheritance tax threshold. And do not pin too much hope on taper relief. It reduces the tax payable, not the taxable value of the gift, so it applies only if the PET is taxable – i.e. above the £285,000 threshold for deaths in 2006–07.

The taxable value of an estate

When you die, your 'estate' consists of:

■ everything owned in your own name (see page 215 for overseas property)
■ your share of any jointly owned property (see overleaf)
■ a payout on your death from a life insurance policy that you took out
■ a gift from which you or your spouse continue to benefit (see page 282) – either a 'gift with reservation' or a 'pre-owned asset' which you have opted to have treated as part of your estate (see page 283)
■ assets in certain trusts from which you have a right to some personal benefit, such as an income (see overleaf)
■ possibly, unused pension fund passed to your family (see page 183)
■ *minus* tax-free legacies (see page 284), such as to a spouse or charity
■ *minus* reasonable funeral expenses (including a headstone)
■ *minus* any money or property owed by you
■ *minus* some forms of compensation, e.g. to holocaust survivors or British prisoners of war in Japanese camps.

ISAs and PEPs become taxable on death

Any investments in a Personal Equity Plan (PEP) or Individual Savings Account (ISA) form part of your estate and lose their tax-free status when you die.

Saving tax on life insurance

Ask the insurance company about getting your policy 'written in trust' for your beneficiaries – the payout will go immediately to them without forming part of your estate. The premiums are a gift to your beneficiaries, but regular premiums are usually tax-free as a gift out of your normal expenditure. Transferring an existing policy also counts as a gift, and under the new rules for trusts tax may be due if it is worth more than the tax-free threshold.

Jointly owned property

The assumption is that joint property is shared equally, in the absence of any documents that say otherwise – e.g. the deeds to a house. But with a joint money account, your share (for inheritance tax purposes) is in line with the money you each contributed to it.

Often, jointly owned assets such as houses and bank accounts are set up so that they pass automatically to the survivor (although the deceased person's share still counts as part of his or her estate). Under English law, this is called a 'joint tenancy'; in Scotland, this is called passing 'by survivorship' (although with a joint bank account, the survivor may operate the account but not necessarily be entitled to the money in it).

Automatic transfer has the advantage of giving the survivor immediate access to the money. However, there can be advantages to owning joint assets as 'tenants in common' (in England) or with no special destination (in Scotland). If this applies, you can leave your share to whomever you wish.

Saving tax on the family home

You might want to leave half your house to someone else, rather than your spouse or civil partner, in order to use up your own tax threshold (£300,000 in 2007–08). You can do this if you own the house as tenants in common rather than joint tenants. But your partner risks having to move if the other owners want to sell on your death.

There are tax-saving schemes involving trusts or giving your house away and then paying a market rent to live in it, but recent changes have made many such schemes ineffective (see page 283). A simpler way to save tax is to move to a smaller home or take out a mortgage, giving away the cash released, but a mortgage may cost more than the tax saved.

Assets in a trust

Trusts – legal arrangements that hold investments or other assets in the care of trustees for the benefit of one or more 'beneficiaries' – have often been used in inheritance tax planning, but changes to their tax treatment in 2006 have removed many of the advantages.

For inheritance tax purposes, these are the main types of trust:

■ Trusts with an 'interest in possession' – where someone has a right to use trust property or receive income from it.
■ Discretionary trusts – ones without an interest in possession, for example where the trustees have discretion over who receives the income.
■ Accumulation and maintenance trusts – with these at least one beneficiary must be entitled to trust assets or income by a maximum age (until which time any income must either be accumulated or used for their maintenance), and the trust must last for a maximum of 25 years unless all the beneficiaries have a common grandparent. It is no longer possible to set up new trusts of this type, but existing ones can continue.
■ Special trusts – discretionary trusts with more favourable tax rules. They include trusts for the benefit of particular groups of employees, trusts for disabled people and some trusts set up in a will.

A gift to all these trusts, except special trusts, now counts as a 'chargeable transfer'. Amounts above the tax-free threshold are liable to an immediate tax charge. Until 22 March 2006, gifts to an interest in possession or accumulation and maintenance trust were treated as a PET, tax-free if you survived seven years.

Tax is also charged every ten years on money in a discretionary trust above the tax-free threshold. This now also applies to new interests in possession and, from 6 April 2008, some accumulation and maintenance trusts, so if you are affected, get professional advice.

Sharing out a tax bill

Any inheritance tax due is paid out of the 'residue' of the estate (what is left after all specific legacies have been paid), unless the will says that a gift should 'bear its own tax' (see Example 13.4). But tax is payable on the loss to the giver, not the benefit to the recipient. So if a gift is intended to be tax-free in the hands of the recipient, it must be 'grossed-up' to find the amount that, after 40 per cent tax, leaves the intended gift. An after-tax legacy of £12,000, say, would actually count as a gift of £20,000 *minus* tax of £20,000 × 40% = £8,000, i.e. £20,000 − £8,000 = £12,000.

Make a will

Think about how any tax will be paid and don't give so much in specific bequests free-of-tax that whoever inherits the residue (e.g. your spouse) has less to live on than you intended. If the recipient can afford it, it is simpler for gifts in a will to bear their own tax.

Example 13.4: **Tax on an estate**

Mr Smith-Jones made no PETs in his lifetime. When he died in May 2007, he left:

- a house worth £300,000 to his wife – this was tax-free as a bequest to his wife
- £200,000 to his son – tax-free as it fell within the tax-free threshold
- the residue of his estate (£250,000), split between his son and his wife. His wife's share is tax-free; his son's share is taxable, but there is still £300,000 – £200,000 = £100,000 of the tax-free threshold to set against it.

If the will says the residue should be divided before tax, his son and his wife will both get £250,000 ÷ 2 = £125,000, and his son will have to pay tax at 40% on £125,000 – £100,000 = £25,000. If it is after tax, the gift has to be 'grossed-up' to include the tax, and the calculations can be very complex.

Deeds of variation

However carefully you do your tax planning, you never know when you will die or what the inheritance tax position will be. Your heirs, however, should bear in mind that they can alter an inheritance after a death, by using a 'deed of variation'. It can also be used if someone dies without leaving a will ('intestate'). A variation allows beneficiaries to disclaim gifts and legacies in favour of their children, say. It must be made in writing within two years of death, but if a beneficiary is a child court approval may be needed, so consult a lawyer. (See the Inheritance Tax Customer Guide on the HMRC website.)

Tax reliefs you can claim

For details of all the following reliefs, see the Inheritance Tax Customer guide on the HMRC website.

Agricultural property relief

Tax relief may be available if you give away agricultural land and property during your lifetime or on your death, provided that you or your spouse or civil partner used it for agricultural purposes for at least two years. If you did not use it yourself, you must have owned it for at least seven years and it must have been tenanted for agricultural purposes throughout.

If the property is let on a tenancy that started after 31 August 1995, 100 per cent relief applies. If not, 100 per cent relief still applies if you have the right to vacant possession within 12 months. Otherwise, the rate of relief is normally 50 per cent.

Business property relief

If you give away a business or a share in a business, or unquoted shares in a business, 100 per cent relief is available provided that you or your spouse owned it for at least two years. However, if you make a lifetime gift of business land, buildings, plant or machinery, or a controlling shareholding in a quoted company, only 50 per cent relief is available.

Relief is not available for pure investment companies, nor is it available for plant or machinery used partly for the business, partly privately. You can claim relief for just part of land or buildings, provided that that part is used exclusively for the business.

Double taxation relief

If you have property or assets abroad, UK inheritance tax is still likely to be payable (see page 215) and the overseas tax authorities may charge the equivalent of inheritance tax on any gift or bequest. If so, you can claim some relief for it against UK inheritance tax.

Quick succession relief

This relief (also known as 'successive charges' relief) applies where someone dies having inherited assets from someone who died in the previous five years. If inheritance tax was paid when the first person died, the tax payable on the second death is reduced.

Insuring to pay inheritance tax

You can take out a life insurance policy to ensure that cash is available to pay inheritance tax. If the policy is 'written in trust' for your beneficiaries, it is not part of your estate and can be paid out before probate is granted (note, though, that new policies for amounts above the tax-free threshold may be affected by the new rules on trusts, see page 288). Alternatively, your beneficiaries may be able to take out a policy on your life.

What to tell HMRC

You do not have to tell HMRC about tax-free gifts or PETs made during your lifetime. Nor do you have to notify them about chargeable transfers you make if they come to £10,000 or less in a tax year, provided that your total chargeable transfers in the previous ten years are £40,000 or less. However, you must tell HMRC if you are liable to income tax on a 'pre-owned' asset, using Question 13 of the main tax return (see page 62).

When someone dies, whoever is handling their affairs has to get legal authority (such as a grant of probate or, in Scotland, grant of confirmation) before they can distribute the assets of the estate. A summary of all the taxable assets of the deceased person has to be sent to HMRC's Inheritance Tax office, and at least part of any inheritance tax paid, before a grant of probate or confirmation is given. This account also covers lifetime gifts, so that HMRC can check whether tax is due on those.

Inheritance tax must be paid within six months of the death, or before you get the grant of probate or confirmation. If the deceased person had money in most bank or building society accounts, or in National Savings & Investments or British Government Stock, this can be used to pay the tax, through what is called the direct payment scheme. And you can opt to pay the tax on some types of asset, such as property, by instalments. Otherwise, the executor or personal representative may have to take out a loan.

Record-keeping

Keep track of the value of your assets in the same way as for capital gains tax (see Chapter 12), and make sure there is documentation to prove the value of any assets at the date you give them away. With jointly owned assets, try to record how much each of you contributed to the purchase price.

You should also keep records of any gifts you have made or received for at least seven years (14 years in the case of chargeable transfers). A dated copy of a letter, saying that it is a gift, is all that is needed. Even if gifts are not taxable, good records are helpful for winding up your estate on your death. Also keep records of any inheritance tax you have paid.

Filling in the forms

Whoever is handling the legal side of things will normally do all this.

The main form is IHT200 *Inheritance Tax Account*, but this is not required for small estates. All the forms are available on the HMRC website, and IHT200 has a working sheet which tells you how to calculate the tax.

IHT200 consists of a main form and supplementary sheets. Figure 13.1 shows the form listing the supplementary sheets. Use it as a guide to the sorts of things you need to keep records of.

Tax-planning hints

1 Most lifetime gifts are tax-free if you survive at least seven years after making them – give early, if you can afford to do so, but do not jeopardise your or your partner's security for the sake of saving tax.
2 Plan ahead to ensure that the cash is there to pay any tax on your

Figure 13.1: Extract from IHT200

D Supplementary pages

You must answer all of the questions in this section, by ticking the box that applies.

If you answer "Yes" to a question you will need to fill in the supplementary page shown. If you do not have all the supplementary pages you need you can download them from the internet (www.hmrc.gov.uk/cto) or request them from the orderline: e-mail (hmrc.ihtorderline@gtnet.gov.uk) or telephone 0845 30 20 900.

		No	Yes	Page
• **The Will**	Did the deceased leave a Will?		✓	D1
• **Domicile outside the United Kingdom**	Was the deceased domiciled outside the UK at the date of death?			D2
• **Gifts and other transfers of value**	Did the deceased make any gift or any other transfer of value on or after 18 March 1986 (including gifts with reservation and gifts involving previously owned assets)?		✓	D3
• **Joint assets**	Did the deceased hold any asset(s) in joint names with another person?		✓	D4
• **Nominated assets**	Did the deceased, at any time during their lifetime, give written instructions (usually called a "nomination") that any asset was to pass to a particular person on their death?			D4
• **Assets held in trust**	Did the deceased have any right to any benefit from any assets held in trust or in a settlement at the date of death?			D5
• **Pensions**	Did the deceased have a pension provision for retirement other than the State Pension?		✓	D6
• **Stocks and shares**	Did the deceased own any stocks or shares?		✓	D7
• **Debts due to the estate**	Did the deceased lend any money, either on mortgage or by personal loan, that had not been repaid by the date of death?			D8
• **Life insurance and annuities**	Did the deceased pay any premiums on any life insurance policies or annuities which are payable to either the estate or to someone else or which continue after death?			D9
• **Household and personal goods**	Complete form D10 in all cases. If the deceased did not own any household goods or personal possessions or they do not have any value, explain the circumstances on form D10.	✓		D10
• **Interest in another estate**	Did the deceased have a right to a legacy or a share of an estate of someone who died before them, but which they had not received before they died?			D11
• **Land, buildings and interests in land**	Did the deceased own any land or buildings in the UK?		✓	D12
• **Agricultural relief**	Are you deducting agricultural relief from the value of any farm or farmland owned by the deceased?			D13
• **Business interests**	Did the deceased own all or part of a business or were they a partner in a business?			D14
• **Business relief**	Are you deducting business relief?			D14
• **Foreign assets**	Did the deceased own any assets outside the UK?			D15
• **Debts owed by the estate**	Are you claiming a deduction against the estate for any money that the deceased had borrowed from relatives, close friends, or trustees, or other loans, overdrafts or guarantee debts?			D16

2   www.hmrc.gov.uk/cto   Helpline 0845 30 20 900

death, and that your partner has enough ready money to live on until your estate can be distributed.

3   Giving assets away in your lifetime (but not cash) may incur capital gains tax. You need to balance this against the potential inheritance tax saving.

4   Make a will – particularly if you are living with someone without being married.

5   Keep good records. It will simplify matters after your death and may mean lower legal bills.

6   A gift to charity in your will is tax-free, but it may be worth more to the charity if made during your lifetime under the Gift Aid scheme.

7   You can make significant inroads into a potential tax bill by using tax-free gifts and the tax-free threshold (£300,000 in 2007–08). Share your wealth with your partner so that he or she can do so too.

8   Your share of jointly owned property forms part of your estate. You may want to own things as 'tenants in common' so that you can leave your share to someone apart from the other owner.

9   There are no foolproof ways of passing on the family home if you are of modest means. The simplest way is to release cash by taking out a mortgage or trading down, and then give away any surplus.

10 If you take out life insurance, consider writing the policy 'in trust' so that the proceeds do not form part of your estate (see page 287).

11 If you have been involved in a trust you may be affected by a change in the rules – get professional advice.

12 Think about 'generation skipping' – leaving money to the next generation, rather than all to your husband or wife – to make better use of your tax-free band (£300,000 in 2007–08).

13 Remember that your family can alter your will within two years after your death, with a deed of variation. This allows your money to be passed on in the way that best suits family circumstances at the time.

14 Beware of 'gifts with reservation' (where you retain the right to benefit from the property). They are still taxed as part of your estate.

15 You may have to pay income tax on assets that you have given away but continue to benefit from (see page 282). If you have made any such gifts since 18 March 1986, take professional advice urgently.

Fact file

Checklist of tax-free income

- Adoption allowances
- Betting winnings, including Premium Bonds and lottery winnings
- Compensation for mis-sold pension products
- Some damages and compensation for personal injury
- Employment grants from some government schemes
- Foreign service allowance paid to servants of the Crown
- Some employee benefits provided by employers (see Chapter 6)
- German and Austrian annuities and pensions for victims of Nazi persecution
- Compensation paid on the dormant accounts of holocaust victims.
- Housing grants
- Most income as a foster carer or adult placement carer
- Interest on damages for personal injuries or death
- Interest on a tax refund
- Interest on British Government Stock if you are not ordinarily resident in the UK (see Chapter 10)
- Interest, dividends and other income from savings and investments in special government schemes (listed on page 230)
- Interest from some National Savings & Investments schemes (see Chapter 11)
- Long-service awards
- Maintenance and alimony
- Overseas income if you are not resident in the UK (see Chapter 10)
- Some payments on leaving a job (see Chapter 6)
- Insurance payouts from a family income benefit life insurance policy, and from some permanent health, personal accident, sickness or income protection policies, and some long-term care policies (see pages 28 and 230)
- Payouts from some life insurance policies (see Chapter 11)
- Some pensions and pension lump sums (see Chapter 8)
- Rental income under the Rent-a-Room scheme (see Chapter 9)
- Scholarship income and bursaries
- Some social security benefits (see Chapter 8)
- War gratuities and bounties, including the annual bounty to Territorial Army members; some payments following injury or death in the Armed Forces; the Armed Forces Operational Allowance.

Form finder

If you have received a tax form you are struggling with, use the table below to find more help.

Form reference	Name/explanation	Where to find more information
	Certificate of deduction of income tax	Chapter 11
64-8	Authorising your agent	Chapter 1
BR735	Notification of taxable amount of state benefits received	Chapter 8
CG34	Application for a post transaction valuation check	Chapter 12
DOM1	Income and chargeable gains – domicile	Chapter 10
EIS3, EIS5	You should receive one of these if you invest in an Enterprise Investment Scheme or fund	Chapters 5 and 11
Form 17	Joint property and income	Chapter 11
IHT200	Inheritance Tax Account	Chapter 13
P2	PAYE Coding Notice	Chapter 2
P9D	Expenses payments and income from which tax cannot be deducted	Chapters 2, 4 and 6
P11D	Expenses and Benefits	Chapters 2, 4 and 6
P38S	Student employees	Chapter 2
P45	Details of employee leaving work	Chapters 2 and 6
P45U, P45(IB)	From Jobcentre Plus when you stop claiming benefits	Chapter 8
P46	PAYE employer's notice to tax office	Chapter 2
P50	Claim for income tax repayments	Chapter 8
P60	End of year certificate	Chapters 2, 4, 6 and 8
P60U, P60(IB)	Statements of taxable amount of Jobseeker's Allowance or Incapacity Benefit paid in a tax year	Chapter 8
P85	Income Tax claim when you have left or are about to leave the UK	Chapter 10
P86	Arrival in the United Kingdom	Chapter 10
P87	Tax relief for expenses of employment	Chapter 6
P91	Form asking for details of your previous jobs	Chapter 2
P160	Employee retiring on a pension paid by employer	Chapter 2
P161	Pension enquiry	Chapters 2 and 8
P810	Tax review	Chapter 2
R40	Tax Repayment Form	Chapters 2 and 4
R85	Getting your interest without tax taken off	Chapters 2 and 11
R86 or R89	Application for an annuity to be paid without tax deducted	Chapters 8 and 11

R105	*Application for a not ordinarily resident saver to receive interest without tax taken off*	Chapter 10
SA300	*Self assessment statement*	Chapter 4
SA302	Notice from HMRC showing how they have worked out your tax	Chapter 4
SA303	*Claim to reduce payments on account*	Chapter 4
SA316	*Notice to complete a tax return*	Chapter 4
	Tax credits forms	Chapter 3

Tax return questions

If you are trying to complete a tax return, you can use this list to find further information that might help you with a particular question.

Question 1	Employment	Chapter 6
Question 2	Share schemes	Chapter 6
Question 3	Self-employment	Chapter 7
Question 4	Partnership	Chapter 7
Question 5	Land and property	Chapter 9
Question 6	Foreign income	Chapter 10
Question 7	Trusts and estates	Chapter 11
Question 8	Capital gains	Chapter 12
Question 9	Non-residence etc.	Chapter 10
Question 10	UK savings and investments	Chapter 11
Question 11	UK pension or Social Security benefit	Chapter 8
Question 12	UK life insurance policies, refunds of additional voluntary contributions	Chapter 11
Question 13	Other taxable income	Chapters 4, 7 and 13
Question 14	Tax relief on pension contributions	Chapters 5 and 8
Question 15	Other reliefs	Chapter 5
Question 15A	Relief on gifts to charity	Chapter 5
Question 16	Blind person's allowance, married couple's allowance	Chapter 5
Question 17	Student Loan Repayments	Chapter 4
Question 18	Calculating your tax	Chapter 4
Question 19	Do you want to claim a repayment?	Chapter 4
Question 20	Tax refunded or set off	Chapter 4
Question 21	Is your name or address wrong?	Chapter 4
Question 22	Other personal details	Chapter 4
Question 23	Additional information	Chapter 4
Question 24	Declaration	Chapter 4
Question 25	Pension charges	Chapter 8

Summary of tax allowances and rates

Income tax	2006–07	2007–08
Personal allowance		
Aged under 65 throughout tax year	£5,035	£5,225
Maximum allowance if aged 65 or over in tax year	£7,280	£7,550
Maximum allowance if aged 75 or over in tax year	£7,420	£7,690
Age allowance income limit	£20,100	£20,900
Minimum where income exceeds limit	£5,035	£5,225
Married couple's allowance (10% relief)		
Either spouse born before 6 April 1935	£6,065	£6,285
Either spouse aged 75 or over in tax year	£6,135	£6,365
Age allowance income limit	£20,100	£20,900
Minimum where income exceeds limit	£2,350	£2,440
Blind person's allowance	£1,660	£1,730
Income tax rates		
Starting rate	10%	10%
On taxable income up to	£2,150	£2,230
Basic rate	22%	22%
On taxable income from starting rate limit up to	£33,300	£34,600
Higher rate	40%	40%
On taxable income over	£33,300	£34,600
Lower rate on savings income and capital gains	20%	20%
Lower dividend rate	10%	10%
Higher dividend rate	32.5%	32.5%

Capital gains tax	2006–07	2007–08
Rate (depending on your taxable income; may be reduced by taper relief)	10%, 20% or 40%	10%, 20% or 40%
Annual tax-free amount	£8,800	£9,200

Inheritance tax	2006–07	2007–08
Threshold for tax-free gifts	£285,000	£300,000
Rate for gifts on death	40%	40%

National Insurance contributions	2006–07	2007–08
Class 1 contributions		
For employees	11% (9.4%*) on earnings between £97 and £645 p.w. 1% on earnings above £645 p.w.	11% (9.4%*) on earnings between £100 and £670 p.w. 1% on earnings above £670 p.w.
Rate for married women who opted for reduced rate before 6 April 1977	4.85%	4.85%
Lower earnings limit (earnings below this give no right to some state benefits)	£84 p.w.	£87 p.w.
For employers	12.8%*on earnings above £97 p.w.	12.8%*on earnings above £100 p.w.
Class 2 contributions for self-employed	£2.10 p.w. on earnings above £4,465 p.a.	£2.20 p.w. on earnings above £4,635 p.a.
Class 3 voluntary contributions to improve benefits	£7.55 p.w.	£7.80 p.w.
Class 4 contributions for self-employed	8% on profits between £5,035 and £33,540, 1% on earnings above £33,540	8% on profits between £5,225 and £34,840, 1% on earnings above £34,840

Tax Credit thresholds	2006–07	2007–08
See page 41 for tax credit rates		
Threshold at which Working Tax Credit starts to be reduced	£5,220	£5,220
If you only qualify for Child Tax Credit, threshold at which child element starts to be reduced	£14,155	£14,495
For Working Tax Credit and child element, amount of credit lost for each extra £ above thresholds	37p	37p
Threshold at which family element of Child Tax Credit starts to be reduced	£50,000	£50,000
Amount of family element lost for each extra £ above thresholds	6.7p	6.7p

* Lower rate if employer has contracted out of the State Second Pension

'Gross' and 'net' figures

When filling in your tax return, you often need to know the gross (before tax) figure of income you receive net (after tax). This is called 'grossing-up'.

For example, the statements from your savings account may show only the net amount of interest received, but the tax return asks for the gross amount and the tax deducted as well. The same applies if you contribute to a personal pension – the amount you hand over is the net amount but the tax return asks for the gross figures.

Ready reckoner for gross and net figures

Rate of tax	If you know the:	Do this:		To find the:
10%	Amount of a share dividend received (i.e. the net amount)	Divide the dividend by 0.9	=	Gross amount before tax
		Divide the dividend by 9	=	Tax credit
20%	After-tax (net) amount of savings interest	Divide the net interest by 0.8	=	Gross amount before tax
		Divide the net interest by 4	=	Amount of tax deducted
22%	After-tax (net) amount of pension contribution or Gift Aid donation	Divide the net payment by 0.78	=	Gross amount before tax
		Multiply the net payment by $^{22}/_{78}$ (in practice it is easier to find the gross amount and deduct the net)	=	Amount of basic rate tax relief

If tax rates change, this is how you can work it out for yourself:
■ Find the relevant rate of tax – 30%, say.
■ To find the amount of tax on income at that rate, multiply the income by that percentage – so income of £200 taxed at 30%, say, is £200 ×

0.30 = £60. This leaves you with net income of £200 × (1 − 0.30) = £200 × 0.7 = £140.

■ If you already know the after-tax amount but want to find the before-tax amount, you simply do the same in reverse. So the gross equivalent of £140, before tax at 30%, is £140 ÷ 0.7 = £200.

■ The foolproof way to find the amount of tax, if you know the after-tax amount, is to work out the gross equivalent and deduct the after-tax amount: £200 − £140 = £60. For some rates of tax, you can do it by simple division of the after-tax amount − see table on page 301.

Capital gains tax indexation factors

Indexation compensates you for any increase in the value of an asset which occurs purely because of inflation. Indexation was frozen from April 1998 and does not apply to periods before March 1982 because only gains made since then are taxable.

You can find the indexed cost of an asset you disposed of after April 1998 by multiplying the cost of the asset by the relevant indexation factor for the month you acquired it. Indexation factors are shown in the table opposite. If, for example, you bought your holiday home in June 1990 for £100,000, the relevant indexation factor is 1.283 and the indexed cost is:

$$£100,000 × 1.283 = £128,300$$

But watch out for two things:

Warning 1: You can use the table opposite *only* if you are working out indexation for periods up to April 1998. If you need to work it out for earlier periods (if, say, you are working out your gain on a parcel of shares and you disposed of part of it before April 1998) you need another set of factors. See the HMRC website for a table of factors for the month of the part disposal. *Warning 2:* These factors give you the *indexed cost*, i.e. the cost of the asset plus the indexation allowance. The HMRC tables give you just the indexation allowance, to be added to the cost − so, in the example above, the HMRC tables would show a factor of 0.283, giving an indexation allowance of £28,300, which you would then need to add to the cost. Both methods give the same result, but our method saves you a step.

Indexation factors – assets disposed of after 31 March 1998

Year	Jan	Feb	March	April	May	June	July	Aug	Sept	Oct	Nov	Dec
1982	–	–	2.047	2.006	1.992	1.987	1.986	1.985	1.987	1.977	1.967	1.971
1983	1.968	1.960	1.956	1.929	1.921	1.917	1.906	1.898	1.889	1.883	1.876	1.871
1984	1.872	1.865	1.859	1.834	1.828	1.823	1.825	1.808	1.804	1.793	1.788	1.789
1985	1.783	1.769	1.752	1.716	1.708	1.704	1.707	1.703	1.704	1.701	1.695	1.693
1986	1.689	1.683	1.681	1.665	1.662	1.663	1.667	1.662	1.654	1.652	1.638	1.632
1987	1.626	1.620	1.616	1.597	1.596	1.596	1.597	1.593	1.588	1.580	1.573	1.574
1988	1.574	1.568	1.562	1.537	1.531	1.525	1.524	1.507	1.500	1.485	1.478	1.474
1989	1.465	1.454	1.448	1.423	1.414	1.409	1.408	1.404	1.395	1.384	1.372	1.369
1990	1.361	1.353	1.339	1.300	1.288	1.283	1.282	1.269	1.258	1.248	1.251	1.252
1991	1.249	1.242	1.237	1.222	1.218	1.213	1.215	1.213	1.208	1.204	1.199	1.198
1992	1.199	1.193	1.189	1.171	1.167	1.167	1.171	1.171	1.166	1.162	1.164	1.168
1993	1.179	1.171	1.167	1.156	1.152	1.153	1.156	1.151	1.146	1.147	1.148	1.146
1994	1.151	1.144	1.141	1.128	1.124	1.124	1.129	1.124	1.121	1.120	1.119	1.114
1995	1.114	1.107	1.102	1.091	1.087	1.085	1.091	1.085	1.080	1.085	1.085	1.079
1996	1.083	1.078	1.073	1.066	1.063	1.063	1.067	1.062	1.057	1.057	1.057	1.053
1997	1.053	1.049	1.046	1.040	1.036	1.032	1.032	1.026	1.021	1.019	1.019	1.016
1998	1.019	1.014	1.011									

HMRC leaflets, helplines and websites

Sources of useful information from Her Majesty's Revenue & Customs (HMRC) and other government bodies are shown below.

■ *Telephone queries.* For general telephone enquiries, either ring the phone number on any correspondence from your tax office, or look in the phone book under 'HM Revenue & Customs'. But HMRC also have a number of specialist helplines, listed on their website at www.hmrc.gov.uk/menus/helpline.htm

■ *Leaflets.* A selection is shown below. They are available from tax offices, from the HMRC Orderline (Tel: 0845 9000 404) or on the HMRC website. Note that HMRC have been reducing their printed guidance and only a few printed leaflets are now available.

■ *Internet.* The website at www.hmrc.gov.uk includes all leaflets and a wealth of other information. HMRC's own internal guidance manuals are at www.hmrc.gov.uk/manuals and there are many forms you can print off or complete online at www.hmrc.gov.uk/allforms.shtml

General

Leaflets and help sheets

AO1 *How to complain about HM Revenue & Customs and the Valuation Office Agency*
CA72 *National Insurance contributions: deferring payment*
CA93 *Shortfall in your NICs: To pay or not to pay?*
CA5603 *To pay voluntary National Insurance contributions*
Code of Practice (COP) 1 *Putting things right: How to complain*
COP10 *Information and Advice*
IR235 *Calculation of Student Loan Repayments on an Income Contingent Student Loan*
Notice 701/7 *VAT reliefs for disabled people*
Tax appeals (Department for Constitutional Affairs leaflet, available from tax offices or the HMRC or DCA websites)

Helplines

National Insurance Contributions	0845 302 1479
Online services	0845 605 5999
Stamp duty	0845 603 0135
Tax and benefits confidential (offers people operating in the hidden economy confidential help and information to help them put their affairs in order)	0845 608 6000
Tax evasion hotline	0800 788 887
Welsh speakers contact centre	0845 302 1489

Websites

HM Revenue & Customs	www.hmrc.gov.uk
Employment status	www.hmrc.gov.uk/employment-status
Married women paying reduced National Insurance contributions	www.hmrc.gov.uk/faqs/women_reduced_rate.htm
Students' area	www.hmrc.gov.uk/students

Self-assessment

Leaflets and help sheets
COP11 *Self assessment. Local office enquiries*
IR160 *Enquries under self assessment*
IR325 *Other taxable income*
SA/BK4 *Self Assessment. A general guide to keeping records*
SA/BK8 *Self Assessment. Your guide*

Helplines
General helpline   0845 900 0444
Orderline for form/leaflet requests   0845 900 0404
Online services   0845 605 5999
Anti-avoidance group   020 7438 6733

Website
www.hmrc.gov.uk/sa/index.htm

Tax credits

Leaflets
COP26 *What happens if we have paid you too much tax credit?*
WTC2 *Child Tax Credit and Working Tax Credit. A guide*
WTC5 *Child Tax Credit and Working Tax Credit. Help with the costs of child care*
WTC6 *Child Tax Credit and Working Tax Credit. Other types of help you may be able to get*

Helplines
Tax credits helpline   0845 300 3900

Website
www.hmrc.gov.uk/menus/credits.htm

Allowances and reliefs

Leaflets and help sheets
IR121 *Income tax and pensioners*
IR340 *Interest and alternative finance payments eligible for relief*
IR341 *Enterprise Investment Scheme – income tax relief*
IR342 *Charitable giving*

Helpline

Charities and Gift Aid   0845 302 0203

Website

Charities   www.hmrc.gov.uk/charities

Employment

Leaflets and help sheets

480 *Expenses and benefits. A tax guide*

490 *Employee travel, a tax and NICs guide for employers*

E24 *Tips, gratuities, service charges and troncs*

IR115 *Income tax, National Insurance contributions and childcare*

IR201 *Vouchers, credit cards and tokens*

IR202 *Living accommodation*

IR203 *Car benefits and car fuel benefits*

IR204 *Lump sums and compensation payments*

IR205 *Seafarers' earnings deduction*

IR206 *Capital allowances for employees and office holders*

IR207 *Non-taxable payments or benefits for employees*

IR208 *Payslips and coding notices*

IR210 *Assets provided for private use*

IR211 *Employment – residence and domicile issues*

IR213 *Payments in kind – assets transferred*

IR216 *Securities as benefits*

IR217 *Securities acquired: post acquisition charges*

IR218 *Employees' shares: operation of PAYE and National Insurance contributions*

IR219 *Securities acquired: from your employment*

IR287 *Employee share and security schemes and capital gains tax*

National Minimum Wage – a short guide for workers (Department of Trade and Industry leaflet from DTI Publications Orderline, 0845 015 0010)

Helplines

National Minimum Wage

  Great Britain   0845 600 0678

  Northern Ireland   0845 650 0207

Websites

Childcare	www.hmrc.gov.uk/childcare
Company cars	www.hmrc.gov.uk/cars
Interest rates	www.hmrc.gov.uk/rates/interest.htm
National Minimum Wage	www.hmrc.gov.uk/nmw
Share schemes	www.hmrc.gov.uk/shareschemes
Vehicle Certification Agency	www.vcacarfueldata.org.uk

Self-employment

Leaflets and help sheets

700/1 *Should I be registered for VAT?*

Notice 1000 (VAT) *Complaints and putting things right*

CF10 *Self-employed people with small earnings*

CIS340 *Construction industry scheme*

IR56 *Employed or self-employed?*

IR220 *More than one business*

IR222 *How to calculate your taxable profits*

IR223 *Rent a Room for traders*

IR224 *Farmers and market gardeners*

IR227 *Losses*

IR229 *Information from your accounts*

IR231 *Doctors' expenses*

IR232 *Farm stock valuation*

IR234 *Averaging for creators of literary or artistic works*

IR236 *Foster carers and adult placement carers*

IR238 *Revenue recognition in service contracts – UITF40*

SE1 *Thinking of working for yourself?*

URN 06/895 *The no-nonsense guide to government rules and regulations for setting up your business* (from DTI Publications Orderline, 0845 015 0010)

Helplines

Construction Industry Scheme (CIS)	0845 366 7899
IR35 (if you are supplying services through a limited company or partnership)	
	0845 303 3535
Employers' helplines (guidance on PAYE, National Insurance and basic VAT registration)	
New employers	0845 607 0143
Established employers	0845 714 3143

National Insurance
    Registering for a National Insurance number   0845 915 7006
    Self Employed helpline   0845 915 4655
Newly self-employed   0845 915 4515
VAT National Advice Service   0845 010 9000

Websites
Business Income Manual   www.hmrc.gov.uk/manuals/bimmanual
Business Link   www.businesslink.gov.uk
Construction Industry Scheme   www.hmrc.gov.uk/cis
HMRC Business Support teams   www.hmrc.gov.uk/startingup/bus_sup.htm
Enhanced capital allowances for environmentally beneficial equipment
      www.eca.gov.uk
Guidance on work in progress   www.hmrc.gov.uk/sa/adinfhelp
Selling goods online or at boot sales   www.hmrc.gov.uk/guidance/selling

Pensions and benefits

Leaflets and help sheets
IR121 *Approaching retirement*
IR310 *War Widow's and dependant's pensions*
SA125(Notes) *Notes on Pensions*

Helplines
Education Maintenance Allowance   0808 101 6219
Pensions Direct   0845 301 3011

Website
Registered pension schemes manual www.hmrc.gov.uk/pensionschemes/rpsm.htm

Land and property

Leaflets and help sheets
IR223 *Rent a Room for traders*
IR250 *Capital allowances and balancing charges in a rental business*
IR251 *Agricultural land*

Website
Non-resident landlords scheme   www.hmrc.gov.uk/cnr/nr_landlords.htm
Property income manual   www.hmrc.gov.uk/manuals/pimmanual

Income from abroad

Leaflets and help sheets

IR20 *Residents and non-residents*
IR211 *Employment – residence and domicile issues*
IR261 *Foreign tax credit relief: capital gains*
IR278 *Temporary non-residents and capital gains tax*
IR300 *Non-residents and investment income*
IR302 *Dual residents*
IR303 *Non-resident entertainers and sports persons*
IR304 *Non-residents – relief under Double Taxation Agreements*
IR321 *Gains on foreign life insurance policies*
NI38 *Social Security Abroad*
DWP leaflet SA29 *Your social security insurance, benefits and health care rights in the European Economic Area*

Helplines

HMRC Residency
  Income tax enquiries   0845 070 0040
  National Insurance enquiries   0845 915 4811

Website

Average exchange rates   www.hmrc.gov.uk/exrate
HMRC Residency   www.hmrc.gov.uk/cnr
Residence Guide   www.hmrc.gov.uk/manuals/rgmanual

Savings and investments

Leaflets and help sheets

IR111 *Bank and building society interest. Are you paying tax when you don't need to?*
IR270 *Trusts and settlements – income treated as the settlor's*
IR320 *Gains on UK life insurance policies*

Helplines

Child Trust Fund   0845 302 1470
Individual Savings Accounts helpline (general queries
  about the tax rules for ISAs)   0845 604 1701
Taxation of bank and building society interest helpline   0845 980 0645

Websites

Child Trust Fund   www.childtrustfund.gov.uk
Enterprise Investment Scheme   www.hmrc.gov.uk/eis/eis-index.htm

Trusts   www.hmrc.gov.uk/trusts
Venture Capital Trusts   www.hmrc.gov.uk/guidance/vct.htm

Capital gains tax

Leaflets and help sheets

CGT1 *Capital Gains Tax – an introduction*
IR277 *Trusts with settlor interest and trusts for the vulnerable: taper and losses*
IR279 *Taper relief*
IR280 *Rebasing – assets held at 31 March 1982*
IR281 *Husband and wife, civil partners, divorce, dissolution and separation*
IR282 *Death, personal representatives and legatees*
IR283 *Private residence relief*
IR284 *Shares and capital gains tax*
IR285 *Share reorganisations, company take-overs and capital gains tax*
IR286 *Negligible value claims and income tax losses on disposals of shares you have subscribed for in qualifying trading companies*
IR287 *Employee share and security schemes and capital gains tax*
IR288 *Partnerships and capital gains tax*
IR290 *Business asset roll-over relief*
IR292 *Land and leases, the valuation of land and capital gains tax*
IR293 *Chattels and capital gains tax*
IR294 *Trusts and capital gains tax*
IR295 *Relief for gifts and similar transactions*
IR296 *Debts and capital gains tax*
IR297 *Enterprise Investment Scheme and capital gains tax*
IR298 *Venture Capital Trusts and capital gains tax*
IR301 *Capital gains from non-resident, dual resident and immigrating trusts*

Website

Capital Gains Manual   www.hmrc.gov.uk/manuals/cg1manual

Inheritance tax

Helpline

Probate and inheritance tax   0845 302 0900

Websites

HMRC Inheritance Tax   www.hmrc.gov.uk/cto
Inheritance Tax Customer Guide   www.hmrc.gov.uk/cto/iht.htm
Pre-owned assets   www.hmrc.gov.uk/poa

Useful addresses

Adjudicator's Office
Haymarket House, 28 Haymarket
London SW1Y 4SP
Tel: 020 7930 2292
www.adjudicatorsoffice.gov.uk

Age Concern England
Astral House
1268 London Road
London SW16 4ER
Information Line: 0800 009966
www.ace.org.uk

Age Concern Scotland
Causewayside House
160 Causewayside
Edinburgh EH9 1PR
Tel: 0845 833 0200
www.ageconcernscotland.org.uk

Age Concern Northern Ireland
3 Lower Crescent
Belfast BT7 1NR
Tel: 028 9024 5729
www.ageconcernni.org

Age Concern Cymru (Wales)
Ty John Pathy
13–14 Neptune Court
Vanguard Way
Cardiff CF24 5PJ
Tel: 029 2043 1555
www.accymru.org.uk

**Association of Chartered Certified
Accountants**
2 Central Quay
89 Hydepark Street
Glasgow G3 8BW
Tel: 0141 582 2000
www.acca.org.uk

**The Association of Taxation
Technicians**
12 Upper Belgrave Street
London SW1X 8BB
Tel: 020 7235 2544
www.att.org.uk

**The Chartered Institute of
Taxation**
12 Upper Belgrave Street
London SW1X 8BB
Tel: 020 7235 9381
www.tax.org.uk

Financial Services Authority
25 The North Colonnade
Canary Wharf
London E14 5HS
Tel: 0845 606 1234
www.moneymadeclear.fsa.gov.uk

Gilts Registrar
Computershare Investor Services
PO Box 2411
The Pavilions
Bristol
BS3 9WX
Tel: 0870 703 0143
www-uk.computershare.com

**The Institute of Chartered
Accountants in England & Wales**
Chartered Accountants' Hall
PO Box 433
London EC2P 2BJ
Tel: 020 7920 8100
www.icaew.com

**Institute of Chartered Accountants
of Scotland**
CA House,
21 Haymarket Yards
Edinburgh EH12 5BH
Tel: 0131 347 0100
www.icas.org.uk

Low Incomes Tax Reform Group
12 Upper Belgrave Street
London SW1X 8BB
Tel: 020 7235 9381
www.litrg.org.uk

The Parliamentary Ombudsman
Millbank Tower
Millbank
London SW1P 4QP
Tel: 0845 015 4033
www.ombudsman.org.uk

The Pensions Advisory Service
11 Belgrave Road
London SW1V 1RB
Tel: 0845 601 2923
www.pensionsadvisoryservice.org.uk

The Pension Service
Future Pension Centre
Tyneview Park
Whitley Road
Newcastle upon Tyne
NE98 1BA
Tel: 0845 3000 168
www.thepensionservice.gov.uk

Student Loans Company
100 Bothwell Street
Glasgow G2 7JD
Tel: 0800 405010
www.slc.co.uk

TaxAid
Room 304, Linton House
164–180 Union Street
London SE1 0LH
Tel: 0845 120 3779 (10.00am–12.00
midday, Monday–Thursday)
www.taxaid.org.uk

TOP (TaxHelp for Older People)
Pineapple Business Park
Salway Ash
Bridport
Dorset
DT6 5DB
Tel: 0845 601 3321
www.taxvol.org.uk

Index

Numbers in bold indicate Tables; those in italics indicate Figures.